An Introduction to Greek Mythology and Modern Society

An Introduction to Greek Mythology and Modern Society

FIRST EDITION

Edited by
Jerrad Lancaster
The University of Akron

cognella®
SAN DIEGO

Bassim Hamadeh, CEO and Publisher
Jennifer Codner, Acquisitions Editor
Albert Liau, Project Editor
Jeanine Rees, Production Editor
Jess Estrella, Senior Graphic Designer
Kylie Bartolome, Licensing Coordinator
Natalie Piccotti, Director of Marketing
Kassie Graves, Senior Vice President of Editorial
Jamie Giganti, Director of Academic Publishing

Cover image copyright © 2019 iStockphoto LP/Svetlana Orusova.
Cover image copyright © 2022 iStockphoto LP/Wirestock.

Printed in the United States of America.

3970 Sorrento Valley Blvd., Ste. 500, San Diego, CA 92121

Contents

Preface

When dating my now wife, one of the early discussions we had (in the get-to-know-you phase) was about my teaching Greek mythology. I had recently visited my nephew's fourth-grade classroom to discuss the mythological references in the *Harry Potter* series, and when she heard this her eyes grew. She loves *Harry Potter*. Over the years following, having listened to the audiobooks and watched all the movies more times than one could count, the connections to Greek myth became more evident. Our discussions of the books/movies and myths grew over time, digging deeper into topics of morals and ethics through social and cultural norms. In Ancient Greece, myths were a way to communicate morality and values and to explain the world. Today, our modern myths, including *Harry Potter*, are often used for the same things. Moral values, including strength through adversity and friendship, are taught through the lens of a growing boy and his friends who face challenges together. Through her encouragement, I began to include the movies in my lectures. Unfortunately, there were no textbooks that incorporated the study of the Greeks with modern connections aimed specifically at *Harry Potter*. This is the influence behind the collection of this anthology.

Greek myths have been collected and studied for generations, and much conversation has been had over J. K. Rowling's use of myths and folktales in her work. In combining the two topics, an overall investigation can arise into the role of myths and how the tales of a culture reflect the norms, ethics, and belief systems present in that society. The works collected here are assembled to reflect the importance placed on mythological tales and as a deeper dive into the people, both past and present, that live(d) with the stories. This author believes that comparing the myths from millennia ago to the *Harry Potter* stories of the past decades can precipitate a better understanding between ourselves and the ancient Greeks. It could even be said that the way we think and relate to the world around us has remained quite consistent over the centuries.

The following selected works are categorized into units that follow the traditional path of Greek mythological study: the study of myths, the Greek gods, and heroes. The units include discussions of the Wizarding World of Harry Potter, creating parallels between the Greek gods and their magical counterparts. First, we will take a macro-level look into the role stories hold and the effects they have on a society. Next, the conversation turns to the main characters in these tales; how they act, what they represent, and the lessons the divine and magical impart as the narratives progress. Finally, we will revisit the heroic exploits of the mortals and semi-divine that adventured far and wide.

This anthology is designed to conjure up a deeper exploration of these themes, journeying into the myths as a reflection on the Greeks themselves and Rowling's work as a mirror of ourselves. We all take meaning from the tales of our own and past generations. The lessons passed down permeate who we are and how we act. Whether from a temple, a book, or a movie, there is so much we can learn by studying those who came before us and the lessons they imparted to their offspring and one another. It is the hope that what is included here can elicit the same discussions my wife and I have enjoyed and, as we still anxiously (albeit less hopefully) await our letters to Hogwarts, continue to have.

Introduction: Greek Myth and Modern Society

· ·

Millennia ago, the Greeks filled their world with mythical beings and creatures to rationalize their fears of nature and conform the world around them with their views of a civilized society. These creations centered on a religious doctrine of belief and worship in divinities with absolute control over virtually everything, from weather to insects. As the years went by, the world changed. Civilizations rose and fell, knowledge and understanding of the world advanced, and today we can understand better why water falls from the sky and how caterpillars can metamorphose so beautifully. Religious devotion to those Greek gods of yesteryear also fell by the wayside, but their place in modern society has persisted, albeit in more peculiar ways.

Millions of miles above us, celestial bodies are orbiting the sun known to us today by their Roman nomenclature: Jupiter (the largest in our solar system and named after the king of the Olympians), the red planet of Mars (for the god of war), and the dwarf planet of Pluto with its largest moon Charon (after the ruler of the underworld and his trusty ferryman) are but a few of our galactic neighbors with divine designation. Back on Earth, our society bombards us with corporate names and iconography influenced greatly by Greek mythology. Nike, perhaps the best known globally, fittingly got its name after the goddess of victory. Plastered on every street corner is the Starbucks logo with its siren beckoning and luring unsuspecting consumers to their coffee. Tire manufacturer Goodyear incorporates the winged shoe of Hermes into their branding, subconsciously connecting their tires to the speedy and reliable messenger of the gods. Pandora, the first woman and whose curiosity released evils into the world, now lives on as both a jewelry retailer and music streaming service.

Hollywood consistently provides a new take on Greek mythology. In 1963, Todd Armstrong starred as Jason who, alongside his Argonauts, encountered many ferocious beasts (come to life in stop-motion animation) and angry gods on his quest for the Golden Fleece. A young Harry Hamlin took the mantle as Perseus in 1981's *Clash of the Titans*, loosely based on the myth and with more stop-motion visual effects. The 2010 remake, and its 2012 sequel *Wrath of the Titans*, enjoyed a much larger budget affording much improved visual effects.

Hercules has been a favorite of the television and movie industries as well. Kevin Sorbo rose to fame as Hercules in five made-for-TV movies created as prequels for the television series *Hercules: The Legendary Journeys*, which aired for six seasons. Although incorporating mythology, this was done loosely around major plot points with notable, and sometimes obscure, Greek gods and heroes. As the series developed, the stories ventured further from the myths, changing Ares to the principal villain before including gods of other cultures, such as Thor (Norse), Gilgamesh (Sumerian), and Krishna (Hindu).

Disney's *Hercules* was the first introduction to Greek myth for an entire generation of children and continues to be a favorite for younger audiences. However, this film too has glaring inaccuracies from the ancient stories, with Hades as the principal villain and Megara (known as Meg) as a love interest and obstacle to overcome, let alone the musical numbers (although historians cannot prove that the Greeks never occasionally broke out into song). In 2014, the world was exposed to no fewer than three movies about the demigod: *Hercules*, *Hercules Reborn*, and *The Legend of Hercules*. The former starred Dwayne "The Rock" Johnson (earning the movie the affectionate moniker of *Rockules*)[1] and went on to box office success. The other two cannot claim the same. *The Legend of Hercules* was almost universally criticized, while *Hercules Reborn* went direct-to-video.

Expectedly, Greek mythology has also been adopted in literary form. In 2005, Rick Riordan released his first book in the five-book, children's fiction series *Percy Jackson & the Olympians*. Set in a modern backdrop, the changes from the traditional stories are evident from the start. Percy, an obvious reworking of Perseus, is the main protagonist, having grown up with a single mother only to discover he is the son of Poseidon. He joins other demigods at Camp Half-Blood, including children of Athena (Annabeth), Hermes (Luke), and a satyr (his best friend Grover). The series incorporates various mythological characters, plots, and locations, but never strictly to the ancient tradition. The first two books, *The Lightning Thief* and *Sea of Monsters*, were adapted into films.

Harry Potter was introduced to the world in 1997 with *Harry Potter and the Philosopher's Stone* (known in the United States as *Harry Potter and the Sorcerer's Stone*). Over the following decade, J. K. Rowling released six additional young adult books as well as created a global franchise unparalleled in the literary world. While not strict adaptations of Greek myth, the influence of mythology becomes easily identifiable. The titular character, Harry, often finds himself in the footsteps of Greek heroes such as Hercules, Perseus, Achilles, and Odysseus. Many of the characters personify qualities of Greek gods and mortals, and in other ways the connection is quite overt: Minerva McGonagall bears the Latin name of Athena, Hermione Granger shares her first name with the daughter of King Menelaus and Helen (of Troy/Sparta), and the ever-watchful caretaker of Hogwarts, Argus Filch, gets his name from the all-seeing giant Argus Panoptes of myth. The connections do not end there. Although the *Harry Potter* stories are not modern versions of Greek mythology as is found

---

1   Monica S. Cyrino, "How the Rock became Rockules: Dwayne Johnson's Star Text in Hercules (2014)," in *The Modern Hercules: Images of the Hero from the Nineteenth to the Early Twenty-First Century,* ed. Alastair J.L. Blanshard and Emma Stafford (Boston: Brill), 650–666.

in the *Percy Jackson* or *Hercules* tales, the ancient myths still form the foundation of the expanding saga that plays throughout Hogwarts and the Wizarding World.

There is more to how and why Hollywood adaptations modernize the Greek myths than purely for entertainment value. While stories created today can be predicated upon absurdities of nature and rely upon a willing suspension of disbelief, audiences maintain a desire to connect to the characters as they overcome the forces that seek to stop them from triumph over evil, falling in love, and their happily ever after. In *Clash of the Titans* (2010), divine Zeus is still the father of Perseus but not through a golden rain while Danaë is imprisoned by her father. Rather, Zeus sires the child with the wife of Acrisius as punishment for the latter's rebellion against the gods. *Rockules* never confirms Hercules's godly parentage, but his demigod powers persist. Harry, while born into a magical family, confronts the same difficulties that we muggles must deal with through childhood and adolescence, such as taking exams, making friends, and gaining the courage to talk to our crush. It is in how the Greek mythology is tailored to our society that provides a reflection upon not only who we are but what we believe, often morally.

Mythology tells us that Acrisius learns of a prophecy that his grandson will kill him. For this, he imprisons his daughter, Danaë, with the aim that a grandchild (Perseus) is never conceived. Upon discovering that Zeus always finds a way, he casts afloat mother and child in a chest to drown; they are later found by a fisherman. With the change in genealogy, *Clash of the Titans* removes the prophecy to better align with the underlying conflict of man versus the gods. Spoilers ahead. The movie revolves around Perseus saving the city of Argos, and its beautiful princess Andromeda, from destruction at the hands, or rather tentacles, of the Kraken. In doing this, our hero does retrieve the head of Medusa, but merely as the tool in which to conquer the beast. This is a reversal from the mythological order in which Perseus's journey is solely for the head of the Gorgon, with the rescue of Andromeda a "side quest" on his return trip home. Why has Hollywood chosen to rewrite the myth in this way? Writers Travis Beacham, Phil Hay, and Matt Manfredi created a story that begins with the rebellion of man against the gods. After generations of fealty and offerings, humanity was tired of the daily struggle of life and the fear of wrath from the gods. While this ideology would be blasphemous millennia ago, it resonates in a modern world with a history of rebellion and in a country founded after a revolution of its own.

Equally modern is the inclusion of a love interest and its alteration from the myth. What adventure would be complete without a love story? The Greek tradition explains that while flying past Ethiopia, the mythological home of Andromeda, Perseus spots the princess chained to a rock by the sea as sacrifice to appease Poseidon for the hubris of Queen Cassiopeia. It is only after securing Andromeda's hand in marriage from her father King Cepheus that Perseus bursts into action with his new favorite weapon. *Clash of the Titans* instead introduces into the myth Io (by tradition a mythological descendent of Perseus) accompanying our hero on his journey. After rejecting Andromeda's offer of marriage and a kingdom, Perseus chooses to live a normal life and is given Io as a companion by his father. As the only female traveler through the quest, it would only serve to disappoint the audience if the protagonist chose the woman (Andromeda) with whom he had no emotional connection. The Greeks would obviously have been befuddled by this choice, not relating to Perseus's rejection of the princess and the throne. We can see in this not only the influences of modern love stories to the ancient adventure but also the evolution of gender roles and relations over time.

Percy Jackson & the Olympians: The Lightning Thief (2010) also modified their godly lineage, although there is some leeway as Percy is not a perfect adaptation of Perseus. The demigod does come from a mortal mother, and his quest (to return the lightning bolt to his uncle Zeus) does lead him to confront Medusa. With her head in hand, however, Percy and friends go on to defeat a Hydra in Nashville and escape lotus-eaters in Las Vegas. This modern motif integrates an odyssean journey with herculean obstacles only heroes the likes of Odysseus or Hercules could overcome. Placing the protagonists in modern society, Riordan also adapts settings and circumstances to that which we would best relate. The Parthenon reconstruction in Tennessee and the Lotus Hotel and Casino in Vegas are two locales that would not be unfamiliar to the average reader or moviegoer. Moreover, Medusa is also portrayed completely anthropomorphized, albeit with snakes for hair. Conversely, the Medusa of *Clash of the Titans* is a woman with a long snake body from the waist down.

What influences the way in which Medusa is represented? Greek Medusa was largely symbolized solely by her head, but she was a mortal woman with a tragic origin story. In *Clash of the Titans*, Medusa was merely a beast to slay (entirely created through CGI animation), while the Medusa of *The Lightning Thief* (played by Uma Thurman) was more developed, telling Percy, "I used to date your daddy" before toppling statues upon him. Medusa's origin is also a part of the mythology that is often overlooked or ignored in modern retellings. Her creature form is a product of rape by Poseidon and subsequent curse by Athena, and Thurman's Medusa provides a spiteful nod to the traumatic tradition in a colloquial phrase of the twenty-first century. When deprived of dialogue or a voice in theatrical form, this aspect can be altogether ignored. Rape, being far from an acceptable act in the ancient world, did not possess the stigma it does at present, and therefore it was not an uncommon part of mythological beginnings. Today, it is an act that carries with it an unbearable weight, and omitting the Greek tradition in this form is more than just a creative choice.

Disney's *Hercules* (1997) is an animated tale obviously aimed at children. We are introduced to a young Hercules, a child of Zeus and Hera raised by mortal parents. He learns of his lineage, destiny, and heroic path before training with a satyr (Phil) and falling for a woman (Meg). His transition from "Zero to Hero" is expedited through a montage, of course accompanied by a jaunty tune, during which he defeats many mythical beasts such as the Erymanthian Boar, Nemean Lion, Minotaur, and Medusa. The young target audience inherently meant that the story had to veer from the myths, but Disney took further liberties. Ignored is Zeus disguised as Amphitryon to sleep with Alcmene; Hercules's descent into madness, invoked by Hera, resulting in the deaths of his wife and kids; and the death-defying labors taking him to the underworld and back. Further, the eponymous leader of the underworld, Hades, takes the mantle as the villain in the tale.

This latter shift from the tradition embodies succinctly the modern influence on the ancient stories. Hades is easily transitioned to the lead bad guy role in present forms of Greek myths. In *Clash of the Titans*, Hades instigates fighting between man and the gods and urges his brother to "release the Kraken." Although not the lightning thief, Hades retrieves the lightning bolt of Zeus, wishing to claim the throne as king of the gods, and proceeds to condemn Percy Jackson, his mother, and friends to the underworld. The gang is saved by Persephone, who only yearns for the time she can be away from her "cruel and abusive" husband. Disney's Hades also plots to become the supreme Olympian god, with the help of the Titans, until Hercules stands in his way. The Greek tradition does not portray a power-hungry Hades with a thirst to rule above ground. Instead, he is content as lord of the underworld and merely wants to keep his subjects within his kingdom once they arrive. The modern correlation of Hades with the Christian Devil has skewed the perception of the Greek god into the go-to villain, when, in fact, if one keeps record of terrible acts on mankind, when compared to his brothers, Hades looks the part of a saint.

In the Wizarding World of Harry Potter, we find much of the ancient tales adapted for modern purpose. Rowling wrote her stories for a young adult audience, and this explains the exclusion of many more vulgar aspects of the Greek myths, especially such topics as rape, incest, and cannibalism. Yet, the manner in which she chooses to construct the divine, semidivine, and mortal beings of mythology into her narrative secures much of the ethics and morality from its original form. Albus Dumbledore, headmaster of Hogwarts and de facto leader of the *Harry Potter* universe, embraces many of the qualities of his Greek counterpart, Zeus. He can remain patient and stoic in the face of grave circumstances yet let anger or empathy lead the way when such emotions are necessary. Early on we question some of the actions Dumbledore takes, especially his inexplicable absences at inopportune times, but we recognize later the "method to his madness." What is not found in the character of Dumbledore are the more immoral or despicable desires and actions, such as rape and vengeful killing, that define Zeus in many ways. The absence of such foundational truths to Greek mythology, particularly everything Dionysus personifies, is not only a choice of Rowling for the audience to which she is writing but also a view to how our society accepts these raw parts of humanity. Perhaps it is because her characters are engrained into us so deeply, but one can only believe that had Rowling written for a mature audience of readers, her stories would not have made as big of an impact as is felt today.

The following readings discuss the placement of myths in ancient and modern societies. They are tools for analyzing, dissecting, and embracing the impact of past and present traditions in forming and shaping the world around us. In recognizing the correlation between myth and ideology, one realizes the power mythological tales can command in a society. However, by examining myths, outside influences can also be identified. Although not present in every reading, many of the following examinations center on the characters and events in the *Harry Potter* tales. J. K. Rowling's stories provide a modern basis of which we can better understand and from which we are more prepared to view the worlds of our past and present and ourselves. What values do we hold dear, and what do we want to gain from our time spent on Earth? What impact do those around us hold, and what is our role within our community? When confronted with danger and fear, how do we overcome the seemingly insurmountable? And when we come out the other side, how have our experiences shaped who we are? These are but a few questions that both the Greeks millennia ago and we ask today. The answers to these questions can be found in the stories that permeate our lives.

Interpreting Myth

Mythology held an important place in the lives of the Greeks millennia ago. These stories not only outlined the underlying qualities of the gods, central to their worship and akin to doctrines of modern religions, but perhaps more importantly the lessons to be learned also included social, ethical, and moral statutes by which the Greeks were to follow. Today, these same standards are more commonly found outside of sacred texts. Secular literature quite often follows the foundational aspects of modern religions, leaving aside the fundamental views of a deity to focus on the daily trials and tribulations of the human experience.

Reading 1.1, "Platform 9¾," addresses how J. K. Rowling's tales of *Harry Potter* were grounded in the humanistic nature of the beloved title character and other members of the wizard community. However, these honorable intentions of Rowling and her characters were overshadowed by criticism and condemnation from religious communities choosing to focus instead on the magical setting in which the stories take place. This reading, in fact, provides a clear comparison between the Magic and Muggle worlds of Rowling with our own in which there is good and evil, right and wrong, and the ways in which those that fall on either side decide to use their abilities and power can be seen to be equally virtuous or deplorable in our history. As Rowling incorporates Greek mythology into her stories, this reading also demonstrates the use of fantastical tales to reintroduce and reaffirm the morality of ourselves in that triumph of good over evil. While reading, recognize not only the impact Rowling's books had upon our society when first published but also the underlying messages woven throughout her tales, keeping this in mind through the rest of the course.

The next reading, "Zeus and Prometheus: Greek Adaptations of Ancient Near Eastern Myths," focuses on the influences of Near Eastern mythology in Greek culture, namely Hesiod. This study is an important companion to discussion of *Theogony*, *Works and Days*, and *Prometheus Bound*, providing a cross-cultural background to the texts. The author discusses the similarities and differences between the Greeks and Near East, emphasizing the cultural role each myth played. It is important to recognize how myths are adapted to suit the society in which it exists; the adoption of Greek myth in the Wizarding World of Harry Potter highlights this point. Also addressed are some unclear aspects of myths, for example: Why do humans suffer from the trickery of the titan Prometheus? This is an important part of studying mythology, in that when confronted with a confusing part of a story, further thought and analysis leads to a better appreciation of the material. Essential to this course, the most puzzling parts of Greek myth often boil down to cultural differences, requiring us to step outside what we know to understand the story, and by extension the world, from a different point of view.

There is regularly more to myths than the basic facts. Zeus disguised himself as Amphitryon. Zeus gave a declaration that his child will rule. Check. Hercules was born and became a powerful warrior. However, also enclosed within these myths are details that carry with them prophetic (whether auspicious or tragic) ramifications. The third reading, "Prologue on Olympus," dissects the tale of the birth of Hercules, bringing forth more nuanced aspects of the story and lending more gravitas to its place in Greek mythological canon. In this reading, pay attention to the themes outlined by the author, which provide a better grasp of the myth and how the Greeks regarded the gods and the half-mortal hero. By delving deeper into the story, the complex nature of Greek myths is easier to recognize and hopefully comprehend, allowing us, thousands of years later, to better understand past societies, for instance in the subjugated role of the mother. It is in this way, through a more detail-oriented and thought-provoking analysis, that this course will attack the Greek myths and their modern, wizard counterparts. Rowling also attaches a prophecy to the birth of Harry Potter. Realize the variations as well that accompany the tales of heroic births and conceptions across time and cultures, harking back to those discussed in the previous reading.

Overall, these readings form a thorough introduction to the study of Greek mythology. Myths fill an important role within a society, and when shared between cultures, adaptations can be altered to serve distinct purposes. It is through in-depth investigation of these myths that the cultures, both of the past and today, can be better understood.

READING 1.1   Platform 9¾

Greg Garrett

> *"Harry Potter was a wizard."*
>
> —Harry Potter and the Chamber of Secrets

> *"Lord Voldemort showed me how wrong I was. There is no good and evil, there is only power, and those too weak to seek it."*
>
> —Professor Quirrell, *Harry Potter and the Philosopher's Stone*

Harry Potter, Gateway to Evil

J. K. Rowling tells a story about an encounter she had in the early years of Harry Potter in New York City; she was in the FAO Schwarz toy store buying gifts for her daughter, when a particular kind of religious man leaned in close to her and spoke. "He said, 'I'm praying for you,'" she remembered, "in tones that were more appropriate to saying 'Burn in hell.'"[1] While this anonymous man never explained his grievance to her, there's little doubt what that grievance was—like many others objecting to the Potter books, he was most probably concerned about the presence of magic in the stories, since in his worldview magic was necessarily dark, a thing of evil.

From the beginning, Harry Potter could not step out of 4 Privet Drive without being accompanied by controversy; for a decade now, the Harry Potter books have been attacked by conservative cultural and religious figures as works promoting witchcraft, Satanism, and antisocial behavior. In 2000 a widely circulated email message spread across the internet, claiming the book was itself a gateway to black magic:

> Harry Potter is the creation of a former UK English teacher who promotes witchcraft and Satanism. Harry is a 13 year old "wizard." Her creation openly blasphemes Jesus and God and promotes sorcery, seeking revenge upon anyone who upsets them by giving you examples (even the sources with authors and titles!) of spells, rituals, and demonic powers. It is the doorway for children to enter the Dark Side of evil. ...

To support these contentions, the "author" of the email had collected several stories of children who had read and been led astray by the books, among them the case of "dear Ashley,"

> a 9-year-old, the typical average age reader of Harry Potter: "I used to believe in what they taught us at Sunday School," said Ashley, conjuring up an ancient spell to summon Cerebus, the three-headed hound of hell. "But the Harry Potter books showed me that magic is real, something I can learn and use right now, and that the Bible is nothing but boring lies."[2]

---

1   Nancy Gibbs, "J. K. Rowling," *Time*, December 19, 2007, http://www.time.com/time/specials/2007/personoftheyear/article/0,28804,1690753_1695388_1695436,00.html.

2   The original email was archived at *Urban Legends*, http://urbanlegends.about.com/library/weekly/aa080900b.htm.

This email, as has been widely noted in print and Web urban legend publications, actually drew its "facts" from an article in the humor publication The Onion (facts such as "dear Ashley," the child inspired and somehow enabled to summon Cerberus the three-headed dog by reading *Harry Potter and the Sorcerer's Stone*), but even after discovering that they had mistakenly quoted a satirical news source that was itself poking fun at Harry Potter hysteria, many opponents of the Potter books said that although that particular source might be bogus, their claims were nonetheless true.[3]

Although Harry has gotten on the wrong side of all sorts of religious and cultural battles, much of the negative has come from conservative Christians. These believers argue that the Harry Potter saga is bad for children because it contains and promotes witchcraft, and the Bible is explicit in its condemnation of witchcraft. To evangelical Christians and others encouraged to read the Bible literally as a record of God's unchanging message to humanity, there seems to be little wiggle room in the way the Bible, particularly the Old Testament, talks about sorcery. Leviticus commands, "You will not practise divination or magic" (Lev 19:23b, NJB). The book of Deuteronomy goes into more detail in its command to eschew magic:

> When you have entered the country given you by Yahweh your God, you must not learn to imitate the detestable practices of the nations there already.
>
> There must never be anyone among you who makes his son or daughter pass through the fire of sacrifice, who practises divination, who is soothsayer, augur or sorcerer, weaver of spells, consulter of ghosts or mediums, or necromancer.
>
> For anyone who does these things is detestable to Yahweh your God; it is because of these detestable practices that Yahweh your God is driving out these nations before you. (18:9–12, NJB)

The rejection of sorcery remains a dogma in the Christian church today, particularly observed among Catholics and evangelicals, and it is from these quarters that many of the strongest condemnations of Harry Potter have emerged. An exorcist at the Vatican recently attacked the Potter novels for their use of magic, calling "fictional wizard-in-training Harry Potter the 'king of darkness, the devil.'"[4] Pope Benedict himself has spoken out against the Potter novels on several occasions. Most recently, in January 2008, the pope argued that Harry's stories were a dark mirror image of the *Lord of the Rings* and *Narnia* stories, often celebrated by Christians. Like other critics, Pope Benedict argues that the Potter books lead children to an "unhealthy interest" in Satanism, and concludes that "despite several positive values that can be found in the story, at the foundations of this tale is the proposal that of witchcraft as positive, the violent manipulation of things and people thanks to the knowledge of the occult, an advantage of a select few."[5]

Similar criticisms of the Potter novels have also come from Greek Orthodox Christians, and from other religious traditions, especially from conservative Muslims, who argue that the depiction of magic and the supernatural in the book is "contrary to Islamic values."[6] The Potter books were banned from schools in the

---

3   *The Onion* article "*Harry Potter* Books Spark Rise In Satanism Among Children" was quoted in both the email and as a source in online postings against the books. *The Onion*, July 26, 2000, http://www.theonion.com/content/news/harry_potter_books_spark_rise_in.

4   "Pope's Top Exorcist Says Harry Potter Is 'King of Darkness,'" *CBC News*, September 3, 2006, http://www.cbc.ca/arts/story/2006/09/03/harrypotter-exorcist-pope.html.

5   "Harry Potter Is 'The Wrong Kind of Hero' According to the Vatican," *Daily Mail*, January 15, 2008, http://www.dailymail.co.uk/news/article-508369/Harry-Potter-wrong-kind-hero-according-Vatican.html.

6   "Emirates Ban Harry Potter Book," *BBC News*, February 12, 2002, http://news.bbc.co.uk/2/hi/entertainment/1816012.stm.

United Arab Emirates, have been attacked by a state-run newspaper in Iran, were pulled from some Muslim schools in Britain because of fundamentalist protests, and have perhaps even been the object of terrorism; in Pakistan in August, 2007, a bomb threat postponed the launch of *Deathly Hallows* at a book store in Pakistan, and police suspect that the threat emerged from religious objections to the Potter books.

And while other religious people (including me) have praised the books for their imagination, the moral values of their heroes, the strong contrast between good and evil, and their similarities to faith narratives (including, in its review of the film version of *Half-Blood Prince*, the same Vatican newspaper that had previously condemned the books), others continue to denounce them in the strongest possible terms.[7] In addition to those recent comments from the pope, Dr. James Dobson, founder of Focus on the Family, released this correction in 2007 when a press account suggested he approved of the Potter books:

> "We have spoken out strongly against all of the Harry Potter products." [Dobson's] rationale for that statement: Magical characters—witches, wizards, ghosts, goblins, werewolves, poltergeists and so on—fill the Harry Potter stories, and given the trend toward witchcraft and New Age ideology in the larger culture, it's difficult to ignore the effects such stories (albeit imaginary) might have on young, impressionable minds.[8]

Following Rowling's post-*Hallows* announcement that Dumbledore was gay, the Christian Coalition and Pat Robertson's Christian Broadcasting Network, which had previously ridden the fence on the Potter books, condemned them strongly. A guest on CBN, Jack Roper, took the opportunity to use the Dumbledore controversy to return to the roots of the argument: "As a cult researcher for many years, I have seen contemporary witchcraft packaged in many seductive forms, and Harry Potter is the best."[9] One needs only look at the comments section of any Christian website publishing a positive assessment of the Potter books to discover that a vocal segment of the faithful still consider the books Satanic, evil, and a negative influence on anyone who reads them. Some have even suggested that they—and books like them—could lead to such horrific violence as the Columbine shootings; when once we invite evil into our schools, they say, who knows where it will stop?

One of those arguing that the Potter books' use of magic actually infected classrooms with evil was anti-Potter activist Laura Mallory, the Georgia housewife who received worldwide attention for her attempts to have the Potter books pulled from her child's school; I first read about her in the London *Daily Mail*. When the school refused, she went to the Georgia Board of Education, then petitioned the state Superior Court, where at last her legal options ended, although her passion did not diminish. Melissa Anelli, Webmistress of the Potter fansite The Leaky Cauldron, went to Georgia to interview Mallory, expecting to find someone who was deranged or paranoid; how could someone claim that God had told her not to read these books that had meant so much to so many?

But Anelli said that what she discovered in Laura Mallory was resolute sincerity and confidence that she was right: "[Harry] is a wizard. Witchcraft is evil ... one day everyone will know that witchcraft is evil."[10] Mallory's reading of Harry Potter told her that it was primarily about magic, and her interpretation of the Bible taught

7   Nick Squires, "Harry Potter and the Half-Blood Prince Praised by Vatican," *The Telegraph*, July 14, 2009, http://www.telegraph.co.uk/culture/film/film-news/5826251/Harry-Potter-and-the-Half-Blood-Prince-praised-by-Vatican.html.

8   "Dr. Dobson: What I Think about *Harry Potter*," *Focus on the Family*, http://listen.family.org/miscdaily/A000000593.cfm.

9   "JK Rowling under Fire from US Bible Belt after Outing Dumbledore as Gay," *Daily Mail*, October 28, 2007, http://www.dailymail.co.uk/news/article-490261/JK-Rowling-US-Bible-belt-outing-Dumbledore-gay.html#.

10   Melissa Anelli, *Harry, A History* (New York: Pocket, 2008), 196.

her that witchcraft—even fictional witchcraft—was an affront to God, and she could not be shaken from that belief. Laura Mallory, and people who believe as she does, cannot be argued with; Anelli certainly tried. But when you consider that this fear of witchcraft grows out of the very real belief that people of goodwill are matched in spiritual warfare with dark forces, then perhaps these sorts of misconceptions and misunderstandings become more understandable, if not excusable. One should not be afraid of a fictional wizard—and the books are, as Rowling insisted, deeply moral. But this continuing controversy has made it possible for the Potter novels to be simultaneously the most-read fiction in history and, according to the American Library Association, the most-banned books of the twenty-first century.[11]

Perhaps the great irony of Dr. James Dobson, the pope, and Muslim fundamentalists finding common ground around their condemnation of J. K. Rowling's works as leading to an unhealthy interest in the occult is that since her earliest interviews about the controversy, Rowling has categorically denied any such intent or content. As far back as 2000 on the *Today Show* with Katie Couric, Rowling had this very clear response to a viewer's question about witchcraft and Satanism:

> **Katie Couric:** Tammy in Kansas was wondering: "What would encourage you to write books for children that are supporting the devil, witchcraft and anything that has to do with Satan?" You've heard that before.
>
> **J. K. Rowling:** Well, nothing would encourage me to do that because I haven't done it so far so why would I start doing it now?
>
> **Katie Couric:** You have heard criticism along those lines ever since the beginning, and I think it also grew since more and more books came out.
>
> **J. K. Rowling:** A very famous writer once said: "A book is like a mirror. If a fool looks in, you can't expect a genius to look out." People tend to find in books what they want to find, and I think my books are very moral. I know they have absolutely nothing to do with what this lady's writing about.[12]

So it is also, perhaps, ironic after chronicling the ongoing contention to suggest that this fuss is primarily the result of bad reading. Rowling's use of magic as an element in her stories is simply a convention of the fantasy and fairy-tale genres and not actually about faith and belief, but rather about power and the willingness to use it. In this chapter, we will explore the world of magic, considering the criticism that Rowling sets up magic as a belief system or presents a Gnostic view of reality in which the magical world and its practitioners are somehow superior to magicless Muggles. And in the process, we will consider the idea that magic is simply an ingredient in the type of story Rowling has chosen to tell, and one that speaks more about our misplaced human desire for power than about any supernatural powers of evil.

---

11 "Harry Potter Tops List of Most Challenged Books of 21st Century," *American Library Association*, September 21, 2006, http://www.ala.org/Template.cfm?Section=News&template=/ContentManagement/ContentDisplay.cfm&ContentID=138540.
12 *The Today Show*, NBC, October 20, 2000. Interview transcribed at http://www.accio-quote.org/articles/2000/1000-nbc-couric.htm.

Magic and the Two Worlds

Magic and Muggles are opposed elements of the Potter story, and it can be easy to misunderstand what Rowling intends to do by creating this contrast. In the course of the Potter narrative, we meet first the horrid Dursleys of 4 Privet Drive, who glory in their suburban normalcy, who have kept Harry under their thumbs for eleven years, and who will continue to make Harry's life a living hell. They are the most Mugglesome of Muggles, "perfectly normal, thank you very much" non-magic people who want no surprises, no changes, and no drama in their lives—except for the drama they themselves create.[13] Vernon Dursley, director of a drill-making firm, is perpetually apoplectic; on the day before his nephew Harry Potter comes to live with them, he "yelled at five different people. He made several important telephone calls and shouted a bit more. He was in a very good mood."[14]

In that first chapter of *The Philosopher's Stone*, we also make the acquaintances of representatives of the Wizarding world: Albus Dumbledore, the headmaster of Hogwarts School of Witchcraft and Wizardry, Harry's future mentor and friend; and Minerva McGonagall, his future teacher and house head, who can't believe Dumbledore truly intends to leave Harry with his non-magical and thoroughly unpleasant aunt and uncle. The two friends are in shock, grieving the great loss of Lily and James Potter amidst the euphoria at the defeat of Lord Voldemort. Then, out of the night, a third representative of the magical world, Hagrid, the Hogwarts gamekeeper, comes roaring in with baby Harry astride Sirius Black's motorbike. Before he gives over the child to be left on the Dursleys' doorstep, he kisses the baby, and grief as outsized as he is boils over at the idea of leaving this child of wizards here in Little Whinging. "S-s-sorry," sobbed Hagrid ... "But I can't stand it—Lily and James dead—an poor little Harry off ter live with Muggles—"[15]

A simplistic division of Harry's life into two distinct worlds—Wizarding and Muggle—is part of the mis-conception of those who believe that magic is the defining element of the Potter stories. In this misreading, there are two worlds, the mundane and the magical, and Harry is an orphan and a misfit in one world but a hero in the other. Certainly one could read the books this way—their beginnings and endings, typically set in non-magical England, show a Harry deeply unhappy at being where he is, while his adventures and acclaim come, at least in the earlier books, entirely in the Wizarding world at Hogwarts School of Witchcraft and Wizardry. This simplistic division between worlds does break down somewhat in later books, however. In *Goblet of Fire*, Harry's great battle with a revived Voldemort occurs in a Muggle graveyard, far from Hogwarts; in *The Order of the Phoenix*, Harry and his cousin Dudley are attacked by Dementors in suburban Little Whinging; in *Deathly Hallows*, Harry, Hermione, and Ron have adventures the length and breadth of the United Kingdom (including a pivotal scene in the Forest of Dean, where Rowling grew up) and return to Hogwarts only for the climactic battle against Voldemort and the Death Eaters. That battle, of course, changes the game for everyone, wizards and Muggles alike; Voldemort is a threat to the entire world.

If we are to read the Potter novels first on a literal level and to place them in an understandable context, then magic is the essential element with which we need to grapple. Are the books *about* magic? Magic pervades the books, certainly, and it would be easy to read them literally and simply assume this. But careful reading suggests an alternative: any simplistic division of Harry's life into two realms, one of which is assumed to be superior

---

13   J. K. Rowling, *Harry Potter and the Sorcerer's Stone* (New York: Scholastic, 1998), 1.
14   Rowling, *Sorcerer's Stone*, 4.
15   Rowling, *Sorcerer's Stone*, 15.

to the other because of its possession of magic, crashes against one of Rowling's most obvious concerns, that of tolerance. The Wizarding world, as will see, is no Utopia; it is only superior to the Muggle world in magic and magical artifacts. It does not surpass the Muggle world in compassion, tolerance, or love; although we have no major Muggle characters who are not Dursleys, we never imagine that Hermione Granger's parents love any less than Ron Weasley's parents do, and conversely, the wizards living in the Wizarding world clearly show that they are no more unified or universally compassionate than those living in the Muggle world. Both "worlds" are disturbingly, hopefully human.

Therefore the notion that wizards and the "reality" they inhabit are somehow superior sounds like an exposition of Grindelwald's, Voldemort's, or Lucius Malfoy's most prejudiced ideas—that magic-using humans are elevated above those who cannot use magic or those magical races who somehow differ from them. As Rowling noted, this reading of the books is in direct conflict with the narrative itself, which dramatically illustrates the evil of prejudice: "Bigotry is probably the thing I detest most. All forms of intolerance, the whole idea of 'that which is different from me is necessarily evil.' ... This world of witches and wizards, they've already ostracized, and then within themselves, they've formed a loathsome pecking order."[16] Two worlds exist, true, but only the villainous characters in either would pretend that their world is superior.

Those who attack the Potter novels as "Gnostic" are probably referring to two distinct aspects of that philosophical and even religious idea: the belief that true salvation comes from secret knowledge held by an elite group, and the concept that there are two realities, with the one we live in being only a shadow of a higher and greater realm. There is, to be truthful, a great deal of secret knowledge in the Potter novels; wizards learn spells and incantations, and since the Statute of Secrecy, they have hidden themselves, their magic, and all magical creatures away from the Muggles. Wizards themselves are secret knowledge. They make this choice, however, not because they inhabit a different world, but because they inhabit the same world, and their secrecy is not simply about preserving secret knowledge; it also serves to protect them—and Muggles—and to preserve the status quo. Hagrid explains to Harry that the Ministry of Magic hides their existence from the country because, "Blimey, Harry, everyone'd be wantin' magic solutions to their problems."[17] And of course as we (and they) remember from the past, fear-filled Muggles do have a penchant for burning the occasional suspected magic-user at the stake. Even if, according to Wizarding history, they tend to burn the wrong people and not to harm the actual witches and warlocks, why stir up such alarm and loathing?

The idea that there are two realities, one more "real" than the other, is an ancient idea, emerging in Greek philosophy, and in religious belief going back at least to the Manichaeans in the first few centuries C.E. It is also a modern idea, found among many religious fundamentalists of various faith traditions who insist that the world we inhabit is completely fallen, and merely a shadow of the true spiritual reality to come. Alister McGrath describes this belief espoused by the Manichaeans as "a fundamental tension between the spiritual realm (which is seen as being good) and the material realm (which is seen as being evil)."[18] One could regard the Wizarding world as a spiritual realm, since much is hidden from the eyes of Muggles, and certainly some wizards believe that they occupy a higher plane of existence. This is the justification used by Voldemort and the Death Eaters to kill Muggles for sport, or by Grindelwald (and the young Albus Dumbledore) to rule over Muggles for "the greater good," as they once plotted together.

---

16 Jeff Jensen, "'Fire' Storm," *Entertainment Weekly*, September 7, 2000, http://www.ew.com/ew/article/0,,85523,00.html.

17 Rowling, *Sorcerer's Stone*, 65.

18 Alister E. McGrath, *Christian Theology: An Introduction*, 4th ed. (Malden, Mass.: Blackwell, 2007), 225.

So if we believe arguments that Muggles are inferior to wizards, then perhaps this radical division of reality makes sense. Certainly Voldemort believes it. At the outset of *Goblet of Fire*, he claims to the caretaker who discovers him in his father's old house that he is not a human (despite his human birth): "I am not a man, Muggle," said the cold voice ... "I am much much more than a man."[19] However, the wizards we most admire in the story—the adult Dumbledore, Arthur Weasley, and others—argue that there is no difference between wizards and Muggles. As with the Jews so reviled by German Nazis, there is no physiological difference between oppressor and oppressed. In Book 7, future Minister of Magic Kingsley Shacklebolt exhorts listeners of the *Potterwatch* broadcast to shelter Muggles from the Dark Lord and his minions by casting protective spells over their dwellings, and concludes, "We're all humans, aren't we? Every human life is worth the same, and worth saving."[20]

Ultimately wizards and Muggles are both human beings, with different gifts; one might have a gene for magic, another a gene for music. But there is no biological distinction between Muggle and magic-user—just prejudice (on both sides) about superficial differences. Just as Harry does not occupy a higher world because of specialized knowledge, he is not somehow superior to the non-Wizarding population because he can cast an "Expelliarmus" charm. Rowling brings these understandings to life for us in a number of ways. First, while Harry's discovery that he is a wizard delights him, becoming a part of the Wizarding community and mastering secret knowledge does not bring him peace or joy in and of itself; it is not a key to redemption or to a higher being. In fact, in some ways, Harry's life for seven years is constantly complicated and endangered because of his knowledge of this other world, and his mastery of magic is not at the core of who he is or even at the heart of his final victory over Voldemort. As Stephen Fry observed to an agreeing Rowling onstage at a talk at the Royal Albert Hall, "It's desperately important that the way Harry solves all his problems is really through his courage, his friendship, and his loyalty and stoutness of heart."[21] Secret knowledge or inhabiting a higher reality do not constitute Harry's redemption; instead, as we will explore in chapter 2, it is the very human joys of love, companionship, and community that give his life meaning.

Second, Rowling draws so many correspondences between the Wizarding world and the Muggle world that there can be little question that she sees them simply as two sides of the same coin, two experiences of the same reality. From the outset of the saga, it seems clear, for example, that the Wizarding world is as full of bad people as is the mundane world, something Rowling demonstrates for us from the beginning of Harry's journey. While the Dursleys are indeed horrible—"You couldn't find two people who are less like us," as Minerva McGonagall says, describing them and their already horrifying little boy—Rowling doesn't mean to suggest that they (and Muggles in general) are uniquely horrible.[22]

There are terrible people in both worlds; the first representative of the Wizarding world that Harry meets (after Hagrid, of course) is Draco Malfoy, who is directly compared to Harry's horrid Muggle cousin: "Harry was strongly reminded of Dudley."[23] Likewise we see Malfoy early in *Chamber of Secrets*, when Harry observes him from a hiding place in Flourish and Blotts, the dark magic store that Harry has entered accidentally. Draco is dragged into the store by his father Lucius, and he behaves precisely as we have seen Dudley behave,

---

19   J. K. Rowling, *Harry Potter and the Goblet of Fire* (New York: Scholastic, 2000), 15.

20   J. K. Rowling, *Harry Potter and the Deathly Hallows* (New York: Scholastic, 2007), 440.

21   "J. K. Rowling at the Royal Albert Hall, 26 June 2003," *Accio Quote!* http://www.accio-quote.org/articles/2003/0626 -alberthall-fry.htm.

22   Rowling, *Sorcerer's Stone*, 13.

23   Rowling, *Sorcerer's Stone*, 77.

sulking, whining, and saying, "I thought you were going to buy me a present."[24] These two boys, Dudley and Draco, are presented as twin bullies, Harry's chief antagonists in the world of his childhood, tormenting him at each of his homes, and they are presented as mirror images so that we might understand that there is no fundamental difference between them.

Draco, who will be a part of Harry's life from their first introduction on, also previews in their first meeting an important element of the Wizarding world which will grow in importance throughout the saga, the completely human bigotry and intolerance of wizards. When Harry meets Draco in Madam Malkin's robe shop, Draco inquires whether Harry's parents were *our* kind," and lets drop that he doesn't believe "they should let the other sort in" to Hogwarts.[25] Rowling intended to plant this focus on Wizardly racism and intolerance from the outset: "It was always there from the beginning, as you saw with Draco—even from [the] first book with Draco Harry discovers him being rude about Muggles."[26]

It is Draco and his family who will carry the banner of "pure-bloods" versus "Mudbloods" and "blood traitors" until Voldemort returns to do it himself, and it is Draco who first utters the insult "Mudblood" to Hermione Granger, although she and Harry need to have it explained to them by Ron: "Mudblood's a really foul name for someone who is Muggle-born—you know, non-magic parents. There are some wizards—like Malfoy's family—who think they're better than everyone else because they're what people call pure-blood. ... It's a disgusting thing to call someone."[27]

In the eyes of the Malfoys and the other Death Eaters, and in Voldemort's own self-loathing prejudice, Muggles are inferior, but even among those in the magical world there are gradations of acceptability, "us" and "them," just as there have always been prejudices in the world you and I inhabit. Wizards who call themselves pure-blooded set themselves up as superior to those who are of mixed blood, or who have no magical abilities at all, just as people have always divided themselves by blood or by race or by culture. These distinctions, though, as Voldemort's own Muggle ancestry suggests, are spurious. As Dumbledore once wrote Lucius Malfoy, explaining a decision not to pull a Muggle-sympathizing story in the *Tales of Beedle the Bard* from the library, there are no purely magical families: "So-called pure-blood families maintain their alleged purity by disowning, banishing, or lying about Muggles or Muggleborns on their family trees. They then attempt to foist their hypocrisy upon the rest of us by asking us to ban works dealing with the truths they deny. There is not a witch or wizard in existence whose blood has not mingled with that of Muggles."[28]

Muggles and so-called pure-bloods are no different, and their worlds are likewise no different. That the magical world is not, in and of itself, intended to be a separate or superior realm may be demonstrated finally by referring to the first chapter of *Harry Potter and the Half-Blood Prince*, when the Muggle Prime Minister is visited by Cornelius Fudge, "The Other Minister," and the Prime Minister tries to express the difficulties of his present moment, only to be brought up short by Fudge:

> "Difficult to know where to begin," muttered Fudge, pulling up the chair, sitting down, and placing his green bowler hat upon his knees. "What a week, what a week. ..."

24 J. K. Rowling, *Harry Potter and the Chamber of Secrets* (New York: Scholastic, 1999), 51.
25 Rowling, *Sorcerer's Stone*, 78.
26 "J. K. Rowling at the Royal Albert Hall," *Accio Quote!*
27 Rowling, *Chamber of Secrets*, 115–16.
28 J. K. Rowling, *The Tales of Beedle the Bard* (New York: Scholastic, 2008), 41.

"Had a bad one too, have you?" asked the Prime Minister stiffly, hoping to convey by this that he had quite enough on his plate already without any extra helpings from Fudge.

"Yes, of course," said Fudge, rubbing his eyes wearily and looking morosely at the Prime Minister. "I've been having the same week you have, Prime Minister. The Brockdale Bridge ... the Bones and Vance murders ... not to mention the ruckus in the West Country."[29]

It seems clear that these leaders occupy the same world, not separate ones, that they struggle with the same challenges although they come at the experience from different directions. Voldemort's rise to power menaces both worlds, Muggle and Wizarding alike, as the film of *Half-Blood Prince* demonstrates dramatically with its Death Eater attacks on the Millennium Bridge, a well-known London tourist attraction, rather than the fictional Brockdale Bridge.

The Prime Minister imagines that because wizards "can do *magic!*" they should be able to sort out anything, but as Fudge and new Minister of Magic Rufus Scrimgeour tell the Prime Minister when they depart his office by flue, magic does not solve all problems, particularly when one's enemies also possess it (any more than, to draw an analogy, nuclear weaponry solves all geopolitical problems for those who control it). It is simply a tool to be used.[30] What matters, ultimately, is not whether one has a magic wand or an M-16: it is what one chooses to do in response to the circumstances of one's birth and upbringing, and the company one finds oneself in because of one's choices. As Fry said with Rowling's assent, the books are less about casting spells that they are about power, what one does with it, with whom, to whom.

Perhaps, finally, the only real difference between the Wizarding world and the Muggle world may be reflected in the type of "magic" people employ to exercise power. Wizards are those who, through an accident of birth, possess some innate mastery of spells; Muggles have developed technology—cars, batteries, escalators, and many other devices—to the great astonishment of Arthur Weasley: "'*Fascinating!*' he would say as Harry talked him through using a telephone. '*Ingenious*, really, how many ways Muggles have found of getting along without magic.'"[31] Other wizards also seem to find Muggle technology estimable. In Book 7, for example, Dedalus Diggle makes much of Uncle Vernon's ability to drive: "Very clever of you, sir, very clever, I personally would be utterly bamboozled by all those buttons and knobs," and he is hardly the only wizard to view technology as something fantastic and barely believable.[32]

All this simply goes to remind of us of the familiar rule formulated by science fiction author Arthur C. Clarke: "Any sufficiently advanced technology is indistinguishable from magic." Just as Sirius is said by the Muggles to be armed with a gun, "a kind of metal wand that Muggles use to kill each other," J. R. R. Tolkien also suggested that there was ultimately little difference between magic and technology.[33] He spoke of the mechanisms used in a world (real or fictional) to project power, whether mechanical, magical, or personal, as "The Machine," and said there was little difference between these methods when they were employed for "the corrupted motive of dominating: bulldozing the real world, coercing other wills."[34] In other words, Hitler's Blitzkrieg of tanks and Stukas is indistinguishable from Voldemort's volley of dark curses; magicians

29   J. K. Rowling, *Harry Potter and the Half-Blood Prince* (New York: Scholastic, 2005), 4.
30   Rowling, *Half-Blood Prince*, 18.
31   Rowling, *Chamber of Secrets*, 43.
32   Rowling, *Deathly Hallows*, 37.
33   J. K. Rowling, *Harry Potter and the Prisoner of Azkaban* (New York: Scholastic, 1999), 38.
34   J. R. R. Tolkien, *The Letters of J. R. R. Tolkien*, ed. Humphrey Carpenter (1981; Boston: Houghton Mifflin, 2000), 145–46.

and Muggles alike employ power, but while wizards have magic wands, charms, and brooms, Muggles have electricity and the plugs and batteries so beloved by Mr. Weasley, who finds them magical. Both are "secret knowledge" to the uninitiated; neither makes for a "superior reality."

The Unforgiveable Curses

When Voldemort launches the Second Wizarding War, all his dark magic (and that of his followers) is marshaled to attain one goal: power. He wants power over others, and ultimately power over death, and magic is his tool in those quests. By eliminating his enemies (including, most especially, Harry) and by taking control of the Wizarding community, Voldemort will be unchallenged and will then be able to exert his will over the non-magical Muggles and other wizards as he desires. His pursuit of a certain powerful magic wand—what we know to be the Elder Wand—in *Deathly Hallows* is in service to these goals; if somehow Harry's wand has stymied Voldemort's every plan to destroy him, then the Dark Lord will simply need to employ a more powerful wand.

Voldemort's followers likewise hope to attain power through the ascent of the Dark Lord; as Voldemort asks the Malfoys after taking over their manor, "Is my return, my rise to power, not the very thing [you] professed to desire for so many years?"[35] This desire is precisely the sort of thing that Augustine was referring to many years ago when he spoke of what he called the disordered desires of human beings; although we desire things strongly, often they are the wrong things, harmful to ourselves and others. More recently, Dr. Martin Luther King Jr. has said that "Much of the evil which we experience is caused by man's folly and ignorance and also by the misuse of his freedom."[36] Dumbledore would, in all likelihood, have concurred with both men: toward the end of his life, he wrote of "The Tale of the Three Brothers" that "the quest for the Elder Wand merely supports an observation I have had occasion to make over the course of my long life, that humans have a knack of choosing precisely those things that are worst for them."[37] For the Malfoys, particularly, their disordered desire for wealth and power leads them to the brink of destruction, for their support of the Dark Lord in pursuit of their goals is almost their undoing, and only too late do they discover that what they care about most of all is not wealth or power but each other.

Those who employ dark magic are traditionally those who most strongly exhibit a will to power; as Harry learns early, most dark wizards have arisen from Slytherin, of whom the Sorting Hat sang, "Those cunning folk use any means/To achieve their ends."[38] However, in their education at Hogwarts, all students are supposed to learn to control their magic and not to use it in ways that are proscribed by the Wizarding community. At the orphanage, for example, Dumbledore says to Tom Riddle (who even this early has been using his power to torment and frighten others):

> At Hogwarts ... we teach you not only to use magic, but to control it. You have—inadvertently I'm sure—been using your powers in a way that is neither taught nor tolerated at our school. You are not the first, nor will you be the last, to allow your magic to run away with you. But you should

35 Rowling, *Deathly Hallows*, 9.
36 Martin Luther King Jr., "Our God Is Able," in *Strength to Love* (Philadelphia: Fortress, 1963), 107.
37 Rowling, *The Tales of Beedle the Bard*, 107.
38 Rowling, *Sorcerer's Stone*, 118.

know that Hogwarts can expel students, and the Ministry of Magic ... will punish lawbreakers most severely.[39]

At Hogwarts and in the Wizarding world at large, there are legitimate uses of magic; it is a tool to be harnessed. It can be used to do daily chores or even to explore the mysteries of the cosmos, but to those of evil inclination, magic becomes something more, a tool for imposing their will upon others, and it is upon this use that the Ministry necessarily sets boundaries.

Many types of magic are regulated by the Ministry of Magic: underaged wizards are not allowed to cast spells; magic-users are not permitted to attack Muggles with their spells or to allow non-magical persons to see them performing magic; and Arthur Weasley is constantly chasing after pranksters who subject Muggles to shrinking door keys and biting kettles and the like. But only three curses are classified as Unforgiveable Curses, and these illegal curses can explain a great deal about the use of magic to project personal power. Certainly the Wizarding community treats these spells as most serious violations; the impostor masquerading as Alastor Moody explains in his Defense Against the Dark Arts class in *Goblet of Fire*, "The use of any one of them on a fellow human being is enough to earn a life sentence in Azkaban."[40] These three curses all represent the most onerous magical projections of one's power onto another, and so we might say that the Imperius Curse, the Cruciatus Curse, and *Avada Kedavra* are magic at its darkest and most dangerous.

The Imperius Curse is a mind-control curse; as "Moody" demonstrates in the classroom, he can order his Imperiused spider to do anything he wishes: swing as though on a trapeze, do a backflip, do a cartwheel, tap dance. The students laugh at this show, but "Moody" is unsmiling. "Think it's funny, do you?" he growled. "You'd like it, would you, if I did it to you?"[41] They wouldn't like it, of course; since the Imperius Curse allows the caster to impose her or his will on the one so cursed, one of the qualities that we hold to be most distinctly human, that of free will, is taken away. The Imperius Curse is rightly condemned, for a successful curse does what not even the most totalitarian regime could ever accomplish: it takes away the option of dissent, hidden though it might be.

Harry and his classmates learn that it is possible to fight the Imperius Curse with one's own will, and Harry proves to be remarkably good at it. But as "Moody" points out, throwing off the Imperius Curse "takes real strength of character, and not everyone's got it."[42] For many in the Potter novels, being Imperiused is a sentence of involuntary servitude that goes on and on, under which they may do many things they would not wish to do. A prime example is in Book 7 when, under the Imperius Curse, Ministry officials are forced to help overthrow the Ministry. When you can force people to act against both their own desires and their own best interests, then you have absolute—if reprehensible—power over them.

The Cruciatus Curse is another means by which the evil wizard imposes his or her will on another. Victims of the torture curse may be induced to act in a certain way or to give information, but the curse can also be used to influence those who may be forced to witness the curse. Harry and Ron would do almost anything rather than listen to Hermione as she is tortured by Bellatrix Lestrange in *Deathly Hallows*, and what parent, lover, or friend could easily stand by as a loved one is subjected to such pain? The Cruciatus Curse also has the

---

39   Rowling, *Half-Blood Prince*, 273.
40   Rowling, *Goblet of Fire*, 217.
41   Rowling, *Goblet of Fire*, 213.
42   Rowling, *Goblet of Fire*, 213.

potential to drive a recipient insane; Bellatrix tortured Neville Longbottom's parents to madness in the First Wizarding War, and that threat of permanent disability adds to the menace of the spell. Torture is defined as the imposition of pain on another, whether to punish, to force speech or action, or for the personal pleasure of the torturer. Whatever the case, it is also an imposition of power on the powerless worthy of its status as unforgiveable.

Finally, the ultimate power is not simply to compel or to harm; it is to destroy, and *Avada Kadavra*, the Killing Curse, gives one that power. The spell is not identified until Book 4, when Hermione answers "Moody's" question about the final Unforgiveable Curse, but we see it in action earlier in *Goblet of Fire*. It is the Killing Curse, of course, that murders the Riddles at their table, the ancient crime of which Muggle gardener Frank Bryce is suspected, and the flash of green light which follows the words Lord Voldemort speaks inside the old Riddle house shows us that it is *Avada Kedavra* that the Dark Lord employs to kill Frank as well. This is, as "Moody" says, the "last and worst" spell, but it requires "a powerful bit of magic behind it—you could all get your wands out now and point them at me and say the words, and I doubt I'd get so much as a nosebleed."[43] Real malice, real evil, and real ambition are needed to harness this spell, of which Harry is the lone survivor in Wizarding history.

These three spells are the ultimate examples in Harry Potter of what Tolkien referred to as The Machine, manifestations of magic that the powerful use to impose their will on the less powerful. But we should not make the mistake of Professor Quirrell, who believed that power was all that matters; Rowling makes it clear that there are such things as good and evil and that use of magic to impose one's power over another is, most definitely, the latter. That is why, after Snape and the Death Eaters take over the school, the changes at Hogwarts are so alarming and contrast so sharply with the reasons Hogwarts has always existed. When Neville tells Harry and the others that Defense Against the Dark Arts is now simply called the Dark Arts, and that students are expected to practice the Cruciatus Curse against their classmates when they are given detentions, we can see that the focus of the school—to teach people to use their magical powers wisely and with respect—has been lost. Power has won out over the notion of good and evil.

Use of any of these curses—ever—is an evil act, and when asked, Rowling has not tried to defend Harry, who employs them on several occasions. At the end of *Order of the Phoenix*, for example, Harry launches the Cruciatus Curse at Bellatrix Lestrange, escaping from her murder of Sirius Black. It knocks Bellatrix off her feet, but she teaches him that—as "Moody" had noted of the Killing Curse—simply mouthing the words does not carry the force of the spell: "You need to *mean* them, Potter! You need to really want to cause pain—to enjoy it—righteous anger won't hurt me for long."[44] Harry attempts the Cruciatus Curse again—twice in *Half-Blood Prince*, when Snape and Draco Malfoy are escaping Hogwarts after Dumbledore's death—and casts it with some success in *Deathly Hallows* at Amycus Carrow after Carrow spits in Professor McGonagall's face. In that novel, Harry also finds himself forced to use the Imperius Curse in Gringott's to control the goblin Bogrod and Death Eater Travers, although he confesses that he hasn't cast it well and has to recast it on both, and Professor McGonagall also uses the Imperius Curse in *Deathly Hallows* against Carrow.

Clearly, even good people can be tempted—or feel the need in these situations—to exercise power over others, and the power that Harry does possess, the power of love, hardly seems equal to the task of protecting him or

---

43   Rowling, *Goblet of Fire*, 217.

44   J. K. Rowling, *Harry Potter and the Order of the Phoenix* (New York: Scholastic, 2003), 810.

overthrowing the Dark Lord. But Harry's awareness that some spells are good and some evil is clear despite his occasional failings, and never is it more clear than when he casts an unknown spell—*Sectumsempra*—on Draco Malfoy in *Half-Blood Prince*. Instantly, Malfoy is stricken:

> Blood spurted from Malfoy's face and chest as though he had been slashed with an invisible sword. He staggered backward and collapsed onto the waterlogged floor with a great splash, his wand falling from his limp right hand.
>
> "No—" gasped Harry.
>
> Slipping and staggering, Harry got to his feet and plunged toward Malfoy, whose face was now shining scarlet, his white hands scrabbling at his blood-soaked chest.
>
> "No—I didn't—"
>
> Harry did not know what he was saying; he fell to his knees beside Malfoy, who was shaking uncontrollably in a pool of his own blood.[45]

Harry is appalled at the force he has unleashed with this unknown spell, which Snape angrily identifies as dark magic. "I'm not defending what I did," Harry later tells Hermione. "I wish I hadn't done it. ... You know I wouldn't have used a spell like that, not even on Malfoy."[46] The film of *Half-Blood Prince* dramatically suggests Harry's remorse by showing him slumped, overcome by emotion, in reaction to Draco's suffering, and by his agreement to get rid of the Half-Blood Prince's potion book, the one from which he took this dangerous spell; in the novel, he hides the Prince's textbook in the Room of Requirement so as to keep it out of Snape's hands but does not dispose of it. But in both cases, Harry knows that what he has done—this power he has attempted to exert over another, even his enemy—is wrong. While, in the heat of emotion, Harry sometimes reacts to provocation by using magic in an evil fashion, there is no suggestion that these misuses of power are acceptable because it is Harry doing them. Rather, as Rowling pointed out, they are reminders that Harry is simply human—and reminders to us all to be on our guard lest we too find ourselves attempting to control, harm, or destroy those with whom we are at odds through the power we have at our disposal.

Magic and the Fantastic

J. R. R. Tolkien recognized that the equation of magic with power was a simple one to make; in his own *Lord of the Rings* saga, he related how Rings of Power—magic rings made with the aid of Sauron, the Dark Lord of his mythos—came into being, and how in his tale, power was an "ominous and sinister word" when applied to anyone except the very gods themselves. In Tolkien's fantasy world, magic could easily become corrupted into evil because of the desire for power, something common to stories of this type.[47] J. K. Rowling's choice of a particular mode of narrative—the children's story, subset fantasy literature—means that she too naturally incorporates a number of traditional story elements. In Harry Potter, the world is filled to overflowing with magical creatures—dragons, gnomes, sphinxes, unicorns, werewolves, giants, and more besides—and with

---

45   Rowling, *Half-Blood Prince*, 522–23.
46   Rowling, *Half-Blood Prince*, 531.
47   J. R. R. Tolkien, "On Fairy-Stories," in *Tales from the Perilous Realm* (Boston: Houghton Mifflin, 2008), 152.

magic of all sorts. Wizards can vanish and reappear, turn teacups into gerbils, transform themselves—or others—into animals. In Rowling's world, wizard-brewed potions can bring good luck or love (or the illusion of it) or cause instant death. Swords, necklaces, journals, and wands can bear fantastic charms or perform powerful magic. Magic is a central—and typical—part of these books, although that does not mean that magic is the point of them.

Fantastic tales have often used this backdrop of magic, and have often conveyed powerful mythic and spiritual meanings in this context. So it is that, before we turn our attention to the way the Harry Potter books deal with life in community, good and evil, heroism, and hope, we will conclude our consideration of magic by discussing the fantasy genre in which Rowling set her tales. Although she writes about a world in which magic is possible and supernatural creatures roam, her characters wrestle, as all of us must, with very human emotions, decisions, fears, and desires. In all of this we can see similarities to classic fairy tales, such as Rowling mimicked in creating *The Tales of Beedle the Bard*, and to fantasy epics such as those written by J. R. R. Tolkien, C. S. Lewis, and others.

In composing the Harry Potter story as a work of children's fantasy, Rowling wrote novels that, as Lisa Miller suggested in *Newsweek*, were new entries into the distinguished tradition of British fantasy, a tradition that cannot seem to help dealing with ultimate questions.[48] As G. K. Chesterton famously said, literature of the fantastic can be moral without moralizing, and this has always been a valuable trait of fantastic literature, whether written for children or enjoyed by all ages. In the Potter novels, Rowling speaks and writes about tolerance; her moral passions do emerge in her writing. So although converting readers is not her aim, in the context of her seven-volume fairy tale, she clearly has issues she wants to explore, and her beliefs have filtered into the way she treats the primary themes of the Potter epic: heroism, sacrifice, community, tolerance, faith. In this, we discover that Rowling is very much like Lewis, who once spoke of how in writing fantasy, one can bring truth to life again by stealing past the "watchful dragons" of piety and convention.[49] (Compare the motto of Hogwarts School of Witchcraft and Wizardry, which contains, as Rowling has said, very practical wisdom, but might also be an account of how stories might work: "*Draco dormiens nunquam titillandus*," that is, "Never tickle a sleeping dragon," or "Let sleeping dragons lie.")

Part of this truth-telling comes because of a tale's mythic quality. Myth has long been recognized as vital in its retelling of ancient stories and ability to convey wisdom. As Karen Armstrong points out, ancient peoples understood the world in two primary ways, *mythos* and *logos*, and both were regarded as attempts to convey the truth about reality. One, *logos*, was empirical and could be verified by observation, but the other, *mythos*, was considered to be equally concerned with truth even though that truth could not be demonstrated by rational means. "Myth," Armstrong says, "was not concerned with practical matters, but with meaning. Unless we find some significance in our lives, we mortal men and women fall very easily into despair. The *mythos* of a society provided people with a context that made sense of their day-to-day lives; it directed their attention to the eternal."[50] Myth helps us make sense of all the aspects of our lives.

While modern life has privileged the fact-based form of knowing, both rational and imaginative understanding are essential. The Scottish fantasy writer George MacDonald acknowledged that perhaps "'the facts

48   Lisa Miller, "BeliefWatch: Christ-Like," *Newsweek*, http://www.newsweek.com/id/32595.
49   C. S. Lewis, "Sometimes Fairy Stories May Say Best What's to Be Said," *Of Other Worlds: Essays and Stories*, ed. Walter Hooper (New York: Harcourt Brace & Jovanovich, 1966), 37.
50   Karen Armstrong, *The Battle for God: A History of Fundamentalism* (New York: Ballantine, 2000), xv–xvi.

of Nature are to be discovered only by observation and experiment.' True. ... We yield you your facts. The laws we claim for the prophetic imagination. 'He has set the world *in* man's heart,' not in his understanding. And the heart must open the door to the understanding."[51] The imagination looks beyond the factual and makes it possible for us to gain some understanding of even those things that are beyond proof. Within the context of a story—even a story filled with the seemingly impossible—we too can be redirected and retaught who we are and what should matter to us, and this moral instruction comes in a way that is fresh and vital because it steals past the dragons. As Lewis said in a review of Tolkien's *Lord of the Rings* saga, "The value of myth is that it takes all the things we know and restores to them the rich significance which has been hidden by 'the veil of familiarity.'"[52]

So it is that in the guise of a story like Harry Potter's, we too can sidestep the veil of familiarity and see the mythic truths again through new eyes. It is essential for our moral development, Stanley Hauerwas argues, "to be introduced to stories that provide a way to locate ourselves in relation to others, our society, the universe." Such stories of moral location, he says, will of necessity be "adventures, for there is no self devoid of adventure."[53] We need adventure to see the shape of a life, but sometimes it can be difficult to see that shape in the adventures of the everyday; while my moral self may be revealed by my quest to finish my grocery shopping, might it not shine out even more clearly if I were trying to get through a dark and magical forest, beset by dangers? In the great fantasy stories of MacDonald, Lewis, and Tolkien, we at once remove ourselves from reality and, as my colleague Ralph Wood notes in his book on Tolkien, are enabled to escape into reality.[54]

The fantastic worlds of magic, combat, and supernatural creatures present the illusion that we are not concerned with the events of the day-to-day, what Armstrong described as one of the primary functions of myth. Yet by the time we conclude our reading, we are often surprised at the way great works of fantastic literature can teach us about our own lives and beliefs. In *The Lord of the Rings*, for example, Tolkien tested Frodo, his hero, to his limits and beyond, and yet, miraculously, all was well: as Tolkien noted, Frodo's "sufferings were rewarded by the highest honour; and his exercise of patience and mercy toward Gollum gained him Mercy."[55] Rowling subjected Harry to tasks that would seem to be beyond anyone, let alone a single teenaged boy, and yet he constantly reaffirmed for us the virtues of love, compassion, and unselfishness. In these fantastic adventures, we can experience these vital human qualities ourselves. Thanks to J. K. Rowling's work, we can gain wisdom and understanding about the hard business of being human.

At the same time, as these examples suggest, amid stories marked by great horror, difficulty, and death, fairy tales and tales of the fantastic often direct us, paradoxically, toward hope, commitment, and life. Foes of fairy tales throughout the ages have condemned them as violent, dark, and bloody and said that while they may be written for children, children should by no means read them. Rowling has had her share of these

51   George MacDonald, *A Dish of Orts*, 1893 (Whitefish, Mt.: Kessinger, 2004), 9.
52   C. S. Lewis, "The Dethronement of Power," *Time and Tide* 36 (October 22, 1955): 1374.
53   Stanley Hauerwas, *A Community of Character: Toward a Constructive Christian Social Ethic* (Notre Dame: University of Notre Dame Press, 1982), 148.
54   Ralph C. Wood, *The Gospel According to Tolkien: Visions of the Kingdom in Middle-Earth* (Louisville: Westminster John Knox, 2003), 1.
55   Tolkien, *The Letters of J. R. R. Tolkien*, 326.

complaints, particularly as the books (in the minds of some critics) grew ever more dark and violent.[56] But Rowling (in the guise of Albus Dumbledore) responds to these critics by pointing out that fairy tales have always been dark, that it is a vital part of their allure and their function. Dumbledore's commentary to the old wizarding tale "The Wizard and the Hopping Pot" mentions the bowdlerizing witch Beatrix Bloxam, who condemned fairy tales such as those in *The Tales of Beedle the Bard* for "their unhealthy preoccupation with the most horrid subjects, such as death, disease, bloodshed, wicked magic, unwholesome characters, and bodily effusions and eruptions of the most disgusting kind." Like many Muggles over the years, in response and outrage, Bloxam wrote versions of these same tales that eliminated any such elements—and any real-world relevance—so that, as Dumbledore notes, Bloxam's "tales" have evoked only a negative response from all those who read them: "uncontrollable retching, followed by an immediate demand to have the book taken from them and mashed into pulp."[57]

This uncontrollable retching is a response to unacceptable sweetness. Tales that are not honest about death, disease, bloodshed, wicked magic, and the like are, first, untrue. However noble the motives for removing ugliness from art, even art intended for children, it is not representative of life. And leaving death out of the story—even a children's story—may be avoiding one's artistic responsibility. J. R. R. Tolkien wrote in his seminal essay "On Fairy-Stories" that while fantastic literature offers escape from the hustle and bustle of modern life, "there are other things more grim and terrible to fly from . ... There are hunger, thirst, poverty, pain, sorrow, injustice, death." In words that might remind us of *Deathly Hallows* and, more particularly, Voldemort's soul-shaping compulsion, Tolkien goes on to say that "the oldest and deepest desire" is "the Great Escape, the Escape from Death."[58] So to write a tale in which—whatever Beatrix Bloxam might say—death is never threatened is to fail as a storyteller who desires both to entertain and be honest. In Rowling's own words, failing to engage death is to fail to engage life: "The real master of Death accepts that he must die, and that there are much worse things in the world of the living. It is not about striving for immortality, but accepting mortality."[59] The responsible author of any work—including fairy or children's tales—must acknowledge this truth.

Moreover, to leave out ultimate crises is to destroy the dramatic potential for those happy endings so usual and so necessary to fairy tales. Tolkien spoke approvingly of "the Consolation of the Happy Ending," and argued that all complete fairy tales must end happily. However true tragedy might be as drama, the fairy tale calls for the precise opposite; Tolkien (as was his wont) actually coined a word to describe the effect we expect at the end of a well-rendered fantastic tale: *Eucatastrophe* ("*Eu*" comes from the Greek prefix for "good," and marks a reversal or transformation of the disastrous events which have gone before). "The eucatastrophic tale," Tolkien said, is the truest fairy tale, and in it we see "its highest function."[60] Thus, in a tale where we come to the point of disaster—and then see that disaster somehow miraculously or magically reversed—we are brought to believe that such reversals are possible, right, and just.

---

56   Rowling has pointed out on many occasions that within the first pages of *Harry Potter and the Philosopher's Stone* we learn of the brutal murder of Harry's parents. Death and loss infuse the entire series, although we do not directly witness deaths of characters who matter to us until *Harry Potter and the Goblet of Fire*, four books into the series.

57   Rowling, *The Tales of Beedle the Bard*, 17, 19.

58   Tolkien, "On Fairy-Stories," 381, 383.

59   "J. K. Rowling Web Chat Transcript," *The Leaky Cauldron*, July 30, 2007, http://www.the-leaky-cauldron.org/2007/7/30/j-k-rowling-web-chat-transcript.

60   Tolkien, "On Fairy-Stories," 384.

Magic in a fantastic story seems to mark a world as somehow unlike our own, putting us at our ease as we read that we are not dealing with our own problems, and thus luring us into engagement with the ideas and issues that emerge from the narrative. As in other fantasy novels and tales, magic in Harry Potter is not a belief system, nor in Rowling's imagination does it delineate a separate, superior world. So in these novels, while magic may be an accepted part of the world, as we've discovered, it is not the point of the world; magic is used in the same sorts of way that we in our world might use science and technology, for good or ill. A responsible reading of the element of magic in Harry Potter shows us that ultimately it is about power—how it is employed, and how it should not be employed. Harry is fortunate to be surrounded by a community of friends and classmates who can help do the work for which Dumbledore suggested Hogwarts exists, that of teaching wizards what is and is not an acceptable use of power. It is in community that we find ourselves, understand our missions, and seek real meaning, and so it is to community and communion that we will turn next in exploring deeper meanings in Harry Potter.

Kurt A. Raalaub

Introduction: The Origins of Evil

Hesiod, a slightly younger contemporary of Homer, is the first Greek poet whom we know by name and life story He tells us of his meeting with the Muses on Mount Helicon who bestowed the gift of song upon him, of his father who emigrated from the Anatolian coast to the miserable little village of Askra in central Greece, and of his quarrel with his brother Perses who continually tried to get a larger share of their inheritance by bribing the aristocratic judges. However we assess the "autobiographical" references in Hesiod's work, his world certainly is one of farmers who work hard to succeed, avoid the public square in the large town with its political and judicial disputes, are suspicious of the "gift-devouring" elite leaders, and seek their support among their neighbors rather than family or elite.[1]

Trying to understand the world in which he lives, Hesiod asks simple but important questions: what are the factors that determine human well-being? What are the main values that sustain a good community? Why is the world full of evils, and who is responsible for human suffering? What qualities must a good leader have, and how can the bad leaders who make the citizens' lives difficult be convinced to change their ways? Despite the traditional poetic form in which he presents his thoughts, Hesiod has an independent mind. He is one of the first political thinkers we know of.[2] His ideas had a deep and lasting impact. He frequently uses stories or myths for an etiological purpose, to explain specific conditions or customs in his own time. Mesopotamian myth often had a similar purpose. The comparison, when we have comparable versions, is illuminating.

Let me illustrate this with the stories that explain the origins of evils in the world. Here is the Sumerian story.[3] The gods have just created humans to do the hard work from which they suffered before. They celebrate this achievement with a party at which they drink too much beer. Two of the most powerful gods, Enki, the god of sweet waters and a very smart problem solver, and Ninmah, the goddess of the earth, start to quarrel. Ninmah challenges Enki in a competition in which one creates human beings with defects, and the other has to find a place for them in society: a man who cannot hold his urine, a woman who is unable to bear children, a being who has neither male nor female organs (presumably a eunuch). Enki is able to place them all. The eunuch serves the king, the barren woman the queen, and so on. When they change sides, Ninmah gets into trouble: for example, Enki creates a person burdened with all the ills of old age for whom Ninmah is unable to find a place. The same happens with Enki's other creatures. Eventually frustrated, Ninmah abandons her efforts. The game and the party are over; the gods leave—but the evils stay. This myth clearly intends to explain

---

1   Autobiographical elements in Hesiod: esp. Hes. *Th.* 22–34; *WD* 27–41, 633–40. For modern discussion, see Gagarin 1974; Nagy 1990: ch. 3. On Hesiod's social context: Millett 1984; Tandy and Neal 1996; Edwards 2004; van Wees 2009.
2   On Hesiod's political thinking: Raaflaub 1988: 215–24; a brief summary in id. 2000: 34–37. See also n. 52 below.
3   On the competition of Enki and Ninmah, see Jacobsen 1946: 161–65; Kramer and Maier 1989: ch. 2.

Kurt A. Raaèlaub, "Zeus and Prometheus: Greek Adaptations of Ancient Near Eastern Myths," *Cultural Contact and Appropriation in the Axial-Age Mediterranean World: A Periplos*, ed. Baruch Halpern and Kenneth Sacks, pp. 17–37, 243, 245–250, 252, 254–259, 262–270, 272, 274–280, 282–283, 287–290, 292–297. Copyright © 2017 by Brill Academic Publishers. Reprinted with permission.

the existence of these evils, for example, all those unpleasant, seemingly unnecessary pains and handicaps that accompany old age. But, as Thorkild Jacobsen emphasizes, it also passes judgement: these evils are not part of the original world order; they came into being when the gods succumbed momentarily to envy and a desire to show off.[4] Humans, we observe, have nothing to do with the origins of evils in this text; created to be the gods' slaves, they are only the victims of the gods' actions.[5]

Not so Hesiod. In his epic the gods create Pandora as a punishment for the offenses of Prometheus, one of the Titans, who twice deceived Zeus, the supreme god. Pandora means "All-gifts" or perhaps rather "All-giver" and her gifts are all evil.[6] In the version of the *Theogony*, Pandora herself is the evil, a beautiful but wasteful woman—in our world, she would be a maniacal shopper—the ancestress of mortal women who (says Hesiod) are a great affliction to men whose life is miserable with or without them. In *Works and Days*, the gods give Pandora a jar in which they pack all imaginable evils; she seduces Prometheus's dumb brother Epimetheus ("he who thinks afterwards," as opposed to Prometheus, who thinks before acting), who ignores explicit warnings in accepting her. She opens the jar and lets all the evils fly out, closing the jar just in time to keep hope or expectation (*elpis*) shut in.[7] Prometheus suffers his own grievous punishment (*Theog.* 521–34, 613–16), and we shall have to ask why humankind has to suffer for Prometheus's offenses. But there is no doubt that Hesiod explains the existence of evils in the world not with divine irresponsibility and arbitrariness but as the result of transgressions that are directly connected with humankind.

The difference between the etiology of evil in Mesopotamian and Greek myth is huge. Moreover, Hesiod says it explicitly, several times: there is no way that anyone can deceive Zeus; his punishment and that of his daughter, Dike, the goddess of Justice, will not fail to meet the evildoer.[8] So the gods are important and play a decisive role as promoters and enforcers of justice, but they do so mainly because there is no sufficiently powerful and just *human* agency to rely upon for such purposes. The problems that Hesiod and other early Greek thinkers tackle fit into an entirely human framework of cause and effect. The gods punish evildoers and their communities and, through seers, poets, or leaders blessed by them, they may offer advice about salutary measures to be taken in a crisis, but they neither cause nor resolve such a crisis. The poet of the *Odyssey* and Solon, the Athenian lawgiver, say it emphatically: the gods are benevolent; they are not the instigators of human suffering beyond what fate (*moira*) has allocated to each. It is the humans, the citizens, who cause social ills and are responsible for their own demise, and they themselves must resolve these problems.[9]

In the case of the origins of the evils, Hesiod's etiological myth and its Mesopotamian counterpart are completely different and thus seem independent of each other. In emphasizing differences, I should add, I generally do not pass judgement: by "different" I do not mean "better" or "worse," I only mean "different." I

---

4 Jacobsen 1946.

5 On humans as the gods' slaves, see n. 45 below.

6 Prometheus and Pandora: Hes. *Th.* 571–612; *WD* 42–105.

7 The latter is not uncontested but, in my view, necessary, not least because of Prometheus's gift of hope to humankind in *Prometheus Bound* (below). For a contrary view, see M. West 1978: 169–71 at *WD* 95–100; for further discussion, not least of the meaning of *elpis*, Pucci 1977: 104–5; Verdenius 1985: 66–71. For a constitutive analysis of the myth, see Vernant 1989, 1990; furthermore Ogden 1998; Clay 2003: ch. 5. On Pandora: Walcot 1966: ch. 3; Pucci 1977: ch. 4; *Brill's New Pauly* 10 (2007): 436–37; *Lexicon Iconographicum Mythologiae Classicae* 7.1 (1994): 165–64 (both with bibliog.).

8 Hes. *Th.* 550–52, 613–16; *WD* 106, 248–67; on the role of Dike and justice in Hesiod, see Gagarin 1973; Erler 1987. Hirzel 1907 remains important.

9 *Odyssey* 1.22–43; Solon, *fr.* 4 West. For the larger implications of these views, see Raaflaub 2005: esp. 255–68.

am sure that in its own cultural context the Mesopotamian explanation of the origins of evil made as much sense as Hesiod's interpretation did to the Greeks. I could even imagine that storytellers offered moral or ethical interpretations in oral performances, but this is a highly contested issue that does not need to be addressed here.[10]

In this essay, I want to focus on the question of how Greek thinkers dealt with ideas that clearly *did* originate in the east. This is a question of considerable importance. For, as is well known, during the so-called "Orientalizing Period" from the late 8th to the early 6th centuries BCE, the Greeks absorbed an enormous amount of outside influences in all areas of culture, coming especially from Anatolia, Mesopotamia, Phoenicia, and Egypt (which I group here together under "the Ancient Near East").[11] This process of cultural dissemination, however, has often been understood too simply, as if it corresponded, so to speak, to a one-way route, on which ship after ship loaded with goods moved from south to north and east to west in the Mediterranean, ending in harbors with warehouses from which the imported goods were distributed and integrated seamlessly into the receiving culture, like bricks in a wall. This view runs into several major difficulties. One, on which I shall focus today, concerns the integration of external impulses into another culture.[12]

Usually, such impulses are adapted (sometimes profoundly) to the conditions prevailing in the receiving society. What results from this process will therefore differ (sometimes substantially) from the "raw material" imported from abroad. On the level of material culture, such differences may have been relatively small: for example, Greek craftsmen could imitate sphinxes and sirens that were typical in the Near East, or learn from itinerant Phoenician artisans the art of making large decorated bronze bowls and plates.[13] Yet even here differences could be substantial: certain Greek statues (the *kouroi*) were obviously based on Egyptian models, and their "archaic smile" recalls that of late Hittite statues, but they underwent rapid artistic change and played in Greek society a role that differed vastly from that of their models in Egypt.[14] On the level of social or political customs and institutions, I suggest, differences were larger and more fundamental.[15] To examine one aspect of this hypothesis, I will look at two myths that reflect such customs and institutions. They are well attested in Mesopotamian literature and play an important role in Hesiod and in a fifth-century tragedy: the myth of the succession of several divine kings and that of the culture hero. That Near Eastern influences play a role especially in Hesiod's epics is obvious and well-known; a famous example is the "Myth of the Ages," characterized by four metals.[16]

---

10   See, for example, Alster 1992 and relevant chapters in Foley 2005; Sasson 1995. See also M. West 1997: ch. 12.

11   For bibliography on the cultural interaction between Greece and the Ancient Near East, see Burkert 1992: 135–52; Raaflaub 1993: VII–XXIII, and, recently, Burkert 2004: 131–42.

12   For more detailed discussion of these issues, see Humphreys 1993; Raaflaub 2008: 33–44; 2009a: 38–39.

13   Kreutz 2004; on sphinxes: Scully 1997: 249–50 (emphasizing changes in the process of imitation); on bronze bowls, Markoe 1985; Hoffman 1997: 32–37 (with n. 21), 125–32. See also Ebbinghaus 2008 on animal-headed vessels.

14   On the *kouroi,* see Hurwit 1985: 186–202; Kyrieleis 1993: 150–51; Fehr 1996; Osborne 1998: 75–85. On the "archaic smile": Işik 2004.

15   For a comparative study of Israelite, Greek, and Roman law codes (unfortunately not including Mesopotamian ones), see Burckhardt et al. 2007.

16   Myth of the Ages: Hes. *WD* 106–201; for eastern parallels, see Walcot 1966: 85–86; M. West 1978 on this section, esp. 172–77; 1997: 312–19; Woodard 2007.

2 Zeus and the Succession Myth

The so-called "succession myth" is recounted in several episodes of the *Theogony*.[17] Uranos (Sky) fathers numerous children with Gaia (Earth) but prevents their birth and causes the mother severe pain. The underlying idea presumably is that earth and sky were not yet separated.[18] Gaia then prompts her eldest son, Kronos, to cut off his father's genitals with a sickle made of the mysterious metal *adamas,* thereby severing their union. Her children can now be born, and Kronos assumes power. He in turn swallows his children immediately after birth to prevent another rebellion. His wife, Rhea, hides the youngest, Zeus, and tricks Kronos into swallowing a stone instead. When he has grown up, Zeus causes Kronos to vomit the stone and his siblings, overthrows him and takes over the kingship of the gods. In a great battle, Zeus and the Olympian gods defeat Kronos and the Titans and imprison them forever in the depths of Tartarus. Another victory, over the Earth-born monster Typhoeus, secures Zeus's power.

Myths told among the Hurrites, Hittities, and other West Asian societies offer remarkable parallels.[19] Here there are four generations of divine kings. After nine years of rule, the first, Alalu is defeated by Anu, the Sky God, who in turn rules for nine years. Kumarbi attacks him, grabs him by his feet when he tries to escape to heaven, bites off his genitals, and swallows them. He thereby is impregnated with three powerful deities. He manages to spit out two of them but fails to get rid of the third, Tessub, the Weather God. Because the following passage is sadly fragmentary, it is uncertain but perhaps likely (because of Hesiod's analogy) that Kumarbi then swallows a stone and tries to eat Teššub after his birth. We *do* know that eventually the Weather God is born, defeats Kumarbi in battle, banishes him and the gods connected with him, and assumes power himself. The story is continued in the myth of Ullikummi, a stone child born of the union of Kumarbi and a rock, who grows up to become a giant monster threatening the gods. Only by using a copper sickle that had served long ago to separate heaven and earth, do the gods succeed in cutting off the monster's feet, toppling and defeating it.

No one will doubt that Hesiod drew on such models when composing the *Theogony*. This raises important and difficult questions. How were such motifs transmitted to Greece? Most of the relevant eastern texts known to us date many centuries before Hesiod: the Hittite texts ca. 1400–1200, the *Enuma elish* in the late 12th century BCE or later.[20] In Mesopotamia, such texts were transmitted in scribal schools far into the first millennium, but Greeks (or their eastern informers) were unlikely to have access to these. Scholars disagree about whether versions of these texts were transmitted orally as well, and how such oral and written traditions might have interacted with each other—although in my view the mere fact that Greek epics reflect much eastern material proves widespread oral traditions that perhaps formed part of a cultural *koinē* in the eastern Mediterranean. Surviving evidence suggests that Mesopotamian epics no less than orally transmitted songs or tales all over the world adjusted to changing conditions. Most likely they were also elaborated in performance. Yet, when-, how-, and by whomever Near Eastern motifs were transmitted to Greece—in the late Bronze Age or early archaic period, via North Syria and the Levant or Anatolia to Crete or the central Aegean and central Greece,

---

17   Succession Myth: *Th.* 116–210, 453–506, 617–735, 820–885. See Brown 1953; M. West 1997: ch. 6.

18   For other explanations, see M. West 1966: 211–14; Hölscher 1968: 51.

19   On the Kumarbi and Ullikummi myths, see Güterbock 1946, 1948, 1952; Hoffner 1998: 40–65; Haas 1994: 82–90, 96–98, 113–15; 2006: ch. 8. On the Storm or Weather Gods of the Ancient Near East, see Schwemer 2001, 2007.

20   For the date of the latter, see Abusch 1995. Halpern, in a personal communication, dates the present form to the 8th century, with forerunners in the 10th.

or via a "cultural *koinē*" in the Eastern Mediterranean—we do not know the versions the Greeks encountered. Inevitably, therefore, we compare what is only partially comparable.[21]

Moreover, on all levels things are more complicated. For example, Kumarbi, the equivalent of Kronos, makes not one but several efforts to overthrow the Weather God, and three of his creatures occupy the divine ruler's throne at least temporarily.[22] Volkert Haas interprets the Kumarbi cycle as a calendar myth that divides the year into the four seasons marking the agricultural year, dominated by the gods of the storm flood (Alalu), sky (Anu), grain (Kumarbi) and weather (Tessub). Kumarbi himself, created before the differentiation between the male and female principles by the separation of Earth and Sky, is sexually undifferentiated, "both father and mother of Tessub."[23] Except for the functions of the Sky (Uranos), Fertility (Kronos), and Weather (Zeus), none of this is found in Hesiod.

More importantly, in the Hittite version the story is told in a straightforward way, without an ethical or political interpretation or purpose. I do not doubt that it too had a deeper cultural meaning but, whatever it was, it is hardly visible in the preserved texts. It is possible, of course, that in oral performance the singer or narrator elaborated on these aspects, but, as said earlier, this aspect is greatly controversial among specialists.[24] In Hesiod's account, such a purpose is unmistakable. The *Theogony* is a hymn to Zeus *and the just world order* he has created (47–74); his rule is embedded from the beginning in the community of gods, and the poet places much emphasis on the justice and fairness of his rule.

By contrast, the rule of Zeus's predecessors appears as violent and unjust. Uranos is a brutal and oppressive ruler. Although Kronos liberates himself and his siblings from such oppression, he "has a crooked cleverness" (*ankylomētēs*), does this in a violent act of usurpation, and commits "a great deed" "out of wickedness" (*atasthaliē*) that will call for revenge (*tisis*, 209–10).[25] Fully aware of this, Kronos fears to be overthrown by his own son, as a prophecy predicts (461–65). So he too suppresses his children. This in turn causes his wife, Rhea, to rebel against him and to save Zeus through deception in order to make Kronos pay for the blood-guilt

21 For a detailed comparison of Greek and Near Eastern versions of the succession myth: Steiner 1958; Schwabl 1962. For continuing adaptation in Near Eastern epic, see, e.g., Cohen 1993: 406–53; for the importance of oral traditions in Mesopotamia, see now Westenholz 2009. For some of the questions raised here, see Mondi 1990; Penglase 1994 (with the review by Scully 1997); M. West 1997: ch. 12; Haubold 2002; Bachvarova 2005, 2008; Bryce 2008; see also earlier discussion by, e.g., Lesky 1950, 1955; Heubeck 1955; Hölscher 1968: 49–82 and, on the traditions preserved by Sanchuniathon and Philo of Byblos, Baumgarten 1981; M. West 1997: 283–86. Regarding the "transmittors," Burkert 1992; 2004 suggests itinerant specialists, including Phoenicians who settled in the Aegean (well attested in Crete: Morris 1992: ch. 1 and 124–49; Hoffman 1997; Stampolidis and Kotsonas 2006). From a West Asian perspective: Grottanelli 1982; Zaccagnini 1983. Even if poets and singers themselves do not seem to have crossed cultural boundaries, regional and supra-regional cults and festivals offered many opportunities for transmission of ideas and stories; see now Bachvarova 2009 and other chs. in Hunter and Rutherford 2009. Niditch 2009 points out tales and characters in early Israelite traditions that recall Greek ones and thinks it important "to acknowledge that more than one epic tradition enlivened the ancient Mediterranean world, and that cross-fertilization between various traditions is to be expected." The question of a cultural *koinē* has been suggested by various scholars and is in urgent need of comprehensive discussion; see, e.g., Seybold and Ungern-Sternberg 1993, 2007; Sherratt and Sherratt 1993; Matthäus 2005.
22 Hoffner 1998: 46ff.; Haas 1994: 85–99; M. West 1997: 103–5. For differences, see also Scully, this vol.
23 Haas 1994: 85, 115.
24 See n. 10 above.
25 For the meaning of *atasthaliē*, see, e.g., *Od.* 1.7, 1.34, 12.300, 23.67; S. West 1988: 72 (with bibliog.).

he has incurred by unmanning her father and swallowing his children (472–73). As a consequence, he too is overthrown, and Zeus rules among the immortals (450–500).

Here we face a problem. Zeus no less than Kronos appears to be a usurper. He defeats and expels Kronos and assumes power himself (490–91, cf. 496). Even worse, Zeus too knows a prophecy that he is fated to be overthrown by an overpowering son (894–98). In order to prevent this, he swallows his first wife, Metis, who is pregnant with Athena. A second pregnancy and its dangerous consequences are now impossible (886–900). Based on these *actions,* at least in his beginnings, Zeus might seem hardly better than Kronos. Yet Hesiod disagrees. He depicts Rhea and Zeus acting upon the prophecy and advice of the oldest and highest authorities among the gods, Uranos and Gaia (469–76, 889). Zeus avenges earlier injustice and replaces a ruler who deserves to suffer divine punishment. He certainly assumes power violently, but this is not represented as an act of injustice: it is never called "wicked." Kronos swallows his children, while Zeus tricks Metis "deceitfully with cunning words" and puts her away in his belly, again on the advice of Earth and Heaven, so that no other god can become king (888–93). Zeus thus integrates Metis into his own body, so that she, "the wisest among gods and mortal men" can "advise him of what is good or bad" (887, 892–93). The word *mētis* means wisdom based on insight and experience, or cunning intelligence.[26] Zeus thus acquires a quality that a good ruler needs to stay in power. And his *mētis* certainly will be straight, not crooked like Kronos'.[27] The intention seems obvious: no stains must appear on Zeus's white shirt![28]

More than that: Zeus goes on to demonstrate his power and leadership abilities by defeating a series of dangerous challengers: the Titans and the monster Typhoeus (629–721, 820–68). In order to do so, he intelligently attracts important supporters: he corrects injustice committed by his predecessor and liberates the Cyclopes, who give him thunder and lightning (139–46, 501–6), and the three Hundred-Armers, superb fighters and prison guards (147–53, 617–735, 815–19). Moreover, by guaranteeing the continuation of honors and privileges to those who held them before and promising proper ones to those who were disadvantaged under Kronos, Zeus proves his willingness to reward his supporters (390–96), as he demonstrates in the case of Styx and her sons: Styx becomes the guarantor of the great oath of the gods, and Zeal, Victory, Power, and Force (Zelos, Nike, Kratos, and Bie) receive homes close to Zeus's own and thus, so-to-speak, form his bodyguard (383–390, 397–401).[29] Hesiod comments: "In the same way Zeus fulfilled his promises to all throughout" (402–3).

After the final victory the gods urge Zeus "to be king and lord of the immortals. And he allotted them privileges (*timai*) satisfactorily" (881–85). The programmatic announcement of the *Theogony's* beginning is fulfilled. Zeus rules not as a usurper and tyrant but with the consent and support of all gods, and based on just principles. Yet there is even more. Applying the methods of his genealogical systematization, Hesiod

---

26 Detienne and Vernant 1991. On the function of this part of the myth, M. West 1966: 401.

27 Just as the judges are supposed to pass straight, not crooked judgements (*WD* 219–26, 250–51. 256–64).

28 See below at n. 52. Peter Rose (oral communication) thinks that the potential for a tyrannical disposition is visible in what he calls "Zeus's mean streak" in his reaction to Prometheus's deception (*Th.* 550–52, but see M. West 1966 on 551) and in his rejoicing in Prometheus's and humankind's punishment (*WD* 59; M. West 1978: *ad loc.* "the cackle of triumph"). Yet, I suggest, this entire episode should also be read in terms of an intense rivalry between two leaders, an experience thoroughly familiar to Hesiod's audiences.

29 M. West 1966: 272 (on *Th.* 384) translates *zēlos* with glory: "not envying but being envied." "Zeal" might fit the context equally well. For a close analogy to the reward offered to Styx' sons, see *Od.* 21.213–16 with Odysseus's promises to the faithful herdsmen, Eumaios and Philoitios: they will become followers and brothers (*hetairoi kai kasignētoi*) of Telemachos and receive a wife and house next to Odysseus's own.

surrounds Zeus with wives and daughters representing personified virtues and values that mark an ideal king (886–917):[30] wisdom and intelligence, adherence to tradition and law, good order, justice, and peace, grace (an indispensable quality of leadership),[31] memory (of tradition and custom) and all aspects of the arts, not least honey-sweet speech that is crucial for success in the assembly—which brings us back to the hymn to the Muses introducing the *Theogony* (80–90).

Overall, then, Hesiod paints a carefully constructed image of a good leader who is able to gain power and popularity and is wise and just enough to maintain his rule. Undoubtedly, this image is intended as a model for elite leaders in human society, presenting a stark contrast to the injustice and corruption that characterizes the "gift-devouring" kings in Hesiod's other epic, *Works and Days*.[32] Hesiod thus reinterprets an old foreign story, integrating it into an ethical and political framework that seems to be absent in the extant Near Eastern "originals."

I should add that in this respect the Babylonion Creation Epic (*Enuma elish*) seems more closely comparable to the *Theogony* (although the succession myth told there is very different from that in Hesiod and the Hittite tradition).[33] Marduk too is elected to power, he is responsible for dividing privileges and setting up the stations for the gods, and he institutes a form of governance that is associated with social harmony and general satisfaction. Despite these important similarities, Hesiod differs from the *Enuma elish* in essential ways that would require a similarly detailed examination. Since Stephen Scully is offering such a study in the present volume, I will only mention a few relevant examples. Some of the differences are mainly due to cultural differences. Thus Marduk's rise to the position of king of the gods, like Zeus's, is approved by the divine assembly. Yet in Hesiod this happens *after* Zeus has proved himself a capable and just leader, and, in distributing functions and privileges, Zeus recognizes existing claims and does not deprive the other gods of their independence. In other words, the gods recognize Zeus's superiority and leadership without submitting to him unconditionally.[34] By contrast, Marduk uses a dire crisis to make kingship a condition for his martial exploits; his creation of a new (and very different) world order too will follow after his elevation. Moreover, the gods subject themselves to his absolute power: together with the power to rule, they also surrender their own autonomy and capacity to support themselves. The type of divine assembly and mode of decision-making, too, differ: here a sober and simple meeting (*agorē*),[35] there a sumptuous feast with much consumption of food and alcohol, followed by solemn coronation rituals and the prostration of the gods before their new king.[36] Overall, then, we have, on the one hand, an absolute, divinely sanctioned king at the top of a strictly hierarchical social order whose position predetermines his power and functions, and, on the other hand, the reflection, typical of the poet's time, of a Greek communal leader, a *primus inter pares*, whose position depends on his *proven* capabilities. A

---

30   For the intricate arrangement of this section, see Ramnoux 1987.

31   MacLachlan 1993; Meier 2000.

32   Clay 2003 rightly emphasizes the organic connection between the two main works of Hesiod. See also Solmsen 1949.

33   The Babylonian *Creation Myth* (*Enuma elish*) is in Foster 2005: 438–86; see Jacobsen 1976: 167–91; Michalowski 1990; M. West 1997: 280–83; for a comparison with Hesiod's *Theogony*, see Brown 1953; Walcot 1966: 27–54; Mondi 1984, and the excellent study of Scully, this vol.

34   Hesiod does not say the latter explicitly but it is a given in Greek epic tradition and belief; see, e.g. *Il* 15.184–217.

35   Scully (this vol.) shows how this detail fits into Hesiod's construction of Olympus as an ideal *polis*.

36   Mary Bachvarova considers it possible that at the end of the Kumarbi-Ullikumini-myth, which is preserved only in fragments, the rule of the victorious king of the gods was also legitimized by the assembly of the other gods (email, Oct. 2, 2005).

similar story but very different, with culturally determined interpretations that do not, in principle, exclude the possibility of the *Enuma elish* having served as a model for Zeus's role in the *Theogony*.

Another difference, though, is more profound and significant to the present discussion. At the end of *Enuma elish,* Marduk's qualities are listed impressively in fifty names or titles. Of these, exactly one mentions Marduk's function as god of justice; only two out of 200 lines are devoted to this topic (Foster 2005: 478):

> who administers justice, uproots twisted testimony, in whose place falsehood and truth are distinguished.

To repeat, Hesiod's story clearly has Near Eastern antecedents but these do not contain the model for his focus on the emergence of Zeus as a *just* leader and creator of a *just* world order although there is no doubt that elsewhere in Near Eastern traditions (for example, in royal inscriptions) justice plays a crucial role. Whatever Hesiod learned from Near Eastern traditions, and however he learned it, he fundamentally reinterpreted it, filled it with new content and meaning and made it serve his purposes and reflect the concerns of his time and society. Hence, if we limit ourselves to finding out what Hesiod borrowed from foreign traditions, we miss the crucial aspects of how he used and transformed these traditions.

3 Prometheus and Myths of Culture Heroes

Turning to a different myth, in extant Greek poetry, Prometheus appears prominently in both of Hesiod's epics and in a fifth-century tragedy, *Prometheus Bound*. Scholars have claimed that Prometheus' character as a trickster and culture hero was essentially borrowed from West Asian myths, by assimilating him to an important figure in the Mesopotamian pantheon, the wise Enki or Ea.[37] As above, let us examine the different versions of this figure.

What I find strangely unclear in Hesiod is Prometheus's relationship to humankind. His troubles begin at the time when gods and humans ceased to live together (that is, probably, at the end of the Golden Age).[38] During a sacrifice, Prometheus tricks Zeus into accepting the larger but worse parts of the sacrificial animal. As a punishment, Zeus hides the fire. Prometheus deceives Zeus again by stealing the fire, thereby prompting the creation of Pandora and all its miserable consequences. Now what does he, son of a Titan, a god, have to do with sacrifices, which are obviously an obligation not of gods but of humans? Why does Zeus punish humankind (first by withholding fire, then by the evils brought into the world by Pandora) for cheating at a sacrifice and stealing the fire—when both offenses were committed not by humans but by the son of a Titan?[39] The story of the fateful sacrifice in the *Theogony* obviously is etiological: it explains why humans sacrifice to the gods at all and why they receive the better parts of the sacrificial animal, and perhaps also why gods and humans are separated and humans no longer live in a Golden Age. But all this does not explain why *humans* suffer for Prometheus' transgressions. The answer to *this* question could be that Prometheus was very early seen as a

---

37   Duchemin 1974; Penglase 1994: ch. 9; S. West 1994. See also Trousson 1964.

38   The Prometheus myth in Hesiod: *Th.* 507–616; *WD* 42–105. For interpretation (including the sacrifice at Mekone), see Walcot 1966: ch. 3; M. West 1966: 305–308; Clay 2003: ch. 5. Further bibliog. in *Brill's New Pauly* 12 (2008): 6–10; *Lexicon Iconographicum Mythologiae Classicae* 7.1 (1994): 531–53.

39   That humankind is punished as a result of Prometheus's actions is said explicitly in *Th.* 550–52, 561–64, 570; *WD* 47–59.

sponsor or protector, or even the creator of humankind, in some ways as "ultimate man" or "superman," and that Hesiod already took this tradition for granted.[40]

The fact that Zeus withholds from humankind the ability to make, preserve, and carry the fire and that Prometheus steals it back from Zeus, proves that fire is essential to humans. The poet does not explain here in what ways this is true, and he does not speak explicitly of technology and civilization but it seems clear enough that by his very act of securing the fire for the humans Prometheus makes them capable not only of simply surviving but of developing their culture. Hesiod's Prometheus, therefore, is at least potentially a culture hero.

Now the idea that the Greek Prometheus is assimilated to the Mesopotamian Enki/Ea seems appealing. In Mesopotamian myth, Ea is the protector and advisor of Utnapishtim, Enki of Atrahasis.[41] These two figures (the counterparts of Noah in the Hebrew Bible and Deukalion in Greek myth) each construct, upon divine advice, an ark, fill it with all types of living beings, survive the great hood, and secure the continuation of humankind and all the animals that would otherwise have perished. In Greek myth Prometheus plays the role of Ea/Enki. It is hardly doubtful that this is a migrating tale originating in the East.

Enki is the Mesopotamian culture hero who, like Prometheus, is responsible for most, if not all, human achievements.[42] In contrast to Prometheus, Enki is one of the most powerful gods in the pantheon. His personality varies from sex maniac and drunkard to wise advisor and resolver of problems. He is a creator god who made a large part of the cosmos; he controls the *me,* the mysterious forces and rules that keep the world order going; he is the god of life-giving waters and fertility.[43] He is also considered the god of craftsmen, artists, and scribes. Let us look at two myths that seem especially illuminating.[44]

Enki and Inanna deals with the organization of the earth and its cultural processes. Placed in charge by the supreme gods, Anu and Enlil, Enki traverses his territory and provides for the essential needs of humans. He bestows fertility on the rivers and the fields irrigated by them. He fills the creeks with fish, the swamps with plants; he fertilizes the oceans, calls up rain clouds on the horizon, and for each of these areas he appoints a divine overseer. Irrigation makes it possible to cultivate the land.

> Enki trained the plow, the yoke, and the team,
>
> great prince Enki furnished them with oxen ...
>
> He opened the mouth of the holy furrow,
>
> made grow the grain in the seeded field.

(317–20, trans. Kramer and Maier 1989: 50)

40   On the creation of humankind: e.g., Walcot 1966: ch. 3; Luginbühl 1992 (224–26 on Prometheus); Clay 2003: ch. 4.
41   On Ea and Ut-napishtim, see tablet XI of the Gilgamesh epic, in Pritchard 1969: 93–97; George 2003: 88–99. On Enki and Atrahasis, Lambert and Millard 1999. Noah: *Gen* 6:5–9:17; Deukalion, son of Prometheus: Hesiod, fr. 2–4 Merkelbach and West; Pindar, *Olympian Ode* 9.49ff.; Epicharmus, *Poetae comici Graeci* I, fr. 113 (p. 73); see also Ovid, *Metam.* 1.336ff.; *Brill's New Pauly* 4 (2004): 321–22; *Lexicon Iconographicum Mythologiae Classicae* 3.1 (1986): 384–85. Generally on the myth of the Great Flood: Dundes 1988; Bottéro and Kramer 1989: ch. 13; García Martínez and Luttikhuizen 1998; see also Scodel 1982.
42   On Enki, see *Reallexikons der Assyriologie* II (1938): 374–79; Jacobsen 1976: 110–16; Kramer and Maier 1989: 1–21; Black and Green 1992: 75; Bottéro 1992.
43   On the *me,* see *Reallexikon der Assyriologie* VII (1990): 610–13; Black and Green 1992: 130; see also Farber-Flügge 1973.
44   For translations of the myths about Enki and Inanna, see Kramer and Maier 1989.

He sows the fields with all kinds of grains and vegetables. Then Enki builds houses, covers the steppes with rich vegetation and herds of wild animals, endows the domesticated animals with milk and fat and protects them in barns and pens. Finally, he builds temples, draws boundaries, and establishes the arts of weaving and sewing clothes.

Although humans profit in multiple ways, this myth is dominated by the perspective of the gods. It is a charter myth praising the great achievements of Enki. Moreover, as mentioned earlier, in Mesopotamian myth humans are slaves of the gods and were created only for this purpose.[45] Enki's care for their well-being therefore ultimately serves the higher purpose of enhancing the well-being of the gods: fat sheep make fat sacrifices.

Enki … filled the dining halls of the gods with luxury …

He packed the houses of the gods with goods.

With Enki they rejoiced and exulted.

(365–68; trans. Kramer and Maier 1989: 52)

Finally, the long catalog of Enki's gifts to earth and humankind does not seem to contain anything that points beyond the subsistence level of a farming community; the god does not pay attention to the values and qualities that make communal life possible on a higher level of culture. This is remarkable, since in the beginning of the story Enki is praised as lord of wisdom who blesses cities, initiates decisions and orders, is experienced in divination, supervises the calendar, knows the number of the stars, assigns the people their places to live, makes them follow their leaders, locks up the weapons in armories and guarantees the people's safety, and realizes justice.[46]

What matters here is even more clearly visible in another tale, *Inanna and Enki,* that tells of the transfer of the sum of cultural factors (*me*) from one city (Eridu) to another (Uruk) and thus explains why one Sumerian city rose to predominance at the expense of another.[47] This story presupposes that from time immemorial there existed a comprehensive catalog of values, abilities, powers, obligations, rules, and norms that concerned the cosmos and the earth, gods and humans, cities and countries, and many aspects of civilized life, and that guaranteed their relations and functioning. The supreme gods entrusted Enki with the administration of these "factors." He kept them in his temple in Eridu. In the story, the protector of Uruk, Inanna, visits her father, Enki. At the end of a long party with much drinking, Inanna persuades Enki to hand all these *me* over to her. She defends them against Enki's multiple efforts to regain them, and brings them triumphantly to her own city, Uruk.

Several times, these factors, around one hundred in total and divided into various categories, are recited. They primarily comprise insignia, abilities, behaviors, and emotions that pertain to royal and priestly rule. A few belong to the sphere of family and farming life, or to crafts or technical skills. What I find most important is that this fixed package of preexisting goods is kept, lost, and traded by the gods, completely independently of the humans who are affected by such machinations.

---

45 See the beginning of *Atrahasis* (Lambert and Millard 1999: 43–67; Dalley 1989: 9–18) or *Enki and Ninmah* (Kramer and Maier 1989: ch. 2) or tablet VI. 1–38 of *Enuma elish* (Foster 2005: 384–85). See also Bottéro and Kramer 1989: 502–40.
46 Lines 1–51, 61–80 (Kramer and Maier 1989: 39–41).
47 Kramer and Maier 1989: ch. 4; Farber-Flügge 1973.

I now turn to the tragedy, *Prometheus Bound,* attributed to Aeschylus. Many scholars doubt its authenticity but still date it to the fifth century.[48] Uniquely, its action unfolds primarily among gods and outside the inhabited world. Prometheus, chained to a rock by Zeus's henchmen, talks with various visitors about his conflict with the new king of the gods and its causes, and hints at the inevitable settlement of this conflict by compromise. Zeus is here sensationally represented as a tyrant. The quarrel between Zeus and Prometheus broke out, we learn, because, after ascending to power, Zeus distributed among the gods their shares of privileges (229–31), but ignored the human race and even planned to eliminate it and to create a new one (231–39). Why he wanted to do so remains unexplained. Nobody had the courage to contradict Zeus. Prometheus alone dared to save humankind from destruction. For this he now suffers bitter punishment. In fact, as it turns out, he did more than that: he expressly acted against Zeus's orders and endowed humankind not only with the fire but with the ingredients of culture.

The play focuses on interactions among gods; humans are only the cause and object of their quarrel. Nor are Prometheus's contributions to the cultural development of humankind important in themselves; they merely illustrate the extent of his rebellion against Zeus's tyrannical orders. Because the conflict between Zeus and his opponent is central to the play, the poet enhances Prometheus's own significance: instead of a cousin of Zeus he is here his uncle, instead of the son of an insignificant Titan he is a direct descendant of the primordial gods (Uranos and Gaia, Sky and Earth), whose wisdom and knowledge of the future he shares. This enables him, before their conflict erupts, to serve as Zeus's clever advisor and help him defeat the Titans. Moreover, his knowledge of the future gives him a trump card: Zeus needs him to survive a son's usurpation threatened by a prophecy (a motif already prominent in Hesiod).[49] Presumably in another play, his conflict with Prometheus must have been resolved, as the latter himself suggests.

The catalogue of cultural achievements Prometheus claims to have given the humans is worth quoting (with my emphasis):

> Of brick-built, sun-warmed houses, or of carpentry,
>
> they had no notion; lived in holes, like swarms of ants,
>
> or deep in sunless caverns; knew no certain way
>
> to mark off winter, or flowery spring, or fruitful summer;
>
> *their every act was without knowledge (gnōmē),* till I came.
>
> I taught them to determine when stars rise or set—
>
> a difficult art. Number, the primary science, I
>
> invented for them, *and how to set down words in writing—*
>
> *the all-remembering skill, mother of many arts*
>
> (*mnēmēn hapantōn, mousomētor' erganēn*).

---

48   On the question of the authenticity of *Prometheus Bound,* see Griffith 1977; Bees 1993. On sources and interpretation, e.g., Lefèvre 2003. On all these issues also Griffith 1983.

49   Prometheus as Zeus's advisor: 199–223, 304–5, 439–40; Zeus's dependence on Prometheus: 167–77, 186–92, 517–25, 755–90, 907–63; see Griffith 1983: 8–9.

I was the first to harness beasts under a yoke

with trace or saddle as man's slaves, to take man's place

under the heaviest burdens; put the horse to the chariot,

made him obey the rein, and be an ornament

to wealth and greatness. No one before me discovered

the sailor's wagon—flax-winged craft that roam the seas.

Such, tools and skills (mēchanēmata) I found for men ...

Now hear the rest of what I have to tell, *what crafts (technai)*

and methods (poroi) I devised—and you will wonder more.

First in importance: if a man fell ill, he had

no remedy, solid or liquid medicine,

or ointment, but for lack of drugs they pined away;

until I showed them how to mix mild healing herbs

and so *protect themselves against all maladies.*

Then I distinguished various modes of *prophecy,*

and was the first to tell them from dreams what Fate ordained

should come about; interpreted the hidden sense

of voices, sounds, sights met by chance upon the road.

The various flights of crook-clawed vultures I defined

exactly ... how to interpret signs in sacrifice ...

So much for prophecy. Next the *treasures of the earth,*

the bronze, iron, silver, gold hidden deep down—who else

but I can claim to have found them first? No one,

unless he talks like a fool. So, here's the whole truth in one word:

All human skill and science (technē) was Prometheus' gift!

(450–506, trans. Vellacott 1961: 34–35)

Prometheus thus mentions the construction of houses, carpentry, distinction of seasons by means of observing the sky, use of numbers and writing, taming wild animals and using them for agriculture and transportation, sailing, medicine, prophecy and the interpretation of omens, and the exploitation of treasures of the earth.

In sum, "all skills came to the humans from Prometheus." This global claim obviously transcends the range of items given in the catalogue, but this hardly matters. The poet, after all, is not a historian or sociologist of technology; Prometheus offers here no more than a set of (carefully selected) examples.

Another statement seems more important: "I caused men no longer to foresee their fate." How so? "I planted firmly in their hearts blind hopefulness." (We immediately think here of Hesiod whose Pandora allows all evils to escape from her jar but keeps hope trapped in it.) This, the chorus comments, is indeed a great and useful benefit. In addition, says Prometheus, I gave them fire. From this, all agree, "the mortals ... will learn many skills" (247–62). For this double offense Prometheus suffers punishment. Finally, he endowed the humans, who were witless like children, with reason and intelligence (443–50). Previously,

> they had eyes, but sight was meaningless;
>
> heard sounds, but could not listen; all their length of life
>
> they passed like shapes in dreams, confused and purposeless.

Now they act with insight and comprehension (*gnōmē*).

Even more: the poet describes the art of writing, invented by Prometheus, as an "all-remembering skill, mother of many arts" (460–61). In other words, writing makes it possible to hx memory and is the foundation of all arts. Prometheus, this means, does not give the humans all the arts but he teaches them the basic skills on which these depend. Nor does he give them wealth, but he teaches them to tame animals that, placed under the yoke or hitched to the wagon, offer them relief and symbolize wealth. This is crucial: what Prometheus gives to humankind is not a bag full of prefabricated elements that he himself disperses on earth, but skills and elementary abilities, reason and intelligence, that help them become human, only *now* in the full sense of the word, and develop their civilization themselves. He helps humans to help themselves: the words the poet uses (*technai, mēchanēmata, poroi*) designate means necessary for achievement. Prometheus is not a producer and distributor, but a teacher and educator. Learning is crucial to this poet: in his story even Zeus, the all-powerful god, has to learn and transform himself in order to survive.[50] In addition, Prometheus takes away knowledge of fate, including fear of death, and gives humans hope, that is, optimism, confidence—for the future and presumably in themselves. This makes possible initiative, development, progress; this results in culture. In this sense Prometheus is right: all skills ultimately come from his gifts!

Why is all this so upsetting to the gods and especially Zeus? I think because thereby the humans receive the potential to transcend their limitations. This interpretation receives crucial support from three aspects that Prometheus mentions at the end of his catalogue (478–504): remedies for illnesses, which means the ability to preserve and extend life; prophecy, that is, the ability to anticipate the future; and the exploitation of minerals, which is equivalent to the potential for technological advancement. I think we are here quite close to the famous "Ode to Man" in Sophocles' *Antigone: polla ta deina* ... But what is missing in Prometheus's list is a crucial factor that both Sophocles in his ode and Protagoras in his famous myth emphasize: human's ability to live together, to be social beings. Scholars presume, plausibly, that the poet of the *Prometheus* did not simply omit these qualities, but that they were bestowed on humankind in the great reconciliation between Zeus and Prometheus that must have followed in a later play.[51]

---

50   Meier 1993: 149–50.
51   Soph. *Ant.* 332ff.; Plat. *Prot.* 320ff., esp. 322c-d; Meier 1993: 152; Griffith 1983: 167–68.

Despite all the liberties that the tragic poet takes with the traditional story told by Hesiod, he constantly presupposes this tradition and plays with it. In Hesiod, Prometheus's trickery at the sacrifice and the subsequent theft of fire are embedded in a specific context of human evolution: the separation of humans from the gods, the end of the Golden Age. In *Prometheus Bound*, humankind is not only expelled, so to speak, from Paradise and compelled to work in order to survive, but threatened by complete annihilation. And Prometheus here does not only help them overcome this threat but gives them the potential of closing the gap to the gods again. This is dangerous and annoying indeed, and it would be even more so if the excessive and stubborn traits in Prometheus's character (178–80, 318–19, 964–65, 1034–35) could be presumed typical of humans as well. Zeus's anger is perfectly understandable from this perspective, quite apart from his tyrannical disposition, and on this even his divine critics agree.

Moreover, Hesiod had been motivated not least by political and social issues agitating his own time (including the injustice and favoritism typical of elite leaders). This had prompted him to portray Zeus as an ideal leader who could serve as a model for judges and leaders in Hesiod's own world. For good reasons, he therefore painted Zeus's predecessors in a negative light and stressed as much as possible the *justice* of Zeus. This made it necessary to plaster over an unclean and disturbing transition in Zeus's early career. We noticed the problem before: how do we get from Zeus, the violent usurper, who in his beginnings is hardly better than his father Kronos, to Zeus, the ideal ruler of gods and the world who is recognized and supported as such by all gods? Zeus the tyrant lurks in the wings of Hesiod's stage but is shut up in a closet.[52] The tragic poet has no such compunctions: he aims his scalpel exactly at this point and focuses with great determination precisely on Zeus's tyrannical potential. This aspect, and Zeus's eventual transformation from tyrant to just ruler, must have been very important to this poet and, presumably to his audience.

We need to remember here that tragedy in ancient Athens was not detached and elitist theater; it was deeply embedded in society. Often the poets enacted on stage problems and conflicts that were of great concern to their fellow citizens. In doing so, they helped the community gain a deeper understanding of such conflicts. The crucial aspects might be highlighted in a way that could not fail to attract the audience's attention. So too in *Prometheus Bound*: whether or not models already existed, it was a daring innovation to apply all the characteristics of a tyrant, with which the audience was thoroughly familiar, to Zeus, who was better known as protector of justice, and to get Zeus involved in a struggle for survival with Prometheus. As Prometheus predicts, this struggle must have been settled by compromise, and Zeus must have changed in a lost play from tyrant to wise ruler. Yet Zeus's unusual characterization in the extant play must have made it clear to the audience that matters of the greatest importance to them were at stake here. This much I consider certain. Unfortunately, what these matters might have been remains uncertain, especially since the play's date and authorship remain contested.[53]

Christian Meier has suggested, however, that in *Eumenides* Aeschylus had also dramatized a conflict between gods and allowed the new gods (Apollo, Athena, Zeus) to be criticized by the old ones (the Furies) as usurpers and breakers of the laws of tradition. Here already the role of Zeus the tyrant was well prepared, and the poet of *Prometheus Bound* only went a logical but decisive step further in this direction. We know the date and political context of the *Eumenides*: 458, four years after crucial reforms that sealed the breakthrough of democracy in

---

52 See above, n. 28.
53 Meier 1993: 137–59 offers a political interpretation of *Prometheus Bound*. Generally on the politics of Greek tragedy, see Meier 1993; Saïd 1998; Boedeker and Raaflaub 2005 (with bibliog.).

Athens but prompted severe dissatisfaction and communal strife. In that situation it made perfect sense to enact on stage a deeply worrisome and potentially lethal conflict between an old and new divine order that could only be resolved by integrating the old order into the new one.[54] Something similar may well underlie the plot of *Prometheus Bo und* but we cannot know this for sure.

At any rate, I hardly need to emphasize how far all this is removed from any possible Mesopotamian models of thought and interpretation. In conclusion, then, the poets of the *Theogony* and *Prometheus Bound* clearly used ancient and foreign Near Eastern myths and reinterpreted them on the basis of the conceptions, needs, and concerns of the time and society in which they lived. Such reinterpretation was largely influenced by the poets' political reflection; the poems are thus immensely valuable testimonies to Greek political thinking. By appropriating and reinterpreting them, the poets made the mythical past significant and useful for the present and at the same time maintained the present's interest in the past—a crucial condition for the Greek historical thinking that emerged at the same time. The poets' portraits of Zeus as the last in a series of divine kings, and Prometheus as a culture hero, are also part of a theory of cultural evolution—another important strand of Greek thought with Near-Eastern antecedents.[55] Yet, and this is crucial: in every respect, what the poets made of foreign models and impulses was distinctly new and different.

Indeed, it is not sufficient to find out what the Greeks borrowed from elsewhere; it is crucial to investigate how they transformed and adapted such borrowings. The next step would be even more fascinating: to ask what values and worldviews caused identical ideas to be interpreted so differently in different cultures. What does this teach us about social structures, hierarchies, relations, pressures, openness and lack thereof? Such a comprehensive comparative analysis would help decisively to overcome the unsatisfactory models of one-sided "influence" and "import" of cultural goods.

Bibliography

Abusch, T. 1995. Marduk. Pp. 1014–26 in *Dictionary of Deities and Demons in the Bible*, 2nd edition, edited by K. van der Toorn, B. Becking, & P.W. van der Horst. Leiden: Eerdmans.

Alster, B. 1992. Interaction of Oral and Written Poetry in Early Mesopotamian Literature. Pp. 23–69 in *Mesopotamian Epic Literature: Oral or Aural?*, edited by M.E. Vogelzang & H.L.J. Vanstiphout. Lewiston, NY: Edwin Mellen Press.

Bachvarova, M.R. 2009. Hittite and Greek Perspectives on Travelling Poets, Festivals, and Texts. Pp. 23–45 in *Wandering Poets in Ancient Greek Culture*, edited by R. Hunter & I.C. Rutherford. Cambridge: Cambridge University Press.

Bachvarova, M.R. 2005. The Eastern Mediterranean Epic Tradition from *Bilgamesh and Akka* to the *Song of Release* to Homer's *Iliad*. Greek, Roman, and Byzantine Studies 45.2: 131–153.

54   Meier's political interpretation of *Eumenides*: 1990: 82–137, 246–70; 1993: 102–37. On the democratic reforms of 462/1: Meier 1987; Raaflaub 2007.

55   For some of these aspects, see Raaflaub 1988, 2000, 2009b. For theories of cultural evolution, see Blundell 1986; Cole 1990.

Bachvarova, M.R. 2008. The Poet's Point of View and the Prehistory of the *Iliad*. Pp. 93–106 in *Anatolian Interfaces: Hittites, Greeks and their Neighbours*, edited by B.J. Collins, M.R. Bachvarova, & I.C. Rutherford. Oxford: Oxbow Books.

Baumgarten, A.J. 1981. *The Phoenician History of Philo of Byblos: A Commentary*. Leiden: Brill.

Bees, R. 1993. *Zur Datierung des Prometheus Desmotes*. Stuttgart: de Gruyter.

Black, J.A. and A. Green. 1992. *Gods, Demons and Symbols of Ancient Mesopotamia: An Illustrated Dictionary*. Austin: University of Texas Press.

Blundell, S. 1986. *The Origins of Civilization in Greek and Roman Thought*. London: Croom Helm.

Boedeker, D. and K. Raaflaub. 2005. Tragedy and City. Pp. 109–27 in *A Companion to Tragedy*, edited by R. Bushnell. Malden, MA and Oxford: Wiley-Blackwell.

Bottéro, J. 1992. Intelligence and the Technical Function of Power: Enki/Ea. Pp. 232–50 in *Mesopotamia: Writing, Reasoning, and the Gods*, translated by Z. Bahrani & M. Van De Mieroop. Chicago: University of Chicago Press.

Bottéro, J. and S.N. Kramer. 1989. *Lorsque les dieux faisaient l'homme: Mythologie Mésopotamienne*. Paris: Gallimard.

Brown, N.O., trans. 1953. *Theogony*. New York: Macmillan Publishing Company.

Bryce, T. 2008. Homer at the Interface. Pp. 85–92 in *Anatolian Interfaces: Hittites, Greeks and their Neighbours*, edited by B.J. Collins, M.R. Bachvarova, & I.C. Rutherford. Oxford: Oxbow Books.

Burckhardt, L., K. Seybold, and J. von Ungern-Sternberg, eds. 2007. *Gesetzgebung in antiken Gesellschaften: Israel, Griechenland, Rom*. Berlin: de Gruyter.

Burkert, W. 1992. *The Orientalizing Revolution: Near Eastern Influence on Greek Culture in the Early Archaic Age*, translated by W. Burkert & M. Pinder. Cambridge, MA: Harvard University Press.

Burkert, W. 2004. *Babylon—Memphis—Persepolis: Eastern Contexts of Greek Culture*. Cambridge, MA: Harvard University Press.

Clay, J.S. 2003. *Hesiod's Cosmos*. Cambridge: Cambridge University Press.

Cohen, M.E. 1993. *The Cultic Calendars of the Ancient Near East*. Bethesda, MD: Capital Decisions.

Cole, T. 1990. *Democritus and the Sources of Greek Anthropology*. 2nd edition. Oxford: Oxford University Press.

Dalley, S. 1989. *Myths from Mesopotamia: Creation, The Flood, Gilgamesh and Others*. Oxford: Oxford University Press.

Detienne, M. and J.P. Vernant. 1978. *Cunning Intelligence in Greek Culture and Society*, translated by J. Lloyd. Chicago: Chicago University Press.

Duchemin, J. 1974. *Prométhée. Le mythe et ses origines*. Paris: Belles Lettres.

Dundes, A., ed. 1988. *The Flood Myth*. Berkeley: University of California Press.

Ebbinghaus, S. 2008. Patterns of Elite Interaction: Animal-Headed Vessels in Anatolia in the Eighth and Seventh Centuries bc. Pp. 181–90 in *Anatolian Interfaces: Hittites, Greeks and their Neighbours*, edited by B.J. Collins, M.R. Bachvarova, & I.C. Rutherford. Oxford: Oxbow Books.

Edwards, A.T. 2004. *Hesiod's Ascra*. Berkeley: University of California Press.

Erler, M. 1987. Das Recht (*DIKE*) als Segensbringerin für die Polis. *Studi Italiani di filologia classica* 3rd series 5: 5–36.

Farber-Flügge, G. 1973. *Der Mythos "Inanna und Enki" unter besonderer Berücksichtigung der Liste der me*. Rome: Gregorian Biblical Bookshop.

Fehr, B. 1996. Kouroi e korai. Formule e tipi dell'arte arcaica come espressione di valori. Pp. 785–843 in *I Greci: Storia Cultura Arte Società*, II.1, edited by S. Settis. Turin: Giulio Einaudi.

Foley, J.M., ed. 2005. *A Companion to Ancient Epic*. Oxford: Wiley-Blackwell.

Foster, B.R. 2005. *Before the Muses: An Anthology of Akkadian Literature*. 3rd edition. Bethesda, MD: University Press of Maryland.

Gagarin, M. 1973. *Dike* in the *Works and Days*. *Classical Philology* 68: 81–94.

Gagarin, M. 1974. Hesiod's Dispute with Perses. *Transactions of the American Philological Association* 104: 103–111.

García Martínez, F. and G.P. Luttikhuizen, eds. 1998. *Interpretations of the Flood*. Leiden: Brill.

George, A.R. 2003. *The Epic of Gilgamesh*. Revised edition. London: Penguin Classics.

Griffith, M. 1977. *The Authenticity of 'Prometheus Bound.'* Cambridge: Camrbidge University Press.

Griffith, M., ed. 1983. *Aeschylus, Prometheus Bound*. Cambridge: Cambridge University Press.

Grottanelli, C. 1982. Healers and Saviours of the Eastern Mediterranean in Pre-Classical Times. Pp. 69–70 in *La soteriologia dei culti orientali nell'Impero Romano*, edited by U. Bianchi & M.J. Vermaseren. Leiden: Brill.

Güterbock, H.G. 1946. *Kumarbi: Mythen vom churritischen Kronos aus den hethitischen Fragmenten zusammengestellt, übersetzt, und erklärt*. Zürich: Europa Verlag.

Güterbock, H.G. 1948. The Hittite Version of the Hurrian Kumarbi Myths: Oriental Forerunners of Hesiod. *American Journal of Archaeology* 52: 123–134.

Güterbock, H.G. 1952. *The Song of Ullikummi: Revised Text of the Hittite Version of a Hurrian Myth*. New Haven: American Schools of Oriental Research.

Haas, V. 1994. *Geschichte der hethitischen Religion*. Leiden: Brill.

Haubold, J. 2002. Greek Epic: A Near Eastern Genre? *Proceedings of the Cambridge Philological Society* 48: 1–19.

Heubeck, A. 1955. Mythologische Vorstellungen des Alten Orients im archaischen Griechentum. *Gymnasium* 62: 508–525. Reprinted in Heitsch 1966: 545–570.

Hirzel, R. 1966. *Themis, Dike und Verwandtes. Ein Beitrag zur Geschichte der Rechtsidee bei den Griechen*. Leipzig: S. Herzel Verlag, 1907. Reprint Hildesheim: George Olms Verlag.

Hoffman, G.L. 1997. *Imports and Immigrants: Near Eastern Contacts with Iron Age Crete*. Ann Arbor: University of Michigan Press.

Hoffner, H.A. Jr. 1998. *Hittite Myths*. 2nd Edition. Atlanta: Scholars Press.

Hölscher, U. 1968. *Anfängliches Fragen: Studien zur frühen griechischen Philosophie*. Göttingen: Vandenhoeck & Ruprecht.

Humphreys, S. 1993. Diffusion, Comparison, Criticism. Pp. 1–12 in *Anfänge politischen Denkens in der Antike. Die nahöstlichen Kulturen und die Griechen*, edited by K. Raaflaub. Munich: Oldenbourg Wissenschaftsverlag.

Hurwit, J.M. 1985. *The Art and Culture of Early Greece, 1100–480 B.C.* Ithaca, NY: Cornell University Press.

Işık, F. 2004. Zur Entstehung der Falten und des Lächelns in der Ägäis. Pp. 127–50 in *Die Aussenwirkung des späthethitischen Kulturraumes*, edited by M. Novák, F. Prayon, & A.-M. Wittke. Münster: Ugarit-Verlag.

Jacobsen, T. 1946. Mesopotamia. Pp. 125–219 in *The Intellectual Adventure of Ancient Man*, edited by H. Frankfort, H.A. Frankfort, J.A. Wilson, T. Jacobsen, & W.A. Irwin. Chicago: Chicago University Press.

Jacobsen, T. 1976. *The Treasures of Darkness: A History of Mesopotamian Religion*. New Haven: Yale University Press.

Kramer, S.N. and J. Maier. 1989. *Myths of Enki, the Crafty God*. New York and Oxford: Oxford University Press.

Kreutz, N. 2004. Fremdartige Kostbarkeiten oder sakraler Müll? Überlegungen zum Stellenwert orientalischer Erzeugnisse in Olympia und zum Selbstverständnis der Griechen im 7. Jh. v. Chr. Pp. 107–20 in *Die Aussenwirkung des späthethitischen Kulturraumes*, edited by M. Novák, F. Prayon, & A.-M. Wittke. Münster: Ugarit- Verlag.

Kyrieleis, H. 1993. The Heraion at Samos. Pp. 125–53 in *Greek Sanctuaries: New Approaches*, edited by N. Marinatos & R. Hägg. London: Routledge.

Lambert, W.G. and A.R. Millard. 1999. *Atra-hasis: The Babylonian Story of the Old Flood.* Winona Lake: Eisenbrauns.

Lefèvre, E. 2003. *Studien zu den Quellen und zum Verständnis des* Prometheus Desmotes. Göttingen: Vandenhoeck & Ruprecht.

Lesky, A. 1950. Hethitische Texte und griechischer Mythos. *Anzeiger der* Österreichischen *Akademie der Wissenschaften* 57: 137–160. Reprinted in Lesky 1966: 356–371.

Lesky, A. 1955. "Griechischer Mythos und Vorderer Orient." *Saeculum* 6: 35–52. Reprinted in Lesky 1966: 379–400; Heitsch 1966: 571–601.

Luginbühl, M. 1992. *Menschenschöpfungsmythen. Ein Vergleich zwischen Griechenland und dem Alten Orient.* Bern: P. Lang.

MacLachlan, B. 1993. *The Age of Grace:* Charis *in Early Greek Poetry.* Princeton: Princeton University Press.

Markoe, G. 1985. *Phoenician Bronze and Silver Bowls from Cyprus and the Mediterranean.* Berkeley: University of California.

Matthäus, H. 2005. Toreutik und Vasenmalerei im früheisenzeitlichen Kreta: Minoisches Erbe, lokale Traditionen und Fremdeinflüsse. Pp. 291–350 in *Crafts and Images in Contact: Studies on Eastern Mediterranean Art of the First Millennium* bce, edited by C.E. Suter & C. Uehlinger. Fribourg and Göttingen: Academic Press.

Meier, C. 1987. Der Umbruch zur Demokratie in Athen 462/61 v. Chr. Pp. 353–80 in *Epochenschwelle und Epochenbewusstsein*, edited by R. Herzog & R. Koselleck. Munich: Wilhelm Fink.

Meier, C. 1990. *The Greek Discovery of Politics*, translated by D. McLintock. Cambridge, MA: Harvard University Press.

Meier, C. 1993. *The Political Art of Greek Tragedy*, translated by A. Webber. Baltimore: Polity.

Meier, C. 2000. *Politik und Anmut: Eine wenig zeitgemässe Betrachtung.* Stuttgart: Hohenheim Verlag.

Michalowski, P. 1990. Presence at the Creation. Pp. 381–96 in *Lingering over Words: Studies in Ancient Near Eastern Literature in Honor of William L. Moran*, edited by T. Abusch, J. Huehnergard, & P. Steinkeller. Atlanta: Scholars Press.

Millett, P. 1984. Hesiod and His World. *Proceedings of the Cambridge Philological Society* 30: 84–115.

Mondi, R. 1984. The Ascension of Zeus and the Composition of Hesiod's *Theogony. Greek, Roman, and Byzantine Studies* 25: 325–344.

Mondi, R. 1990. Greek and Near Eastern Mythology. Pp. 141–98 in *Approaches to Greek Myth*, edited by L. Edmunds. Baltimore: Johns Hopkins University Press.

Morris, S.P. 1992. *Daidalos and the Origins of Greek Art.* Princeton: Princeton University Press.

Nagy, G. 1990a. *Greek Mythology and Poetics.* Ithaca, NY: Cornell University Press.

Nagy, G. 1990b. *Pindar's Homer: The Lyric Possession of an Epic Poet.* Baltimore: Johns Hopkins University Press.

Ogden, D. 1998. What Was in Pandora's Box? Pp. 213–30 in *Archaic Greece: New Approaches and New Evidence*, edited by N. Fisher & H. van Wees. London and Swansea: Classical Press of Wales.

Osborne, R. 1998. *Archaic and Classical Greek Art*. Oxford: Oxford University Press.

Penglase, C. 1994. *Greek Myths and Mesopotamia: Parallels and Influence in the Homeric Hymns and Hesiod*. London: Routledge.

Pritchard, J.B., ed. 1969. *Ancient Near Eastern Texts, Relating to the Old Testament*. 3rd edition with Supplement. Princeton: Princeton University Press.

Pucci, P. 1977. *Hesiod and the Language of Poetry*. Baltimore: Johns Hopkins University Press.

Raaflaub, K.A. 1988. Die Anfänge des politischen Denkens bei den Griechen. Pp. 189–368 in *Piper's Handbuch der politischen Ideen*, I: *Frühe Hochkulturen und europäische Antike*, edited by I. Fetscher & H. Münkler. Munich: Piper.

Raaflaub, K.A. 1993. ed. *Anfänge politischen Denkens in der Antike. Die nahöstlichen Kulturen und die Griechen*. Munich: Oldenbourg Wissenschaftsverlag.

Raaflaub, K.A. 2000. Poets, Lawgivers, and the Beginnings of Political Reflection in Archaic Greece. Pp. 23–60 in *The Cambridge History of Greek and Roman Political Thought*, edited by C. Rowe & M. Schofield. New York: Cambridge University Press.

Raaflaub, K.A. 2005. Polis, 'the Political,' and Political Thought: New Departures in Ancient Greece, c. 800–500 bce. Pp. 253–83 in *Axial Civilizations and World History*, edited by J.P. Arnason, S.N. Eisenstadt, & B. Wittrock. Leiden: Brill.

Raaflaub, K.A. 2007. The Break-through of *demokratia* in Mid-Fifth-Century Athens. Pp. 105–54 in *Origins of Democracy in Ancient Greece*, edited by K.A. Raaflaub, J. Ober, & R.W. Wallace. Berkeley: University of California Press.

Raaflaub, K.A. 2008. Zeus und Prometheus: Zur griechischen Interpretation vorderasiatischer Mythen. Pp. 33–60 in *Christian Meier zur Diskussion: Autorenkolloquium am Zentrum* für *Interdisziplinäre Forschung der Universität Bielefeld*, edited by M. Bernett, W. Nippel, & A. Winterling. Stuttgart: Franz Steiner Verlag.

Raaflaub, K.A. 2009. Early Greek Political Thought in Its Mediterranean Context. Pp. 37–56 in *A Companion to Greek and Roman Political Thought*, edited by R.K. Balot. New York: Wiley-Blackwell.

Ramnoux, C. 1987. Les femmes de Zeus: Hésiode, *Théogonie*, vers 885 à 955. Pp. 155–64 in *Poikilia: études offertes à Jean-Pierre Vernant*, edited by M. Détienne, N. Loraux, C. Mósse, & P. Vidal-Naquet. Paris: Editions de l'Ecole des hautes études en sciences sociales.

Saïd, S. 1998. Tragedy and Politics. Pp. 275–95 in *Democracy, Empire, and the Arts in Fifth-Century Athens*, edited by D. Boedeker & K.A. Raaflaub. Cambridge, MA: Harvard University Press.

Sasson, J.M, ed. 1995. *Civilizations of the Ancient Near East*. 4 vols. New York: Charles Scribner's Sons.

Schwemer, D. 2001. *Die Wettergottgestalten Mesopotamiens und Nordsyriens im Zeitalter der Keilschriftkulturen*. Wiesbaden: Harrassowitz Verlag.

Schwemer, D. 2007. The Storm-Gods of the Ancient Near East: Summary, Synthesis and Recent Studies, pt. I. *Journal of Ancient Near Eastern Religions* 7: 121–168.

Scodel, R. 1982. The Achaean Wall and the Myth of Destruction. *Harvard Studies in Classical Philology* 86: 33–50.

Scully, S. 1997. Whose Greece? *International Journal of the Classical Tradition* 4: 247–255.

Seybold, K. and J. von Ungern-Sternberg. 1993. Amos und Hesiod. Aspekte eines Vergleichs. Pp. 215–39 in *Anfänge politischen Denkens in der Antike. Die nahöstlichen Kulturen und die Griechen*, edited by K.A. Raaflaub. Munich: Oldenbourg Wissenschaftsverlag.

Seybold, K. and J. von Ungern-Sternberg. 2007. Zwei Reformer: Josia und Solon. Pp. 103–61 in *Gesetzgebung in antiken Gesellschaften: Israel, Griechenland, Rom*, edited by L. Burckhardt, K. Seybold, & J. von Ungern-Sternberg. Berlin: de Gruyter.

Sherratt, S. and A. Sherratt. 1993. The Growth of the Mediterranean Economy in the Early First Millennium b.c. *World Archaeology* 24: 361–378.

Solmsen, F. 1995. *Hesiod and Aeschylus.* New York: 1949. Reprint Ithaca, NY: Cornell University Press.

Stampolidis, N.C. and A. Kotsonas. 2006. Phoenicians in Crete. Pp. 337–60 in *Ancient Greece: From the Mycenaean Palaces to the Age of Homer*, edited by S. Deger-Jalkotzy & I.S. Lemos. Edinburgh: Edinburgh University Press.

Tandy, D.W. and W.C. Neale. 1996. *Hesiod's Works and Days: A Translation and Commentary for the Social Sciences.* Berkeley: University of California Press.

Trousson, R. 1964. *Le thème de Prométhée dans la litérature européenne.* 2 vols. Geneva: Librairie Droz.

van Wees, H. 2009. The Economy. Pp. 444–67 in *A Companion to Archaic Greece*, edited by K.A. Raaflaub & H. van Wees. Malden, MA and Oxford: Wiley-Blackwell.

Vellacott, P. trans. 1961. *Aeschylus: Prometheus Bound, The Suppliants, Seven Against Thebes, The Persians.* Harmondsworth: Penguin Publishing Group.

Verdenius, W.J. 1985. *A Commentary on Hesiod: Works and Days, vv. 1–382.* Leiden: Brill.

Vernant, J.-P. 1989. At Man's Table: Hesiod's Foundation Myth of Sacrifice. Pp. 21–86 in *The Cuisine of Sacrifice among the Greeks*, edited by Marcel Detienne & J.-P. Vernant, translated by P. Wissing. Chicago: University of Chicago Press.

Vernant, J.-P. 1990. The Myth of Prometheus in Hesiod. Pp. 183–201 In *Myth and Society in Ancient Greece*, translated by Janet Lloyd. New York: Zone Books.

Walcot, P. 1966. *Hesiod and the Near East.* Cardiff: University of Wales Press.

West, M.L. 1966. *Hesiod: Theogony. Edited with Prolegomena and Commentary.* Oxford: Oxford University Press.

West, M.L. 1978. *Hesiod: Works and Days, Edited with Prolegomena and Commentary.* Oxford: Oxford University Press.

West, M.L. 1988. The Rise of the Greek Epic. *Journal of Hellenic Studies* 108: 151–172.

West, M.L. 1994. Ab ovo: Orpheus, Sanchuniathon, and the Origins of the Ionian World Model. *Classical Quarterly* 44: 289–307.

West, M.L. 1997. *The East Face of Helicon: West Asiatic Elements in Greek Poetry and Myth.* Oxford and New York: Oxford University Press.

Westenholz, J.G. 2009. Historical Events and the Process of Their Transformation in Akkadian Heroic Traditions. Pp. 26–50 in *Epic and History*, edited by D. Konstan & K.A. Raaflaub, 26–50. Malden, MA, and Oxford.

Woodard, R.D. 2007. Hesiod and Greek Myth. Pp. 108–50 in *The Cambridge Companion to Greek Mythology*, edited by R. Woodard. Cambridge: Cambridge University Press.

Zaccagnini, C. 1983. Patterns of Mobility among Ancient Near Eastern Craftsmen. *Journal of Near Eastern Studies* 42: 245–264.

Maurizio Bettini and Emlyn Eisenach

Legend has it that on the very day that Alcmene was supposed to give birth to Heracles in Thebes, Zeus addressed himself to all the gods, making the following boast:[1]

> Listen to me, all gods and all goddesses, as I say what the heart in my chest commands. Today Eileithyia, the goddess who brings labor pains, will reveal to the light a man who will rule all who dwell around him, one of the men who by lineage and blood descend from me.

1. The Cunning Interlocutor

Zeus, however, failed to take into account the extraordinary ingenuity of his wife, Hera, "the goddess who has devious thoughts." These are the words she spoke to him in reply:[2]

> You will be a liar, and you will never make your words come true.[3] So come on, swear to me now, Olympian, a solemn oath: swear that a man who on this day falls between a woman's feet will rule all those who dwell around him, one of the men who descend from the blood of your lineage.

Zeus did not realize the trap concealed in Hera's words and he swore a solemn oath, just as she requested. This is precisely the moment that the mind of Zeus was "blinded by Ate,"[4] or, in more practical terms, the moment when Zeus made a terrible mistake. As soon as he swore the oath, Hera went to work:[5]

> She leaped away from the peak of Olympus and quickly reached Argos in Achaea, where she knew the noble wife of Sthenelus, a descendant of Perseus, was carrying a son, and it was her seventh month. But Hera made the child come into the light even though it was not the proper month, while she interrupted Alcmene's labor and held back the goddesses of childbirth, the Eileithyiai. Then she herself gave the news to Zeus, the son of Kronos: "Father Zeus, god of the flashing lightning, I will give you a message to consider. A noble man has now been born who will rule the Achaeans, Erystheus, the son of Sthenelus, a descendant of Perseus. He is your kind; it is not unfitting for him to rule the Achaeans.

---

1   Homer *Iliad* 19.101–5.

2   Ibid., 19.107–11.

3   Hera employs a rarely used expression here, *pseustéseis*, as noted in Mark W. Edwards, *The Iliad: A Commentary*, vol. 5, *Books 17–20* (Cambridge: Cambridge University Press, 1985), 250, on lines 19.107–9. She is thus able to insinuate that Zeus will be proved to be a liar. Hera's taunt compels Zeus to restate his claim so that he is trapped, but at the same time her words unmistakably anticipate what is actually going to happen. Zeus's words will not turn out to be true after all, given that they are "falsified," as it were, by Hera's own intervention.

4   Homer *Iliad* 19.113: *aásthe*.

5   Ibid., 19.115–24.

Eurystheus could in fact claim to be a descendant of Zeus: his father, Sthenelus, was the son of Perseus, and Perseus in turn was the son of Zeus and Danaë.[6] The problem was precisely that Zeus had left behind quite a number of mortals who could claim to be his descendants. Hera prevented Alcmene from giving birth to Heracles while at the same time inducing labor in Nikippe, the wife of Sthenelus,[7] and in this way she was able to fulfill the solemn vow that Zeus had made before all the gods on Olympus while at the same time frustrating his firm intention to make Alcmene's son Heracles lord over all the Achaeans. As soon as Zeus realized what had happened, he was grief-stricken, and in a rage he cast Ate out of Olympus, whereupon she came to dwell among mortals instead.[8]

But what about the suffering of Alcmene? To tell the truth, Homer does not supply us with a detailed account of Alcmene's labor. All he says is that Hera "interrupted Alcmene's labor and held back the Eileithyiai," the goddesses who presided over childbirth.[9] The scholia commenting on this passage explain that the Eileithyiai were simply a figurative way to say "labor pains."[10] This turns Homer's story into something easy enough to understand (in the mind of one ancient scholiast at least), but also makes it far less meaningful: the Eileithyiai are indeed labor pains, but they are also goddesses, possessed of supernatural powers.[11]

Apparently, Homer was not especially interested in describing the precise way that the Eileithyiai were "held back," even though the story of Alcmene is not complicated to explain—as we will see later, the rhetorician Libanius was able to tell a perfectly acceptable version of the story in a few simple sentences. Homer could have done so just as well, except he did not want to. This is why, in order to find out what happened to Alcmene when Hera played her trick on Zeus, in later chapters we will have to turn to other versions of the story that are more generous with details. These are stories told not by a bard who sings the bloody adventures of heroes, but by storytellers who are instead represented (on more than one occasion) as women. The difference is remarkable.

2. The Four Themes of Homer's Story

Even if we must wait for other authors to supply us with the details of Alcmene's story, Homer's account of the intricate prologue among the gods still merits our attention, and it introduces four distinct themes for our consideration. The first concerns the way that Zeus formulates his initial pronouncement: why is it, after all, that Zeus instead of saying simply "my son" uses such a complex formulation: "one of the men who by lineage and blood descend from me"? The second matter is this: independent of how it was formulated, what is the meaning of this solemn declaration? Why must the birth of the child be preceded by this sort of prenatal

---

6   See the family tree below.

7   Her name is reported in Apollodorus *Library* 2.4.5.

8   Homer *Iliad* 19.125ff.

9   They are called "daughters of Hera" in the *Iliad*, 11.270–71, and in Hesiod *Theogony* 922. In Homer, we find both the singular Eileithyia and the plural Eileithyiai; in yet other versions of the story, as we will see, they are associated with other goddesses, the Moirai and the Pharmakides. See the remarks in Antoninus Liberalis, *Les Metamorphoses*, ed. and trans. Manolis Papathomopoulos (Paris: Les Belles Lettres, 1968), 134; and the detailed analysis of Paul Baur, "Eileithyia," *Philologus Supplement-band* 8 (1899–1901): 452–512; and Semeli Pingiatoglou, *Eileithyia* (Würzburg: Königshausen und Neumann, 1981). For Eileithyia in Latin poetry, see Hubert Petersmann, "Lucina Nixusque pares," *Rheinisches Museum* 133 (1990): 157–75.

10   Homer *Iliad* 19.119; and the relevant scholia in Hartmut Erbse, ed., *Scholia Graeca in Homeri Iliadem* (Berlin: De Gruyter, 1969–88), 4:603.

11   For a discussion of Eileithyia as a religious representation of labor pains, see chap. 4, sec. 3.

"decree"? The third topic we must address is the particular way that Hera distorts Zeus's solemn declaration, and the crafty use she makes of his words.

Finally, there is a more general issue to consider, one that has to do with the importance that Zeus, and thus also Hera, attaches to the particular day a child is to be born: it is the man who will be born *today*, Zeus declares, who will rule over the neighboring peoples. Much of this story depends on the element of timing and the manipulation of the precise time at which a child is to be born. The child born tomorrow will not have the same destiny as the one who was born yesterday.

3. The Secret Twins and the Fateful Decree

In many situations the Homeric gods appear to be driven by quite human emotions, as seems to be the case here. Given that Hera was standing right there, Zeus could not openly declare that he was about to have a son by another woman, much less that he had destined this son for greatness. Hera was jealous of Zeus's women,[12] and one of the reasons for her jealousy was precisely the fact that he did not make her a mother, denying her the chance to bear him "a son fine and strong."[13] Hera's husband preferred to make other women the mothers of his sons, or even to bear children himself.[14] The first element of Homer's story—Zeus's vague periphrastic reference to Heracles as "one of the men who by lineage and blood descend from me"—can thus probably be explained as a matter of reticence. In another setting—that is, if Hera had not been there—Zeus could have been more outspoken and therefore less ambiguous in his choice of words.

Zeus, in any case, was cautious about what he said. The required qualifications of the future ruler of "all who dwell around him" are carefully defined. The child Zeus intends must be born at a precise time, "today," and among all the other children born "today" he is further marked by belonging to those who descend from the "lineage and blood" of Zeus. And Zeus introduces one final detail: in addition to the child's belonging to "lineage and blood," Zeus adds that he must be "from me" (*ex emeû*). The use of the personal pronoun seems to signal the fact that there must be a direct and personal link between him and the designated child.[15] Would it not have sufficed to say born "from my lineage"? How many other descendants of Zeus could be expected to be born "today,"

---

12   See Diodorus Siculus *Library of History* 4.9.4, where Hera is explicitly said to be jealous of Alcmene, *zelotupoûsa*. On the anthropomorphic qualities of the Homeric gods, see the classic remarks of M. I. Finley, *The World of Odysseus* (London: Chatto & Windus, 1956), 147–51.

13   Editor's note: Zeus and Hera are known to have had children together, most importantly Ares, Hebe, Eileithyia, and (according to most myths) Hephaestus. However, neither Ares or Hephaestus were considered "fine and strong" by Zeus or Hera.

14   Hera's jealous reaction to her husband's infidelity is mentioned twice in the *Homeric Hymn to Apollo*, with reference to the birth of Apollo at lines 90–106 and the birth of Athena at lines 300–362. See the discussion in Massimo Pizzocaro, *Il triangolo amoroso: La nozione di "gelosia" nella cultura e nella lingua greca arcaica* (Bari: Levante, 1994), 53–58; and Marcel Detienne, *L'écriture d'Orphée* (Paris: Gallimard, 1989), 29–40. The motif of the "jealous wife" and the "persecuted rival" is found in many cultural traditions, as discussed in Alfred Nutt, *The Celtic Doctrine of Rebirth*, vol. 2 of *The Voyage of Bran, Son of Febal, to the Land of the Living; an Old Irish Saga*, ed. and trans. Kuno Meyer (London: David Nutt, 1897), 56 and n. 1.

15   Once again, it seems that the scholiasts risk impoverishing the text in their efforts to explain it: in this case, the scholia would posit the phrase "from my" (referring back to the "blood"), *ex emoû*, in place of *ex emeû*, "from me" (see the scholia to Homer *Iliad* 19.105b in Erbse 4:599, with a discussion in the apparatus ad locum). See also the observations of F. A. Pailey in *The Iliad of Homer* (London: Whittaker, 1871, 2:255, line 105), and Edwards, *Iliad*, 250–51. The scholia to *Iliad* 19.105c (in Erbse, 4:600) already notes that Zeus's words seem to refer ambiguously both to his sons and to all his descendants.

making it necessary for him to add that additional qualification, "from me"? Yet, as we will see, the problem is precisely that on that day at least two children would be born descended from Zeus, and not just one, because of a rather embarrassing aspect of Zeus's affair with Alcmene. As we learn from a poem once attributed to Hesiod, Alcmene had conceived one child with Zeus but also another child with her mortal husband, Amphitryon:[16]

> [Alcmene], submitting to the god, and to the man far best of men in Thebes of the seven gates, bore twin sons, whose hearts and spirits were not alike; it is true they were brothers, but the one was a lesser man, and the other a man far greater, a dread man and strong, Heracles the powerful. This one she conceived under the embraces of Zeus, the dark clouded, but the other one, Iphicles, to Amphitryon of the restless spear; seed that was separate; one lying with a mortal man and one with Zeus, son of Kronos, marshal of all the immortals.

In ancient Greece and Rome (as in medieval Europe) twins were often considered to be the result of adultery, as we see here in the case of Heracles and Iphicles.[17] Yet the situation is made even more complicated by the fact that Iphicles, the son of Alcmene and Amphitryon, could also be said to have at least a drop of Zeus's blood in his veins, given that Iphicles was a distant descendant of Zeus, much like Heracles' rival Eurystheus, the son of Sthenelus and Nikippe. Zeus was unbeatable at tangling genealogies: the father of Iphicles, Amphitryon, was in turn the son of Alcaeus, the son of Perseus, who was the son of Zeus. And even Alcmene, Iphicles' mother, was the daughter of Elektryon, who was himself a son of Perseus, an altogether complicated situation, as this genealogical chart reveals:[18]

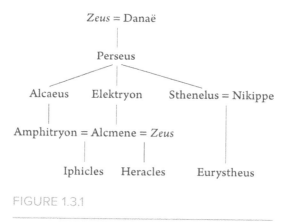

FIGURE 1.3.1

16 (Pseudo-) Hesiod *Shield of Heracles* 48–56 (translation from Hesiod, *Hesiod: the Works and Days, Theogony, the Shield of Herakles*, trans. Richard Lattimore [Ann Arbor: University of Michigan, 1959], 193–94). For the interpretation of the phrase *homà phronéontes* in line 50, compare Homer *Iliad* 5.440.

17 For twins as the outcome of adultery, see Francesca Mencacci, *I fratelli amici: La rappresentazione dei gemelli nella cultura romana* (Venezia: Marsilio, 1996), 10–14. There might also have been a link assumed between Alcmene's supposed (albeit involuntary) adultery and her extraordinary labor pains and difficult delivery. In some cultures, a woman having a difficult labor was interrogated about any possible adultery and it was believed that she would not be able to give birth until she confessed. On this, see Hastings *ERE*, s.v. "Birth," esp. p. 638b.

18 The chart is based on the genealogies found in Apollodorus *Library* 2.4.5. The inventory of Perseus's descendants is basically the same in the mythographers, with the most important difference having to do with the greater or lesser degree of kinship that is posited between Alcmene and her husband Amphitryon. See R. Raccanelli, *Prima di Plauto: Il racconto di Anfitrione* (Tesi di laurea, University of Venice, 1987, 126–61).

Zeus had thus seduced his own great-granddaughter, Alcmene, who was herself married to one of his great-grandsons, Amphitryon. As a result, the night Zeus spent with Alcmene in Thebes made quite a mess of things: not only his own son, Heracles, but also Heracles' twin brother, Iphicles, the son of Amphitryon, could be considered descendants of Zeus by "lineage and blood." Iphicles, the lesser of the twins, was actually related to Zeus twice over, on both his mother's and father's sides. Adding "from me" is hardly overdetermination; if anything, it is the bare minimum required to identify Heracles as the descendant Zeus has in mind.

Thus, although Zeus is being reticent, he is nevertheless choosing his words with care in order to distinguish between the twins. Regardless, however, of the reasons Zeus might have had for choosing these particular words, how are we to understand the second, more basic, issue raised by the Homeric narrative? That is, why must the birth be marked by a solemn prenatal decree? The fact, as we have seen, that Zeus's public pronouncement has something to do with needing to distinguish between the two twins born to Alcmene, Heracles and Iphicles, may help us to understand.

As Claude Lévi-Strauss has shown at great length in one of his more recent works, distinguishing between twins is a complex cultural problem.[19] There are, for example, many Amerindian myths in which two twins show themselves to have different characteristics and abilities, as in the story of Maire-Ata told by a Brazilian tribe (a story recorded as early as the seventeenth century). Maire-Ata had married a woman from his village, and she became pregnant. But when the woman was out traveling about, she was also impregnated by Opossum, and conceived a son "who kept company in her womb with the first one." The woman was then killed by members of an enemy tribe, but before eating her they threw the twins away with the trash. Another woman found and raised them, and the boys vowed that one day they would avenge their mother's death. The two boys were not identical, however: the son of Opossum proved to be invulnerable, while the son of Maire-Ata was not.[20] As in the case of Heracles and Iphicles, these are twins with two different fathers, one twin superior to the other.

What could be the basis for this kind of story? It appears that twin birth presupposes distinct and separate fathers, a situation that must somehow be immediately narrated and described. By denying the possibility of identical, perfectly equal, "doubles" as suggested by the twins, and by insisting instead on marked differences between them—and on their different fathers—these stories reaffirm the rule of uniqueness.[21]

Lévi-Strauss's observations become even more interesting if we link them to the sort of prenatal "sentence" that is issued by Zeus at the beginning of Alcmene's story. For example, Lévi-Strauss includes a type of myth in which a prenatal, fateful sentence is addressed directly to an unborn child: "If you are a girl you will live, but

19   Claude Lévi-Strauss, *The Story of Lynx*, trans. Catherine Tihanyi (Chicago: University of Chicago Press, 1995).

20   Ibid., 46–47.

21   To summarize his approach very briefly, Lévi-Strauss argues that in Amerindian mythology, twins are *not* in fact identical, because they are supposed to have different fathers; moreover, twins do not even exist in many cultures because they are immediately separated at birth and one of them is killed. In this context, the twins thus appear to be a good way to "think" about identities that appear to be the same but that are actually composed of different elements, as in such pairs as Sun/Moon or Europeans/Natives. These binary pairs are composed of elements that are in some sense equivalent but which are actually not the same and can never be equated with one another. Therefore, in cases where twins are posited at the beginning of two different lineages (as in the case of the European and Native peoples), the meaning that emerges is quite complex: the myth tells us that the Europeans and the Indians do constitute a perfect binary pair, just like twins, but at the same time emphasizes that in reality these categories are not identical, as is also the case with twins. According to Lévi-Strauss, this understanding of the twins is not typical of Indo-European culture, where it is instead often the case that the twin pair is linked to an actual duplication of the same identity. For a discussion, see Mencacci, *I fratelli amici*, 56–107.

if you are a boy you will die." There are many things that might drive someone to make this type of decree. For example, an oracle might have made an unfavorable prediction, or a father might be terrified by the possibility that a son would carry off all his possessions, and so on. In any case, the fact remains that the sentence pronounced prior to birth serves in some way to distinguish, to identify a being who will be born but who does not yet exist.

There is a similar motif in a myth told by the Kutenai, a tribe that lived in the foothills of the Rocky Mountains. Yaukekam, the founding hero of the tribe, was sent to visit his grandmother when he was still an infant. When Yaukekam arrived at his grandmother's house, the old woman was sleeping. When she woke up she realized that a child had been in the house, but: "No one knows if it's my grandson or my granddaughter," she exclaimed. The old woman identified the child as follows: she put out a tiny bow and a tiny basket and then went back to bed. Based on whether the baby Yaukekam upon his return chose the bow or the basket, that is, the toy for boys or the toy for girls, she would receive her answer.[22] This is the problem: the being that has come into her house has for the moment only a virtual identity. In order to acquire its own particular identity, its individuality, the identity must be revealed and it must be done according to certain rules that are established before the moment of identification takes place.

In a sense the child that is not yet born, or who is not yet seen, exists as a sort of "twin to itself," a pair of possibilities, one of which must be separated from the other.[23] From this perspective, the sentence, the condition set at the birth of a still-unknown child, is no different from the proof that two twins give of themselves at the moment of their birth, openly declaring their respective paternities and therefore their precise identities. Thus Zeus's solemn decree, made at the time of Heracles' birth and meant to distinguish between the paternal identities of the twins, seems to belong to the general category of fateful sentence, which in Amerindian myth is made at a birth for a certain reason or because of some doubt or uncertainty.

Heracles' identity, moreover, must be affirmed not only by Zeus's prenatal decree, but also by a proper identity test. Aelian tells us, for example, that as soon as "Heracles was delivered ... [he] at once began to crawl."[24] The son of a god displays exceptional qualities that immediately distinguish him from the sons of mortal fathers.[25] In a version of the story told by Pherekydes, we find an even more explicit test of Heracles' identity.[26] After Alcmene gave birth to twins, Amphitryon let loose two snakes in the bed where the babies

---

22 In comparative terms, this is essentially the same motif that we find in the story of Odysseus detecting Achilles when he has been sent into hiding disguised as a girl.

23 Lévi-Strauss, *Story of Lynx*, 60.

24 Aelian *On the Nature of Animals* 12.5 (translation from Aelian, *On the Characteristics of Animals*, trans. A. F. Scholfield [Cambridge, MA: Harvard University Press, 1958–59]).

25 On the exceptional behaviors displayed by the hero immediately after his birth, see Alwyn Rees and Brinley Rees, *Celtic Heritage: Ancient Tradition in Ireland and Wales* (London: Thames & Hudson, 1961), 223–24, 241, 244–51. The Rees brothers propose a paradigm for the Celtic hero's conception, birth, and postnatal demonstrations of prowess that is strikingly similar to the story of Heracles. In a late Byzantine version of the *Alexander Romance* (for a discussion of the various Greek versions of the story, see n. 44 below), the newborn Alexander immediately begins to speak and prophesy to his mother about his future conquests. For a discussion of this episode of the story as a sign of Alexander's divine "election," see Corinne Jouanno, "Le Romance d'Alexandros ou l'enfance d'un héros," in *Enfants et enfance dans les mythologies: Actes du VIIe colloque du Centre de recherches mythologiques de l'Université de Paris-X (Chantilly, 16–18 septembre 1992)*, ed. Danièle Auger (Paris: Université de Paris X-Nanterre, 1995), 272.

26 Pherekydes 3 F 68 (in Felix Jacoby, *Die Fragmente der griechischen Historiker* [Berlin: Weidmann, 1923–40; Leiden: Brill, 1941–]), 2:79 = Apollodorus *Library* 2.4.8 (translation from Apollodorus, *The Library*, vol. 1, trans. Sir James George Frazer [Cambridge, MA: Harvard University Press, 1921], 175); also, the scholia to Pindar *Nemean Odes* 1.65. We will see

were sleeping "because he would know which of the two children was his son, and when Iphicles fled in fear, and Heracles stood his ground, he knew that Iphicles was begotten of his body" (fig. 1.3.2).

FIGURE 1.3.2   Baby Hercules strangling two serpents. An ancient Roman fresco in the Casa dei Vettii, Pompeii, Italy. Photograph: Scala/Art Resource, New York.

4. Ate and Hermeneutics

Zeus is in a difficult position. He must describe a highly complex situation (two twins who are both in some way connected to him, whom he must distinguish from each other) and do so in a setting that is rather hostile. It is thus not surprising that he has recourse to a sort of linguistic compromise, a construction equal parts calculation and ambiguity.[27] Zeus is clever, but he makes one serious error: he takes the element of timing for

later that the weasel is an animal implicated in this drama of prenatal identification. In the *Physiologus latinus* (Francis J. Carmody, ed., *Physiologus Latinus Versio* Y [Berkeley: University of California Press, 1941], 34), it says that the weasel gives birth through the ears, producing male babies from her right ear and female babies from her left ear. For a discussion of the weasel in different versions of the *Physiologus*, see chap. 7, sec. 6.

27   See, for example, Sigmund Freud's definition of this phenomenon in "Der Wahn und die Träume in Wilhelm Jensens 'Gradiva,'" in vol. 8 of *Gesammelte Werke: Chronologisch Geordnet*, ed. Anna Freud et al. (Frankfurt: S. Fischer Verlag, 1961–83); Italian translation: "Il delirio e i sogni nella Gravida di Wilhelm Jensen," in *Opere*, vol. 5 (Torino: Boringhieri, 1972): see esp. pp. 326–28. See also the excellent comments of Francesco Orlando in *Illuminismo e retorica freudiana* (Torino: Einaudi, 1982), 3–28.

granted. "Today," he says, completely confident that he knows what he is talking about. What could be surer than a birthday for identifying a child? We regard the date of our birth with the same confidence, recording it on our identifying documents. The problem, however, is that Zeus is not the god in charge of birth and birthdays: this is Hera's domain. Hera is the mother of the Eileithyiai, and they, not Zeus, are the divinities who decide precisely when a woman brings an end to her labors and gives birth.[28] Precisely this element will play a crucial role in the third aspect of Homer's story that we need to consider: the way that Hera was able to turn the words of Zeus's solemn oath to her advantage.

Alcmene's troubles are thus the result of this hermeneutic contest between Zeus and Hera. Hera restates her husband's words and asks the fateful question: Is this really what you mean to say? It is a question of meaning and interpretation. Hera asks her husband to swear by a solemn oath that he really said what he said, and as she makes this demand, she restates bit by bit what Zeus had said, asking whether he is willing to endorse their meaning once again. The trick, however, depends on the fact that there is a tiny difference between Hera's version of Zeus's words and what he actually said. The notorious pronoun "from me" vanishes from Hera's version, and is replaced by an adjective. Hera does not say "one of the men who by lineage and blood descend from [you]," but instead "one of the men who descend from the blood of your lineage" (*hoì sês ex haímatos ... genéthles*).[29] Zeus does not exercise critical listening skills and fails to notice the small difference between his words and Hera's when he swears to her version. When Ate gets involved in hermeneutics, the result cannot help but be a disaster (*pollòn aásthe*): as Homer says of Zeus's oath, the poor man was "seriously blinded."

In addition, Hera has changed the way the birth is to take place. Zeus had originally said that "today Eileithyia, the goddess who brings labor pains, will reveal to the light a man ..." We could call this the usual way to refer to childbirth in Homeric language: the goddess of childbirth will make the baby come into "the light." But in Hera's formulation, the baby will "fall between a woman's feet." It is an odd expression. Why is it that in Hera's version the baby cannot be "revealed to the light" by the usual goddess, but instead is destined to "fall between the feet" of its mother?[30] Modern commentators confronting this problem have taken Hera's words to be a kind of "naive" expression, or even a "primitive" description of childbirth. In other cases, the commentators simply consider this to be an allusion to the mother kneeling in order to give birth and make no further conjectures.[31] Only the commentators Ameis and Hentze put forward a more insightful observation:[32] "This phrase is used in place of Zeus's words (19.103) because the birth of Eurystheus, as Hera intends, is not

---

28 For the Eileithyiai as the "daughters of Hera," see n. 9 above.

29 Homer *Iliad* 19.111. For the interpretation of this line and its "piled up genitives," see Edwards, *Iliad*, 250–51. In Homeric criticism, the discrepancy between lines 19.111 and 19.105 has been understood as a textual problem that must be "fixed," and it has even been proposed that the two lines should be made to agree, which would surely be a mistake (see, for example, the long discussion in C. G. Heyne, "Variae lectiones," in Homer, *Homeri carmina cum brevi annotatione*, ed. C. G. Heyne [Leipzig: Weidmann, 1802], vol. 7, and also G. D. Montbel, *Observations sur l'Iliade d'Homère* [Paris: Didot, 1830], 2: 157–58).

30 For the woman in childbirth, see chap. 3, sec. 1.

31 See Pailey, *Iliad of Homer*, 255 ("a primitive expression for delivering by quick travail"); W. Leaf, *The Iliad* (Amsterdam: Hakkert, 1902), 326 ("a naive expression = be born"); and Edwards, *Iliad*, 250 ("come to birth ... a kneeling position for childbirth indicated at Hymn. Ap. 117–18"). Yet if we consider Hera's words in a more anthropological framework, this motif of the baby "falling" turns out to be of considerable significance. There are many cultures in which birth is associated with a "fall" which is juxtaposed with the ritual "picking up" of the baby by the father who in this way acknowledges the baby's legitimacy. For a discussion of birth as a "fall," see *Enciclopedia*, ed. Ruggiero Romano (Torino: Einaudi, 1980), vol. 9, s.v. "Nascita." In Hesiod *Theogony* 460 we find the remark that Cronus devoured "every baby that fell out from the womb of the sacred mother [Rhea] between her knees."

32 Homer, *Homers Ilias*, ed. and trans. Karl Friedrich Ameis and Karl Hentze (Leipzig: Teubner, 1878), on line 19.110.

carried out with the help of Eileithyia." In other words, the Eileithyiai cannot attend Nikippe, the mother of Eurystheus, since they will instead be at Alcmene's side, "held back" there, as Homer puts it.

But aside from the presence or absence of the Eileithyiai during Nikippe's labor (a problem that is already overly positivistic), there is no doubt that there was something hurried and unexpected about Eurystheus's birth, driven by the necessity of Zeus's determination that "today" was when the child must be born. Nikippe was only seven months pregnant, but Hera was nevertheless ready to bring the child into the light before his time. Given that she was not expecting to go into labor, Nikippe had not arranged for anyone to assist her, which could account for the baby "falling between her feet." Perhaps she was taking a walk and grabbed hold of a tree for support when she was suddenly struck by the unexpected labor pains. Or perhaps she suddenly collapsed. Who knows?[33] What matters is that Hera has taken charge of Eurystheus's birth, and she is the one who decides when and how his mother, Nikippe, will go into labor. Although Zeus was able to turn time to his advantage, as myth tells us, making the night he spent with Alcmene last as long as three nights,[34] in this case it is Hera who makes use of time. And when Hera comes back to Olympus to tell Zeus about the birth of Eurystheus and to have him designated as the future ruler of the neighboring peoples, her interpretation of Zeus's infamous oath is so brief and blasé as to be insulting: the boy is "your kind," she says, and worthy to rule the Achaeans. In the end, Zeus's elaborate, evasive formulas have been reduced to a single phrase, *sòn génos*, "your kind." Blame it on Ate.

5. Unless the Child Comes Out through My Side

So far we have considered three of the different themes involved in Homer's story. We now have some idea of why Zeus chose to express the identity of the unborn child in such ambiguous and complicated terms, and why this birth had to be marked by this sort of precautionary decree. In addition, we have also found some of the factors that made it possible for Hera to so adroitly propose a false interpretation of Zeus's pronouncement, turning it to her own purposes. There remains a fourth and final aspect of Homer's story that deserves our consideration: the meaning of time itself, and of the timing—the precise timing—of a baby's birth.

It is the baby born "today" (and not some other day) who will become a great hero. Of course, the specificity or excellence of one day as opposed to another day does not depend only on the word of Zeus. There are,

---

33 In the Western tradition there was, however, another very famous baby who was destined to "fall to the ground" at the moment of his birth: Alexander the Great, whose extraordinary birth is narrated in the so-called *Alexander Romance*. In this case his mother, Olympias, was condemned to give birth unaided by any helping hands. Not that she was alone: Nectanebo, the Egyptian magician who had seduced her, was standing by, but he was busy reading the astrological signs so that the most auspicious moment could be chosen for Alexander's birth. For the Greek versions of this story, see n. 44 below. In the Latin versions, Olympias gives birth while seated. See Julius Valerius *Res Gestae Alexandri Macedonis*, in Bernard Kübler, ed., *Iuli Valeri Alexandri Polemi Res gestae Alexandri Macedonis translatae ex Aesopo graeco* (Leipzig: Teubner, 1888), 6, and the version of Leo Archipresbyter, *Historia Alexandri Magni (Historia de preliis): Rezension J1*, ed. Alfons Hilka and Karl Steffens (Meisenheim am Glan: A. Hain, 1979), 9, where the baby is also said to fall on the ground. For depictions of the birth of Alexander in illustrated manuscripts, see D. J. A. Ross, "Olympias and the Serpent," in his *Studies in the Alexander Romance* (London: Pindar Press, 1985), esp. 347ff. Ross notes that in the later iconographic tradition, the depiction of Olympias giving birth while sitting on a birthing chair (*díphros*) is gradually replaced by a depiction in which she is shown lying on a bed, the birth position more familiar to a European audience.

34 Apollodorus *Library* 2.4.5.

in fact, various ways that the propitiousness of a given day could be determined. In archaic Greece, Hesiod indicated that some days of the month were good for conceiving boys and other days for girls; moreover, he explained the character or qualities that could be expected from someone born on a given day of the month.[35] As for Heracles, he not only failed to be born on the propitious day determined for him by his father but also was finally born on a day that was traditionally unlucky, the fourth day of the month. According to Philochorus of Athens, people like Heracles born on the fourth of the month "work only so that others can enjoy the fruits of their labors."[36]

In addition to the days of the month, there are, of course, the stars: nothing can match the complicated conjunctions of the heavenly bodies for determining the lucky or unlucky quality of a particular day or particular time for a baby to be born. Suetonius, for example, tells us that when Augustus was born, Octavius, his father, was late arriving to the Senate because he had stayed at home to attend his wife's delivery of the child. It was the day that the Senate was debating what to do in response to the Catiline conspiracy, and a great expert in soothsaying and astrology "learning of the reason for [Octavius's] tardiness and being informed also of the hour of the birth, declared that the ruler of the world had been born."[37]

It is worth comparing here the Annunciation, in which Mary was informed about the coming birth of Christ:[38]

> And, behold, thou shalt conceive in thy womb, and bring forth a son, and shalt call his name Jesus. He shall be great, and called the son of the Highest: and the Lord God shall give unto him the throne of his father David: And he shall reign over the house of Jacob forever.[39]

The angel's pronouncement seems to follow the same basic pattern as the horoscope made by the ancient astrologers on the occasion of a child's conception.[40] Needless to say, the narrative of Christ's nativity later involves the famous star seen in the east, which was a sign to the Magi that a king of the Jews was about to be born.[41] Given the significance attributed to astrological signs, it was considered important to record precisely

---

35   Hesiod *Works and Days* 782ff. These lines in Hesiod are often considered to be the first evidence of "astrological" belief in Greek literature; see comments in T. A. Sinclair, ed., *Hesiod: Works and Days* (Hildesheim: Olms, 1966), 84 on lines 788–89. Herodotus attributed similar beliefs to the Egyptians, *Histories* 2.82.

36   Philochorus 328 F 85 (in Jacoby, *Fragmente*, 3b:123). Philochorus attributes a proverbial value to this expression: "you were born on the fourth of the month" means that you work for others.

37   Suetonius *Divus Augustus* 94.5 (translation from Suetonius, *Suetonius*, vol. 1, trans. J. C. Rolfe [Cambridge, MA: Harvard University Press, 1998]). There are also predictions made by the *mathematicus* Scribonius on the occasion of Tiberius's birth (Suetonius *Tiberius* 14). For the importance of astrology in the Roman world, see A. Bouché-Leclercq, *L'astrologie grecque* (Brussels: Culture et Civilisation, 1963), 542ff. In yet another example of the legendary coincidence that can accompany the birth of a hero, Suetonius (*Augustus* 94) reports that the Roman Senate had decreed that all the babies born in the year in which Augustus was born were to be killed and that fathers who were expecting the birth of a child had prevented the decree from being published (the similarities to the birth story of Christ are obvious). For a discussion of the widespread belief that "everyone has a star in the sky" or "he was born under a lucky star," see Franz Cumont, *After Life in Roman Paganism: Lectures Delivered at Yale University on the Silliman Foundation* (New York: Dover, 1959), 92–93.

38   Luke 1:31–33 (King James Version).

39   On the conception of Christ through the ear, see chap.7, secs. 6 and 7.

40   J. Weiss in an oral communication reported in Franz Boll, "Die vierte Ekloge des Virgil," in his *Kleine Schriften zur Sternkunde des Altertums* (Leipzig: Koehler & Amelang, 1950), 332.

41   Matthew 2:1–2. On the star seen by the Magi, see the discussion in F. C. Conybeare, *Myth, Magic, and Morals: A Study of Christian Origins* (Boston: Beacon Press, 1925), 193. Augustine returned to this topic repeatedly in his writings, because it seemed to sanction the practice of astrology; for a discussion of Augustine's response, see Lynn Thorndike, *A*

the dates of both a child's conception and its birth (although there was much debate among the astrologers as to which of these pieces of data was more relevant).[42] According to Godfrey of Viterbo, for example, at the moment of the conception of Arthur, son of Igierna and Uther Pendragon (who had disguised himself as Gorlois, Igierna's husband), the "night, day, and hour" that this event took place were scrupulously recorded.[43] In some stories, the astrologer was supposed to have been present in person at the moment of birth, which was also the case at real births (and when the astrologer was not present, the task of inspecting the heavens was simply assigned to the midwife).[44] In other cases, the astrologer is not only present at the moment of birth but in a certain sense manages the entire process, as in the legend of Alexander the Great.[45]

As in the story of Eurystheus's birth, Alexander's birth involved not simply the coincidence of the birth of a hero with a specific astral conjunction that occurs naturally at the time of the birth, but rather a situation

---

History of Magic and Experimental Science (New York: Columbia University Press, 1964), 1:518–19. There are also Jewish legends based on the motif of a natal star which are similar to the story of Christ's nativity. For example, on the night when Abraham was born, the astrologers and wise men of Nimrod saw a great star rise in the east which crisscrossed the heavens and devoured the four other stars that marked the cardinal points. See Louis Ginzberg, *The Legends of the Jews*, trans. Henrietta Szold (Philadelphia: Jewish Publication Society of America, 1909–38), 1:34–36.

42   On this debate, see Bouché-Leclercq, *L'astrologie grecque*, 372ff.; Richard Kieckhefer, *Magic in the Middle Ages* (Cambridge: Cambridge University Press, 1989), 125–31; Valerie I. J. Flint, *The Rise of Magic in Early Medieval Europe* (Princeton, NJ: Princeton University Press, 1991), 92–101.

43   Godfrey of Viterbo *Pantheon* XVIII (in Migne *PL*, 198:1005).

44   See Renate Blumenfeld-Kosinski, *Not of Woman Born: Representations of Caesarean Birth in Medieval and Renaissance Culture* (Ithaca, NY: Cornell University Press, 1990). For a discussion of the timing of the birth for future monarchs, see Bouché-Leclercq, *L'astrologie grecque*, 438ff.; Kieckhefer, *Magic*, 125–31; and Flint, *Rise of Magic*, 92–101. For the midwife-astrologer inspecting the heavens to identity the baby's lucky star, see *HDA*, s.v. "Hebamme" (3:1594). For a depiction of the astrologer-obstetrician, a bearded old man looking at the sky through a window in the room in which the expectant mother is about to give birth (attended by midwives), see Rueff, *De conceptu et generatione hominis*, cited in Thomas Rogers Forbes, *The Midwife and the Witch* (New Haven, CT: Yale University Press, 1966), 114. There are also legends of animals using the stars as a guide for giving birth. According to the *Physiologus*, the ostrich (referred to by the name *asida*) looks at the sky in order to see the rising of the star called Virgilia, and only at this moment does she lay her eggs; see Francis J. Carmody, ed., *Physiologus Latinus: Éditions preliminaires versio B* (Paris: Droz, 1939), 27.

45   The story is told by Pseudo-Callisthenes Historia Alexandri Magni 1.12.1ff. (*recensio L*, in Helmut van Thiel, ed. and trans., *Leben und Taten Alexanders von Makedonien: Der griechische Alexanderroman nach der Handschrift L* [Darmstadt: Wissenschaftliche Buchgesellschaft, 1983]). The Greek tradition of the *Alexander Romance* is extremely complicated. It consists of the so-called *recensio vetusta*, from the third–fourth century C.E., edited by Wilhelm Kroll, *Historia Alexandri Magni: +Recensio vetusta* (Berlin: Weidmann, 1958); and the so-called b recension, from the fifth century, edited by Lief Bergson, *Der griechische Alexanderroman: Rezension b* (Stockholm: Almquist & Wiksell, 1965); followed by *recensio L*, which can be roughly dated to the seventh–eighth century, edited by Van Thiel. There are two other Byzantine versions that are not particularly relevant for the story of Alexander's birth: Juergen Trumpf, ed., *Anonymi byzantini: Vita Alexandri regis Macedonum* (Stuttgart: Teubner, 1974); and K. Mitsakis, ed., *Der byzantinische Alexanderroman nach dem Codex vindob. theol. gr. 244* (Munich: Institut für Byzantinistik und Neugriechische Philologie der Universität, 1967). The story of Alexander's birth is very similar to the story told about the birth of the founder of the Sassanid dynasty, Ardashir-Artaxerxes. There was an obscure cobbler living in Persia named Papak who was actually an extraordinary astrologer, knowing all the stars and their secrets. By means of his astrological knowledge, Papak had discovered that Sasan, a soldier in the Persian army, could father a son destined to achieve incredible power. Moreover, Papak had identified the precise moment at which the hero, Ardashir-Artaxerxes, must be conceived in order for him to win his fortune. It was on the basis of Papak's minute observations of the stars that the hero's birth was brought about. The story is found in Agathias Histories 2.27.1ff. For a discussion, see C. Questa, "Il morto e la madre: Romei e Persiani nelle Storie di Agatia," *Lares* 55 (1989): 375–405.

in which the baby is compelled to be born at a particular moment, just as Nikippe was compelled to give birth to Eurystheus prematurely in order to meet the temporal specification imposed by Zeus's temporal decree, "today," while Alcmene's labor was blocked precisely so that Heracles would not be born on that auspicious day. According to the author of the *Alexander Romance*, the astrologer Nectanebo had predicted to Olympias, the wife of Philip, king of Macedon, that she would give birth to a son fathered by the god Ammon. Then, making use of his magical powers, Nectanebo had seduced the queen disguised as this god. The queen conceived and together the two of them were awaiting the moment when she would give birth (fig. 1.3.3).

FIGURE 1.3.3   Birth of Alexander. From the *Alexander Romance*, an ancient Greek manuscript (Ms. f. 14v.). Photograph: Istituto Ellenico di Studi Bizantini e Postbizantini di Venezia, Italy. Source: "Birth of Alexander," Alexander Romance, 338

When the time came, Olympias sat herself on the birthing chair and her labor pains commenced. Nectanebo stood by to assist her, observing the movements of the constellations in the sky and urging her not to be too quick in giving birth. Nectanebo, with his magical knowledge, kept the situation under control, ordering the queen to delay the delivery: "Woman, restrain yourself and fight your natural urges. For if you give birth now, you will produce a slave, a prisoner of war, or a terrible monster." Olympias was stricken with terrible labor pains, but Nectanebo continued, "Endure for a little longer, woman. For if you give birth now, your child will be an ineffectual eunuch." In addition to these verbal exhortations, Nectanebo indicated to her that she should use her hands to keep the baby back, while he himself used his magic powers to delay the delivery. Finally, watching the paths of the stars, Nectanebo saw that the sky was in perfect equilibrium and was suffused with a light as bright as the noonday sun. At that moment, Nectanebo said to Olympias: "Make the birth-cry now!" And as he nodded his head, he allowed the birth to take place: "Now you will bring forth a king who will rule the world." Olympias screamed, louder than the bellowing of a cow, and gave birth to a baby boy who fell to the ground as thunderclaps boomed and lightning flashed in the sky, and the entire universe was shaken.

Other versions of the story provide even more elaborate descriptions of this scene, in which the astrological details are presented in lengthy and complex detail.[46] For example, at one point Nectanebo turns his attention to the circle of the zodiac and says,

> Get up from your (birthing-) chair and take a little walk. Scorpio is dominating the horoscope and the bright Sun, when he sees the beasts of heaven yoked together and going backward, will turn one who is born at the hour altogether out of heaven. Take a grip of yourself, your majesty, and wait for this star as well. Cancer dominates the horoscope.

There then follow descriptions of the other constellations, together with continual exhortations to Olympias to hold back her delivery.

> Next is the lion-like rage of Mars. He is a lover of horses and war, but was exhibited naked and unarmed by the Sun on his adulterous bed. So whoever is born at this hour will be a laughing-stock. Wait also for the passing of Mercury, your majesty, the goat horned next to the ill-omened one:[47] or you will give birth to a quarrelsome pedant.

Finally Nectanebo says to the queen,

> "Sit down now, your majesty, on the chair of benefaction, and make your labors more frequent and energetic. Jupiter, the lover of virgins, who was pregnant with Dionysus in his thigh, is now high in the clear heaven,[48] turning into horned Ammon between Aquarius and Pisces, and designating an Egyptian world-ruler. Give birth NOW!" And as the child fell to the ground, there were great claps of thunder and flashes of lightning, so that all the world was shaken.[49]

---

46   Pseudo-Callisthenes *Historia Alexandri Magni* 1.12.1ff. (in *recensio L*, Van Thiel; translation from Richard Stoneman, trans., *The Greek Alexander Romance* [New York: Penguin, 1991], 43–44). For a discussion, see Ross, "Olympias and the Serpent," 347ff. Unfortunately the text of this recension is rather corrupt and often difficult to understand. There is an excellent analysis in Boll, "Die vierte Ekloge," 351–56. For a discussion of the other miraculous events associated with Alexander's birth, see Jouanno, "Romance d'Alexandros."

47   According to Boll, "Die vierte Ekloge," 353, this would be a reference to the constellation of the Monkey.

48   For the interpretation of this passage, see ibid., 354.

49   The Syriac version of the story is equally rich in astrological details, although they are arranged in yet another configuration. See Pseudo-Callisthenes, *The History of Alexander the Great, Being the Syriac Version of the Pseudo-Callisthenes*, ed. and trans. Ernest A. Wallis Budge (Cambridge: Cambridge University Press, 1889), 11–12.

Once again, we have a hero who "falls between the feet of a woman," the words used for the birth of Eurystheus in Homer's *Iliad*.[50] The point, of course, is that the baby "fell to the ground" at precisely the right moment: now. Like Nikippe, the mother of Eurystheus, and Alcmene, the mother of Heracles, Olympias is also a woman whose delivery has been changed from its natural course in order to coincide with a particular moment in time. In this case, the birth coincides not with a time decreed by Zeus in heaven, but with a particular astral moment determined by the astrologer's science. The celestial code of astrological signs provides the map of Alexander's destiny.[51] When a hero is born, the heavens cannot remain indifferent, but must in some way reflect the extraordinary dimensions of the event that is taking place down below on earth. Albertus Magnus provides a particularly interesting discussion of the cosmic dimensions of Alexander's birth:[52]

> Hippocrates and Galen say that every substance is connected to a conjunction of the planets, the star signs, and to the combination of the four elements. For this reason, Nectanebo, the natural father of Alexander, joined himself to Alexander's mother Olympias taking careful account of the time, so that he did so when the Sun was entering into Leo and Saturn was entering Taurus: he wanted for his son to acquire the features and powers of these planets.

---

50   For the position of the woman in labor, see chap. 3, sec. 2. There are a number of representations of the birth of Alexander that show his mother, Olympias, seated on a *díphros*, or birthing chair, while the baby can be seen lying on the ground. A number of illustrations are reproduced in Ross, "Olympias and the Serpent," 347ff. According to Ross, the scene reproduced in fig. 2 belongs to the "Egyptian" iconographic tradition, since the baby is propped on papyrus scrolls in the Egyptian custom.

51   It is also worth noting that the stars played a part when Zeus fathered Heracles with Alcmene, since he caused the stars to stand still in the heavens so that he could enjoy a triple night of love. For the details of this story, see Diodorus Siculus *Library of History* 4.9.2; Pherekydes F 13 c (in Jacoby, *Fragmente*, 1:63–64); Plautus *Amphitryon* 271–83; Propertius *Elegies* 2.21; Ovid *Amores* 1.13.45–46; and Lactantius Placidus *Commentary on Statius's Thebaid* 9.424 and 12.301 (in Richard Jahnke, ed., *Lactantii Placidi qui dicitur Commentarios in Statii Thebaida et Commentarium in Achilleida* [Leipzig: Teubner, 1898]). In the medieval tradition, the motif of the "triple night" was applied to the birth story of King Arthur (a story which shares many of its details with the story of Heracles' birth). See, for example, the version in William di Rennes, *Gesta Regum Britanniae*, 2923–2927 (in Franchisque-Michel, ed., *Gesta regum Britanniae: A Metrical History of the Britons Of The XIIIth Century Now First Printed from Three Manuscripts* [Bordeaux: Cambrian Archaeological Association, 1862]), although the corresponding episode in Geoffrey of Monmouth (*Historiae Regum Britanniae* 137) does not mention the triple night, which seems to have been added directly by William to his version. For a discussion, see John S. P. Tatlock, *The Legendary History of Britain: Geoffrey of Monmouth's Historia Regum Britanniae and Its Early Vernacular Versions* (Berkeley: University of California Press, 1950), 313–18; Rosemary Morris, *The Character of King Arthur in Medieval Literature* (Cambridge: D. S. Brewer, 1985), 25, and "Uther and Igerne: A Study in Uncourtly Love," in *Arthurian Literature* 4 (1982): 70–92.

52   Albertus Magnus *De animalibus* 22.7 (in H. Stadler, ed., *De animalibus libri XXVI* [Munster: Aschendorff, 1920], 1352): "Ypocras etiam dicit ut ibidem Galienus, quod omnis substantia sit legata et coniuncta in planetis et signis et nexibus quattuor elementorum. Et ideo Nectanebus naturalis Alexandri pater cum matre sua Olympiade tempus observans coivit Sole Leonem intrante et Saturno in Taurum, e quibus planetis suum filium volebat recipere figuram et potestatem." The source cited by Stadler is Pseudo-Galen *De spermate* 14. For a discussion, see Thorndike, *History of Magic*, 1:562–63, and also Albertus Magnus, *Man and the Beasts (De animalibus, Books 22–26)*, trans. James J. Scanlan (Binghampton, NY: Medieval & Renaissance Texts and Studies, Center for Medieval and Early Renaissance Studies, 1987), ad locum. The influence of astrological signs at the moment of birth is also discussed in the *De secretis mulierum*, a treatise once attributed to Albertus Magnus. See Helen Rodnite Lemay, ed. and trans., *Women's Secrets: A Translation of Pseudo-Albertus Magnus's De Secretis Mulierum, with Commentaries* (Albany: State University of New York Press, 1992), 27–32, 78–95.

The Greek and Latin versions of the *Alexander Romance* do not contain any astrological observations regarding the time at which Nectanebo seduced Olympias, but this element will occur in the Arabic version of Alexander's birth, to which we will turn shortly.[53] The *Romance* tells us only that as soon as Nectanebo reached Philip's palace he was asked by the queen to give a prediction regarding the future of her marriage with Philip. Nectanebo therefore asked Olympias to tell him the details of her birth and that of the king, but he then made a comparison of his own birth with that of Olympias in order to see "if their stars coincided."[54] Albertus Magnus is not the only medieval thinker to make an explicit connection between astrological observations and conception. Thomas Aquinas reports that demons also carefully "observe celestial signs" so that when they take a man's sperm (lying with him in the form of a succubus) they can implant this sperm at the right time in the right woman (lying with her in the form of an incubus) in order to spawn human beings of exceptional strength and power.[55]

Returning to the comparison of Alexander and Heracles, as we have seen, Heracles is forced to serve Eurystheus, the baby born prematurely to Nikippe, because Hera's intervention slowed Alcmene's labor. Alexander differs from Heracles in that he lacks a rival like Eurystheus for the right birth moment. Surveying the wide range of late antique and medieval stories, however, it is not surprising that this motif of "rivalry" did in fact make its way into a version of Alexander's birth, a tale attested in an Arabic encyclopedia, the *Hayat-al-Hayawan*. This work, an immense zoological encyclopedia famous in both East and West, is the work of an eminent Islamic theologian, scholar, and writer named ad-Damiri, who was born in Cairo in 1341 and died in that same city in 1405.[56] In it we find the following account of Alexander's birth, in which Alexander is referred to by the name Dhû'l-Ḳarnain, a name regularly used to refer to Alexander in the Islamic tradition:[57]

> There is a difference of opinion with regard to the pedigree (origin) and name of Dhû'l-Ḳarnain. The author of *Ibtilâ'l-akhyâr* states that the proper name of Dhû'l-Ḳarnain was Alexander, and that his father was the most learned man out of the people of the earth in the science of astrology; nobody had observed the movements of the stars as he. God had extended the period of his life. He said one night to his wife, "Want of sleep has very nearly killed me; let me alone that I may sleep

53 For the Arabic version of Alexander's birth, see above, sec. 5.

54 Pseudo-Callisthenes *Historia Alexandri Magni* 1.4.7 (*recensio vetusta = recensio L* 1.4); Julius Valerius, *Res gestae Alexandri Macedonis* 1.4. Although in the Greek version this episode is limited to a few phrases, in the Latin version it is considerably longer. It is also worth noting that in his polemic with the astrologers Augustine referred somewhat obscurely to the adventures of an otherwise anonymous *vir doctus* who had chosen a certain time at which to sleep with his wife in order to give birth to an extraordinary son (*City of God* 5.7.1). According to Thorndike, *History of Magic*, 1:516, this reference in Augustine is "an inaccurate allusion to the story of Nectanebus." It was said that the emperor Frederick II waited to consummate his marriage to Isabella until an auspicious time had been indicated to him by astrologers (see Kieckhefer, *Magic*, 120–31). For the legend of King Arthur's conception, see above, sec. 5.

55 Thomas Aquinas *De potentia* 6.8 (in P. Bazzi et al., eds., *Quaestiones disputatae. Volumen II* [Torino: Marietti, 1965], 181): "et tamen possibile est quod per talem modum [*scil.* since the demons collect male sperm by taking the form of succubi, and then transfer the sperm into a woman's womb by taking the form of incubi] homines fortiores generentur et maiores, quia demones volentes in suis effectibus mirabiles videri, observando determinatum situm stellarum, et viri et mulieris dispositionem possunt ad hoc cooperari." For a discussion of other influences that can have an effect at the moment of conception (e.g., a baby can be influenced by the appearance of a painting that the woman is gazing upon at the moment of conception), see the discussion in Maurizio Bettini, *Il ritratto dell'amante* (Torino: Einaudi, 1992), 221–22.

56 See B. Lewis et al., eds., *The Encyclopedia of Islam* (Leiden: Brill, 1965), s.v. "al-Damiri"; K. Ranke, ed., *Enzyklopädie des Märchens* (Berlin: De Gruyter, 1981), s.v. "Damiri."

57 Ad-Damiri, *Hayat al-hayawan: A Zoological Lexicon*, ed. and trans. A. S. G. Jayakar (London: Luzac, 1908), 2:48–49.

for a time, and do you watch the sky (for me); when you see a (certain) star rising in this place," pointing with his hand the place of its rising, "wake me up, that I may compress you, and you may conceive a son who will live to the end of time." Now, her sister was listening to his words. The father of Alexander then slept, and the sister of his wife kept up watching for the star; and when the star rose, she informed her husband of the affair, and he compressed her, with the result of her conceiving al-Khiḍr, so that al-Khiḍr was the son of Alexander's (maternal) aunt; he was his wazîr (too). When Alexander's father woke up, he saw that the star had descended into a sign of the Zodiac other than he was watching, so he said to his wife, "Why did you not wake me up?" She replied, "I was ashamed." He then said to her, "Do not you know that I have been watching for this star for forty years? By God, I have wasted my life without any profit; but at this moment there will rise in its steps another star, and I shall compress you then, so that you will conceive a son who will possess the two horns of the sun." He had not waited long when the star rose, upon which he compressed her, and she conceived Alexander, who and the son of her maternal aunt, al-Khiḍr, were born on the same night. Then God bestowed on Alexander his firm possession of the earth; he conquered countries, and his career was such as is known to have been.[58]

The character al-Khiḍr (or al-Khaḍir) plays an important role in the culture and legends of the Islamic tradition and appears in the Koran itself.[59] In the story of Alexander, al-Khiḍr was the legendary companion of Dhû'l-Ḳarnain and led the advance guard in Alexander's march into the wilderness searching for the fountain of youth.[60] In the version of Alexander's birth cited by ad-Damiri, al-Khiḍr plays a role that is identical to that played by Eurystheus in relation to Heracles. Once again, a rival "robs" the hero of the privileges granted by the timing associated with the birth and acquires the benefits that were supposed to belong to the hero instead.

The narrative structure of the Islamic version is, naturally, somewhat different from the story of Heracles and Eurystheus. In place of the desired coincidence created by the word of Zeus, the Islamic story substitutes an astrological coincidence, a precedent that had already been established in the Greek and Latin versions of Alexander's story. In addition, it is no longer a god who fathers the heroic child, but an astrologer of supernatural powers—although unlike the Greek and Latin versions, this Arabic version has the astrologer observing the stars at the moment of Alexander's conception, not at his birth.[61] Finally, the woman who is actually responsible for the trick is not an omniscient Greek goddess jealous of her philandering husband and his heroic offspring, as we saw in Homer, but is instead a timid wife's ambitious sister, who heard the words of the astrologer without being detected, a scene that might almost have been taken from a comedy.

---

58 In the Western tradition of the *Alexander Romance*, Alexander lost his chance at immortality through sheer carelessness, failing to realize that he had in fact found the fountain of eternal youth. Instead, the only person in his army to realize what had happened was the cook, who shared the elixir of life with Alexander's daughter. As punishment, Alexander's daughter was turned into a Nereid and the cook into a sea monster, as told in Pseudo-Callisthenes *Historia Alexandri Magni* 2.39ff. (*versio L* in Van Thiel). The hero Gilgamesh also failed to gain possession of the plant of eternal life because of carelessness. See G. Pettinato, ed., *La saga di Gilgamesh* (Milano: Rusconi, 1992), 227ff.
59 Koran, Sura 18.60–82.
60 In some versions of this story, al-Khidr actually becomes the central character, overshadowing Alexander. See the discussion in the entry "al-Khidr" in *Shorter Encyclopaedia of Islam* (Ithaca, NY: Cornell University Press, 1967), ed. H. A. R. Gibb and J. H. Kramers, 232.
61 For the conception of the hero, see above, sec. 5.

The story, however, is still fundamentally the same, and the central elements of its plot—the coincidence of the birth with certain external determinants, the trick played on the father of the future hero, the loss of privileges suffered by the son—remain the same. In the Arabic version, the wise man finds himself unaccountably distracted, much like Zeus blinded by Ate, and in both cases there is a cunning woman standing by, ready to seize the moment. It is notable that in this account of Alexander's birth, he is able to recover at least part of his lost birth privilege by means of a secondary intervention that granted him earthly powers, much as Heracles succeeded in eventually overcoming his subordination to Eurystheus so that in the end he was even able to take his place among the immortals in heaven.

Over time, of course, cultural models shift and change, but certain deep patterns of thought and narration remain, such as the coincidence of a child's birth with external determinants that insure his heroic destiny, the connection between the mother's labor pains and the timing of this coincidence, and the existence of a determining power that arranges this situation. These are cultural motifs that seem to have a widespread and long-lived existence.

Over a thousand years after Homer composed the *Iliad*, in a quite different cultural context, we find this same kind of story played out once again in the ancient Celtic epics, even farther removed from Homer than the *Alexander Romance*. The hero's name is now Conchobar, and he is the son of a woman named Ness:[62]

> Assa, as she was first called, had twelve guardians, but they were killed by the druid Cathbad during a raid. She decided to seek revenge, and armed a group of men to go raid in turn the lands of her enemy. She changed her name, and was now called "Nihassa," or "Ness," because of her prowess and strength. After a while, however, Cathbad surprised her when she was unarmed and bathing in a spring, and she agreed to marry him in order to save her life.[63] Ness thus became the wife of Cathbad. During the night, Cathbad was thirsty and asked Ness to bring him some water: she returned with a cup and offered it to her husband, but Cathbad realized that inside the cup there was not only water, but two worms. Afraid that Ness was trying to kill him, Cathbad compelled her to drink from the cup: Ness drank, and afterward became pregnant.[64] The situation was made even more complicated by the fact that Ness had a secret lover, Fachtna Fathach, and the child she bore was actually his. Ness and Cathbad set out on a journey, and at a certain point Ness went into labor. Cathbad entreated her to wait: "O wife," says Cathbad, "would it were … in

---

62   This version of Conchobar's birth is recorded in a manuscript dating to the fifteenth century (Stowe ms. n. 992) that was published and translated by Kuno Meyer, "Anecdota from the Stowe Ms. N. 992," *Revue Celtique* 6 (1884): 173–86. It is a more recent version of a shorter version of the story found in the *Book of Leinster* 106a–107b (in R. I. Best, O. Bergin, and M. A. O'Brien, eds., *The Book of Leinster* [Dublin: Dublin Institute for Advanced Studies, 1954], 400–404). For a discussion and bibliography, see C. J. Guyonvarch, "La naissance de Conchobar, version A," *Ogam* 11 (1959): 56–65. See also Nutt, *Celtic Doctrine*, 72ff., and Rees and Rees, *Celtic Heritage*, 216ff.

63   Rees and Rees (*Celtic Heritage*, 235) note that this meeting at the spring recalls the widespread folktale motif in which a mortal surprises a girl/swan at a spring, steals her swan attire, and makes her his wife. For a discussion of this motif, see Edwin Sidney Hartland, *The Science of Fairy Tales: An Inquiry into Fairy Mythology* (London: Walter Scott, 1891), 255–332.

64   Worms are frequently a cause of conception and pregnancy in Irish folklore. The births of CúChulainn and Conall Cernach were likewise attributed to the ingestion of worms by the future mothers. See Edwin Sidney Hartland, *The Legend of Perseus: A Study of Tradition in Story, Custom and Belief*, vol. 1, *The Supernatural Birth* (London: David Nutt, 1894), 116ff.; and Edwin Sidney Hartland, *Primitive Paternity: The Myth of Supernatural Birth in Relation to the History of the Family* (London, David Nutt, 1909–10), 1:9ff. On the subject of supernatural impregnation, see above, sec. 6.

thy power ... not to bring forth the child that is in thy womb till tomorrow, for thy son would then be king of Ulster, or of all Erinn [Ireland], and his name will last in Erinn for ever, for it is ... of the same day that the illustrious child will be born whose glory and power has spread over the world, namely Jesus Christ, the son of God everlasting." Ness replied, "I will do so. If it does not come out through my side, it shall not come out any other way until that time arrive." Having said this, Ness lay down on a great stone on the bank of the river Conchobur and waited until the next day. The baby was born with a worm in each hand, and you can still see today the stone on which Conchobar was born.

This story of Conchobar's birth has much in common with the birth of Heracles. Above all, we are dealing with two heroines, Ness and Alcmene, who have suffered basically the same kind of travail.[65] Yet there is a new element in Conchobar's story that deserves our attention: in order to establish Conchobar's heroic future, Cathbad seeks to insure that the baby's birth coincides with that of Jesus Christ. The auspicious day is thus not established by the word of a god directly (as in the story of Heracles) or by the calculations of an astrologer (as in the story of Alexander), but by a correspondence with the date of another famous birth.

Given the extraordinary success enjoyed by the *Alexander Romance* in the medieval period, and its intricate and various textual variants,[66] it is entirely likely that the story of Conchobar's birth could owe something to this ancient model, with the druid Cathbad as a later incarnation of the astrologer Nectanebo. In any case, the narrative context in which the birth occurs is quite different from the context of Alexander's story. Here Cathbad is the legitimate husband of Ness, while Nectanebo was an illegitimate lover of Olympias (the role assigned to Fachtna Fathach in Ness's story).[67]

---

65 Further, in other versions of the myth Alcmene may have also been the victim of a deadly raid carried out by the man who would become her husband; see Maurizio Bettini, "Il racconto di Alcmena e Anfitrione: Un'analisi antropologica," *Dioniso* 63 (1993): 59–76. Alcmene's name, in fact, is etymologically similar to Ness, both of which mean "strength" (Alkmene). Likewise, each woman was impregnated by someone other than her husband (Zeus, in the case of Alcmene, as opposed to the two worms and the secret lover in Ness's story), which precedes their extended labor pains. There even seems to be an analogy between the motif of Heracles' strangling the snakes in his cradle while still an infant and Conchobar's being born with a worm in each hand. Finally, the name Ness is also one of the names for the weasel in Irish and, as we will soon see, the weasel is one of the most significant characters in Alcmene's story. See Guyonvarch, "La naissance de Conchobar," 58 n. 7, following a suggestion first made by Rudolf Thurneysen, *Die irische Helden- und Königsage bis zum siebzehnten Jahrhundert* (Hildesheim: Olms, 1980), 273. For the connection between the name Ness and the weasel, see M. Joynt, *Contribution to a Dictionary of Irish Language* (Dublin: Royal Irish Academy, 1941); and Ernst Windisch, *Irische Texte mit Wörterbuch* (Leipzig: Hirzel, 1886), 76. The sources for this connection are the *Prisciani codex Sancti Galli*, in which the word *ness* is glossed as *mustella, mus longa* (cited by J. C. Zeuss, *Grammatica celtica: Editio altera*, ed. H. Ebel [Berlin: n.p., 1871], 49); and King Cormac of Cashel, *Sanas Chormaic: Cormac's Glossary*, ed. Whitley Stokes, trans. John O'Donovan (Calcutta: Irish Archaeological and Celtic Society, 1868), 126. See also J. Vendryes, *Lexique etymologique de l'irlandais ancien* (Paris: C.N.R.S., 1960), n. 11, although he does not give a detailed listing of the sources.

66 For a "brief survey" (that is anything but) of the sources of the Alexander legend in the Middle Ages, see George Cary, *The Medieval Alexander*, ed. D. J. A. Ross (Cambridge: Cambridge University Press, 1956), 9–74.

67 There is a similar link between the birth of a hero and the birth-day of Christ in the *Voyage of Bran*, in which the birth of the hero Mongan is narrated. The text and a translation can be found in Séamus MacMathúna, *Immram Brain: Bran's Journey to the Land of the Women* (Tübingen: M. Niemeyer, 1985), n. 48. For a discussion, see Nutt, *Celtic Doctrine*, 13ff.; J. Carney, *Studies in Irish Literature and History* (Dublin: Institute for Advanced Study, 1955), 282; and esp. P. MacCana, "Mongan mac Fiachna and Immram Brain," *Eriu* 23 (1972): 102–42.

Conchobar was not the only Irish hero whose mother had to painfully delay her delivery in order to secure her son's heroic destiny; a similar story is told about the birth of the hero Fiacha Broad-Crown:[68]

> The night before he was killed in battle Eogan, the king of Munster, slept with the daughter of a druid in order to have a child by her. A baby boy was conceived, and when it was time for the woman to give birth, the druid told his daughter that if the delivery could be delayed until the next morning, the baby would become the most powerful man in Ireland. The woman told her father that the baby would not be born that night unless it came out of her side. She sat astride a stone, in the middle of a ford, ordering the stone to hold back the baby. When she finally gave birth on the next day, she died, and the head of the baby was pressed flat by the stone, which is why he was called Fiacha "of the broad crown."

Once again we are dealing with the motif of the timing of a birth to coincide with a desired moment or event and with a delayed delivery in order to secure the child's heroic future. And once again, the mother of the hero uses the same striking formula to describe the complete blockage of her womb: the only way that the baby will be born against her will is if it is taken "from her side."[69] Given that in antiquity and the early Middle Ages a baby could be extracted from its mother's "side" only after her death, it is possible that this expression simply means "unless I die and the baby is taken from my side."[70]

Perhaps the most famous example of this motif of birth through the side is not in the human world, but in the legendary world of animals. Female vipers supposedly gave birth through the side, as Pliny the Elder explains: "The viper is the one terrestrial animal that bears egg inside itself ... on the third day the eggs open inside the womb, and after this the mother gives birth each day to one of the babies, until they number about twenty. At this point the others, impatient at the delay, burst through her sides, killing the mother."[71] Aelian describes the same process in terms of "bursting through to make a passage."[72] The birth of the viper—the mother's side is burst by babies that share her vicious nature—provides a paradigm of unnatural birth because

---

68 Standish H. O'Grady, ed. and trans., *Silva Gadelica (I–XXXI): A Collection of Tales in Irish with Extracts Illustrating Persons and Places* (London: Williams & Norgate, 1892), 1:314 and 2:354; and Rees and Rees, *Celtic Heritage*, 220.

69 In comparative terms, it is worth noting that the motif of a woman giving birth through her side is found in various cultures. For example, the Buddha was said to have entered the womb of his mother through her right side and to have emerged from her right side when he was born (Hartland, *Legend of Perseus*, 1:130–31). There is also a Coptic magical papyrus with an incantation to facilitate delivery that contains the motif of birth "through the side," cited by W. H. Worrell, "Coptic Magical and Medical Texts," *Orientalia* 4 (1935): 1–37 (including references to a similar expression found in Rashi's commentary on the Babylonian Talmud).

70 Blumenfeld-Kosinski, *Not of Woman Born*, 21–32; and Danielle Gourevitch, *Le mal d'être femme: La femme et la médecine dans la Rome antique* (Paris: Les Belles Lettres, 1984), 188–89.

71 Pliny *Natural History* 10.170: "terrestrium eadem sola intra se parit ova ... tertia die intra uterum catulos excludit; dein singulis diebus singulos parit, XX fere numero; itaque ceteri tarditatis impatientes perrumpunt latera occisa pariente."

72 Aelian *On the Nature of Animals* 15.16 (translation from Aelian, *On the Characteristics of Animals*, trans. Scholfield); see also 1.24. Aelian explains that the *thalattía belóne* gives birth in the same way. According to Herodotus *Histories* 3.109, viper young eat their mother after they are born, a belief also reported in the *Physiologus*, as in this version of the *Physiologus latinus* (in Carmody, Y, 12): "cum autem creverint filii eius in utero matris sue, non habens illa sinum unde pariatur, tunc filii adaperiunt latus matris suae, et exeunt occidentes matrem."

it is driven and violently directed from inside, against the mother's will, by unborn creatures who refuse to wait in the womb and instead open up an unnatural birth canal in order to come into this world.[73]

Returning to the world of human legend, the motif of the delayed delivery is found not only in the lives of Irish heroes, but also in saints' lives. In these stories, of course, the career of the child born on the required date, at great suffering to his mother, is not destined to be a terrestrial hero, but a worthy servant of God. In the life of St. Lasrianus (or Molaissus), the druid is replaced by a prophet, a figure who is better suited to this new religious context.[74] The substance of the story, however, does not change: the prophet asks the mother of the future saint to delay his birth until the following day "so that a son will be born who will be honored by one and all." Thus, "God closed her vulva and she did not give birth until the light had returned to the sky the next day." It is now the God of Christianity who has unexpectedly taken the place of the Homeric Eileithyia or the Egyptian astrologer Nectanebo, using his powers to close up the womb so that little Lasrianus will not emerge before the auspicious moment arrives. The text self-consciously insists: "God did not delay the time of the baby's birth in order to coincide with the constellation of heavenly bodies, but in order to fulfill his own plan."[75] The explicit reference to astrology as a reason for delaying the child's birth naturally recalls the story of Alexander, whose birth story seems to have cast its shadow on the legends of the Irish saints.[76]

Finally, it should be mentioned that the practice of retarding childbirth in order to coincide with astrological conjunctions or other events was not only a literary and mythological motif. This was something that could also happen in real life. We know, for example, that as recently as the nineteenth century, in some regions of France the midwife would hasten or delay the birth of a child in order to prevent the birth from taking place between the hours of eleven o'clock and midnight, which was considered an extremely ill-omened time of day. Indeed, given that labor has a tendency to begin in the middle of the night, it might well be that in past centuries the practice of hastening or delaying birth was a common practice.[77] Returning to the Irish legends, both the hero Fiacha Broad-Crown and the saint Lasrianus had to wait through the night until the morning to be born, with the mother holding back the child until the "light" of the next day had appeared.

---

73 A similar motif is associated with the birth of the Antichrist, who is supposedly born by Caesarean section, thus "bursting" through the side of the mother in a way that resembles the viper's birth. According to Rabanus Maurus, there were many points of contact between the legends of these wicked creatures; see the discussion in Blumenfeld-Kosinski, *Not of Woman Born*, 120ff., esp. 135–36.

74 Charles Plummer, ed., *Vitae sanctorum Hiberniae: Partim hactenus ineditae, ad fidem codicum manuscriptorum* (Oxford: Clarendon, 1910), 1:cxxii and 2:131–32.

75 Ibid.: "non tamen ideo Deus tempus pariendi puerum propter aliquam corporum celestium costellacionem expectavit, set ut beneplacitum suum adimpleret."

76 For the importance of astrology at the moment of birth in Ireland, see Hastings *ERE*, s.v. "Birth (Celtic)," 645. After a baby was born, the mother "waited for a lucky hour for the child," probably in order for the horoscope to be cast. Likewise, the druid Cathfaidh observed the astrological signs, the clouds, and the phase of the moon immediately following the birth of Deirdre.

77 Jacques Gélis, *L'arbre et le fruit: La naissance dans l'Occident moderne, XVIe–XIXe siècle* (Paris: Fayard, 1984), 273ff. Even today, hospitals will hasten deliveries to prevent them from coinciding with less favorable days, no longer because some days are "lucky" or "unlucky," but simply because of overriding organizational arrangements.

6. The Hero Is Not Born Alone

The best way to label all the stories that we have considered so far is that they are stories of identity. The obsession with insuring a certain determining coincidence, even at the cost of the mother's pain and suffering, is connected with an explicit concern to establish the future identity of the child, hoping that it will be the highest and most glorious identity possible. The *dies natalis*, the day of birth, is in and of itself a means of identification: "I" am who I am because I was born on "this" day, a day that serves as a primary certification of who I am. In Roman culture, the *dies natalis* was linked to a celebration of the *genius* of a given person. In other words, the birthday celebrated the manifestation in a divine form of that person's identity and vital force.[78] Since the *dies natalis* has a supernatural dimension that marks one particular day as privileged over other days, the normal identifying function of the birthday takes on a mythical quality and is able to designate a newborn baby as a future hero. This exceptional guarantee must be obtained at any cost, regardless of the agony the expectant mother might have to endure. In all the stories that we have looked at so far, the mother has had no choice: whether she wants to or not, she is forced to participate in the heroic dimension of her son's identity, even at the risk of her own life. As in other cultural practices, the woman here is reduced to a passive participant in the process of reproduction. She is a mere receptacle for the male seed at the moment of conception, a field to be cultivated during the growth of that seed during gestation, and, even at the moment of her labor and delivery, expected to submit to the will of the men who surround her.[79] The mother did not pass her identity on to the child either in biological or institutional terms. The identity of the child derived from the father and from his blood.

The story of the birth of Heracles is also a myth of identity, just like the stories of Alexander and the Irish heroes. Moreover, in the light of those other stories, we can perhaps now see some meanings of the Heracles legend that were not entirely clear before. The other stories were based essentially on the demand that a woman delay giving birth in order to make the birth of the child coincide with an external determinant. In the Heracles story, however, we see the position of the woman refracted into two different possibilities: there is a woman, Nikippe, who is required not to delay but to accelerate her delivery in order to coincide with the external sign, competing with Alcmene, a woman who is compelled by external forces to delay her delivery, but this time the delay causes a failure to coincide with the external sign. The elements in play are basically the same—a significant day, a birth, a destiny linked to the coincidence of the birth and the day—but the way that the Heracles myth assembles these elements is unusually complex. The suffering of the woman and the child, who are compelled to postpone the moment of their mutual liberation from one another, is transformed into a competition between two babies and two mothers, who are both obliged by

---

78   See Roscher *GRM*, s.v. "Genius" (vol. 1, pt. 2, 1613–25), and S. Mattero, "The Gluttonous Genius: Yearning for Vitality and Fertility," *Arctos* 26 (1992): 85–96. See also the classic study by Nicole Belmont, *Les signes de la naissance: Étude des représentations symboliques associées aux naissances singulières* (Brionne: Berard Monfort, 1971), 181–92.

79   There is abundant evidence from ancient Greece and Rome that the woman was considered only the container for the male seed, as in Aeschylus *Eumenides* 658ff. For a general discussion, see Erna Lesky, *Die Zeugungs- und Vererbungslehren der Antike und ihr Nachwirken* (Wiesbaden, 1950), 54; and G. E. R. Lloyd, *Science, Folklore, and Ideology: Studies in the Life Sciences in Ancient Greece* (Cambridge: Cambridge University Press, 1983), 86ff. See also Jean Pierre Vernant, "Hestia-Hermes," in his *Mito e pensiero presso i Greci* (Torino, 1970), 99–100; and Nancy H. Demand, *Birth, Death, and Motherhood in Classical Greece* (Baltimore: Johns Hopkins University Press, 1994), a book that has been a valuable source of information and ideas and to which I will make frequent reference throughout this study.

a superior power to violate the anticipated birth of the baby and end of the mother's pregnancy. The story is, as it were, doubled.

This motif of the doubling of the hero deserves our further attention, before we turn our attention from Heracles to his mother, Alcmene, and the weasel. Because of the doubling of the narrative in the Heracles legend, the question of coincidence expands from the coincidence of time ("today") to the fact that two different babies are born in specific relation to one another: Eurystheus, the son of Nikippe, and Heracles. Turning again to Irish heroic legends, we find what seems to be a similar motif. When a hero is born, it is often the case that an animal is born at the same time: a colt is born at the same time as Pryderi; two colts are born at the same time as CúChulainn; the birth of Finn is accompanied by the birth of a dog; and the hero Lleu has a brother-fish, while the twelve "half brothers" of Lug turn into seals.[80] This multiplication of animal births around the birth of the hero can perhaps be connected with a folk practice found in various northern European cultures in which a colt born at the same time as a baby would be dedicated to that baby, as would a weapon that had been forged at the same time as the baby's birth.[81] The hero is not born alone; his birth casts shadowy reflections around him. It is as if his generation were not single, but already multiplied, so that those animals who are born together with him, or those weapons that are forged at the moment of his birth, come into existence as further representations of the hero, expanding to express his multiple identity.

In this context, it is worth citing one more Irish legend.[82] The god Manannan wanted to seduce the wife of Fiachna the Beautiful, so he disguised himself as Fiachna, and it was as a result of this union that the hero Mongan was born. Thus, like Heracles, Mongan was a hero who had two fathers, and one of his fathers was a god who had disguised himself as the human father, just as Zeus disguised himself as Amphitryon in order to seduce Alcmene.[83] Moreover, on the very night when Mongan was born, the wife of An Damh, Fiachna's shield-bearer, also gave birth to a son, Mac an Daimh. The two boys were baptized together, and Mac an Daimh became a faithful companion during Mongan's adventurous career. Finally, also on that same fateful night Fiachna the Black, a warrior who ruled jointly with Fiachna the Beautiful, gave birth to a daughter, Dubh-Lacha ("Black Duck"). Mongan and Dubh-Lacha were immediately betrothed to one another and married.

Thus as a result of Mongan's birth, two pairs were created (one single-sex pair and one of both sexes), intersecting in the person of the hero: Mongan + companion-in-arms and Mongan + wife. The birth of Mongan was doubled and then redoubled in other human births that coincided with his own: the hero, once again, is not born alone; instead, his identity is multiplied at the moment of his birth.

---

80   Rees and Rees, *Celtic Heritage*, 231; see also Nutt, *Celtic Doctrine*, 42.

81   See H. Munro Chadwick and N. Kershaw Chadwick, *The Growth of Literature* (Cambridge: Cambridge University Press, 1968), 1:219ff., who offer a comparison of the gifts presented at the births of Achilles and CúChulainn.

82   The text is from a fifteenth-century manuscript, translated by Kuno Meyer, *The Voyage of Bran, Son of Febal, to the Land of the Living: An Old Irish Saga* (London: David Nutt, 1895–97), 2:42ff. For a discussion, see Rees and Rees, *Celtic Heritage*, 213ff.

83   On the analogies between these two myths, see the unhelpful discussion in T. O'Broin, "Classical Sources of the Conception of Mongan," *Zeitschrift für Celtische Philologie* 28 (1960–61): 262–71; and the sober rejoinder by MacCana, "Mongan mac Fiachna."

7. Fecal Doubles, or the Holiness of "This" and "That"

Like the birth of the Irish hero Mongan, the birth of Heracles was also accompanied by a doubling and a redoubling. Heracles was born together with his twin, Iphicles, who became his faithful shield-bearer, and his birth was also linked to that of Eurystheus, his rival.[84] Now that we see the structural potential for the hero's birth to be accompanied by a helper-twin and a rival-twin, we can see that al-Khiḍr played both roles in the Arabic version of Alexander the Great's birth: he served as Alexander's vizier and adviser, but he was also Alexander's rival and stole from him the right to immortality.[85] In short, the identity of the hero—doubled, redoubled, refracted, and multiplied—exceeds the norm because in this way the hero has the capacity both to be himself and to be someone else. It is as if the hero at the moment of his birth had to come into existence as a double of himself.

This double nature can be expressed in the form of a double paternity, as in the case of Heracles or Conchobar, and also those of Theseus, who was supposed to be the son of Aegeus and also of Poseidon,[86] and Pollux, the son of Zeus and Tyndareus,[87] among others. The same can also be said for Alexander, whose paternity is even more complex, involving Philip, the king of Macedon and husband of Olympias, Nectanebo, and the god Ammon.[88] Based on the model of Alexander, similar claims for double paternity were made at Rome, as in the case of Scipio Africanus, who was considered to be the son of Jupiter, or Augustus, who was considered the son of Apollo.[89] Even culture heroes such as Plato and Pythagoras were later considered to have multiple fathers, with the god Apollo taking his place beside the natural fathers

---

84   In a previously published analysis of these materials (Maurizio Bettini, "Eracle, Alessandro e la mitologia irlandese," in Mencacci, *I fratelli amici*, vii–xliii), I suggested the possibility that this multiplication of the hero's identity could be understood in terms of the narrative mechanism of triplification, common in folktales. See V. J. Propp, *Morfologia della fiaba* (Torino: Einaudi, 1972), 102ff.; A. Olrik, "La costruzione del racconto: Le leggi epiche," *Uomo e cultura* 11–12 (1973), 197ff.; and a wide array of materials in Hermann Usener, *Dreiheit: Ein Versuch mythologischer Zahlenlehre* (Hildesheim: Olms, 1966), 1–48, 161–208, 321–64. As has often been observed, folktales frequently incorporate threes: there are three brothers (two are intelligent, one is a fool, or two foolish brothers and one wise one), the hero is accompanied by three helpers (a dog, a cat, and a snake, for example), he overcomes three different obstacles using three different magical objects, making three attempts each time, and so on. On this, see E. M. Meletinskij, *La struttura della fiaba* (Palermo: Sellerio, 1977), 132ff. Rather than enumerating the hero's qualities in a list, the folktale unfolds them in narrative form, using triplification to make these different aspects of the hero's identity part of the structure of the story itself.

85   For the Arabic version of the birth of Alexander, see above, sec. 5.

86   Apollodorus *Library* 3.15.7; and Hyginus *Fables* 37.

87   According to legend, Zeus, disguised as a swan, seduced Leda, who also slept with Tyndareus that same night. Zeus was thus the father of Pollux and of Helen, while Tyndareus fathered Castor and Clytemnestra, although the outcome is reported variously in the sources (Apollodorus *Library* 3.10.7; Hyginus *Fables* 77; and Pindar *Nemean Odes* 10.79ff., among others).

88   For the gossip about Alexander having been fathered by Ammon, see Arrian *Anabasis* 3.3.2 and 7.30.2; for his birth from Nectanebo as narrated in the *Alexander Romance*, see above, sec. 5. According to Robert McQueen Grant, *Miracle and Natural Law in Graeco-Roman and Early Christian Thought* (Amsterdam: North-Holland Publishing, 1952), 176, the story of Nectanebo and Alexander is a rewriting of the more ancient legend that considers Alexander to be the son of Ammon.

89   For Scipio, see Livy *History of Rome* 26.19.7; for Augustus, see Suetonius *Augustus* 94.

of the philosophers.[90] And, of course, the central example of this phenomenon is the double paternity attributed to Jesus Christ.[91]

Finally, the hero's birth can also be linked to the simultaneous birth of an animal, as we saw in the case of the colt born at the same time as the Irish hero Pryderi, the dog born with Finn, and so on. Our first impulse might be to consider this a reflex of the practice of animal totemism,[92] but I think that in this case we should take a different approach, or at least consider what would have to be called a *sui generis* variety of totemism. As anthropologists have known for some time, among the Kujamat Diola people of Senegal it is believed that at a certain point in life a person can defecate an animal, which immediately runs away and hides in the bushes.[93] The animal that comes into existence in this extraordinary fashion is called the *ewúúm*, and from the moment of its birth it serves as a "double" of the person who produced it. If the animal is wounded in some part of its body, it causes the human member of the pair to suffer; indeed, the human being suffers more from wounds inflicted on the animal than the animal suffers from wounds that might be inflicted on the human. This is, in some sense, a kind of totemism, but it is a totemism of a decidedly metonymical rather than metaphorical nature.[94] In addition to serving as a kind of physical double, the fecal double also has a sociological identity. As soon as it is born, the *ewúúm* takes refuge in the region where the human partner's maternal relatives live, in the case of a man or an unmarried woman, but if the human partner is a married woman, the *ewúúm* dwells in the region where her paternal relatives live.

In the cultural imagination of the Kujamat Diola, the presence of these animal doubles realizes the impossible desire of each person to be both himself and someone else, making it possible to embody both identity and alterity in reference to a single person. The situation is very much like that of the mythical hero who, in the context of a patrilineal society, needs to have a double paternity, so that he can achieve another identity that the rules of kinship and filiation would normally exclude. The Kujamat Diola limit the significance of their animal doubles to the physical and sociological plane, but the mythical hero can even aim higher, combining human nature with the nature of a god, remaining "himself" while at the same time achieving the "otherness" of a god.

We can thus take one last look at Heracles, the hero whose legendary birth started us on this long journey along the paths of myth. Heracles is in every way the prototypical hero: the son of two fathers, accompanied by a faithful twin and a rival who is his would-be twin, Heracles is also explicitly considered an embodiment of both human and divine nature—so much so that after his death he was both possessed of a shade in Hades,

---

90   For Plato, see Diogenes Laertius *Lives of the Philosophers* 3.2 and Origen *Against Celsus* 1.37. For Pythagoras, see Porphyry *The Life of Pythagoras* 2; and Iamblicus *On the Pythagorean Life* 2.4–7. See also Grant, *Miracle and Natural Law*, 173–74.
91   See Klaus Schreiner, *Vergine, madre, regina* (Rome: Donzelli, 1995), 17–52; Walter Bauer, *Das Leben Jesu im Zeitalter der neutestamentlichen Apokryphen* (Darmstadt: Wissenschaftliche Buchgesellschaft, 1967), 39–40; and Hans Joachim Schoeps, *Theologie und Geschichte des Judenchristentums* (Tübingen: Mohr, 1949), 71–74 (cited in Grant, *Miracle and Natural Law*, 170). Jesus's multiple paternity was a subject of ridicule for both pagan and Jewish critics of Christianity. Celsus, probably using a Jewish source, explained the so-called virgin birth by arguing that Mary had in fact had a love affair with a Roman centurion named Panthera (cited by Origen *Against Celsus* 1.39). See also P. Saintyves, *Les vierges mères et les naissances miraculeuses* (Paris: E. Nourry, 1908), 260; Grant, *Miracle and Natural Law*, 177; and Marina Warner, *Alone of All Her Sex: The Myth and the Cult of the Virgin Mary* (New York: Knopf, 1976), 35 and n. 4.
92   For the modern debate on totemism, see chap. 11, sec. 2; for the category of "individual totemism" (which is what we could be dealing with here), see Claude Lévi-Strauss, *Il totemismo oggi* (Milan: Feltrinelli, 1964), 65.
93   J. D. Sapir, "Fecal Animals," *Man* 12 (1977): 1–21.
94   Ibid., 5.

just like other mortal men, and enjoyed an immortal existence among the gods on Mount Olympus.[95] Heracles is both "this" and "that" at one and the same time. Or, in the words used by the Rees brothers to describe the identity of the hero in Celtic mythology: "It is along this knife-edge line between being and not-being that the god appears."[96]

---

95   Homer *Odyssey* 11.601–4; Lucian *Dialogues of the Dead* 11. On the Alexandrian critique of Homer's lines (which were considered to be interpolations), and above all on the possibility that a single person could have two souls, see Plutarch *De facie lunae* 29.944–45; and Plotinus *Enneads* 4.3.32 and 4.4.1, among others. See also Félix Buffière, *Les mythes d'Homère et la pensée grecque* (Paris: Les Belles Lettres, 1956), 404–9.
96   Rees and Rees, *Celtic Heritage*, 235–37.

Comprehension

Directions: Refer to the readings to respond correctly to the questions below.

1. What is J. K. Rowling's response to the religion-backed critiques of her work?
2. In the Succession Myth of Zeus, what cultures has Hesiod borrowed from? Although the actions of Zeus parallel many of those in the Greek and Western Asian myths, he is not considered an immoral or unjust god. Why does Hesiod portray Zeus as a just god as compared to his predecessors?
3. What mistakes does Zeus make in his prophetic declaration of the birth of Hercules?

Critical Thinking

Directions: Think about the ideas presented in the readings as you form your own answers to the questions below. When possible, use these ideas to support your answer.

1. How do you feel about the backlash received by religious leaders to the publication of the *Harry Potter* books? Are these views justified; why or why not? Should parents be weary of the content of Rowling's books?
2. How do you rationalize the acts of Prometheus with the punishment afflicted to humans? Do you feel Prometheus is deserving of the title of "sponsor or protector" of humankind knowing his actions resulted directly in the suffering of man?
3. What is your opinion of Hera in light of the myth of the birth of Hercules? Do you see her actions as one of trickery (in thwarting the plans of the king of the gods) or cleverness (in justifiable manipulation of an unfaithful husband)?

UNIT II

· ·

Gods and Wizards

As we learn about the gods and their place in the Greek world, certain qualities and themes take shape. While all powerful and immortal, the gods and goddesses fall prey to many of the same shortcomings as humanity: greed, lust, anger, and wrath. The myths in which the gods take the starring role often go beyond their origin story, detailing their core character and, more importantly, why they should be feared. Deep within the myth, however, are morals and lessons that resonate just as strongly as guidelines for how mortals should live their own lives.

When confronted with the opportunity to achieve everything one desires, most of us would likely weigh the consequences before acting. In Reading 2.1, "Heaven, Hell, and Harry Potter," Jerry L. Walls debates the moral implications to desiring ultimate wealth and immortality, and in doing so he confronts the role (via Christianity) of deities and the demand of human morality. The Greek gods equally demanded moral choices in the lives of their mortal counterparts, Zeus being the most adamant of this in his position as god of justice and hospitality, though not always living up to the same standards themselves. Myths then often served as cautionary tales of giving in to such desires. Think for a moment the impact of immortality on Endymion (with Selene) and Tithonus (with Eos). Walls also explores modern naturalism, a contemporary version of Greek humanism, and the place of love in moral philosophy. Love is a complex notion that traverses varying levels of interpersonal relationships and basic human action. While reading, consider the love found in Greek myth, namely Aphrodite, with that understood in our society and written in the *Harry Potter* books.

Also prevalent in mythology are the social structures as defined by the gods and goddesses. Led by the relationship between their king and queen, Zeus and Hera, and touched upon in Reading 1.3, the male-dominated kingdom of the gods served as model for Greek society. The opposite, however, was written by Rowling, as Mimi R. Gladstein shows in Reading 2.2, "Feminism and Equal Opportunity," in the importance of Hermione Granger and other strong female characters of the Wizarding World. This reading serves to provoke thought in the role of women in a society and as seen in that society's myth. While the roles of Greek men and women were clearly defined in the canon of their mythology, these roles have become less demarcated today. Gladstein demonstrates that Rowling's work takes this a step further in which her character's gender is "irrelevant to the question of one's moral fiber." As Greek myth was a mirror on ancient society, evaluate how the witches and wizards of *Harry Potter* reflect our own.

The Greek mythological world was divided into three parts: gods, demigods and mortals, and the in-between (nymphs, gorgons, etc.). Underlying much of the mythos are the relationships within these communities, like that found in the Rowling's stories. In Reading 2.3, "The Order of the Phoenix," Greg Garrett discusses the impact of community to Harry Potter and the students of Hogwarts. The bond of family and friendship is a central influence on Harry across the books/movies, one that can be easily recognized in our own lives. This influence can also be found in Greek mythology, especially within the heroic exploits of the *Iliad* and *Odyssey*. It is family that leads to Hector's sacrifice in front of the walls of Troy and inspires Odysseus's decade-long trek home. It is friendship that thrusts Achilles back to the battlefield from his cocoon of anger and provides Odysseus support in the bloodbath of the suitors. Even in the basic similarities between the Greek and magical worlds, recognize also the kindness, compassion, and love that underscore the modern stories.

The readings in this unit are foundational to understanding the role of myth to the Greeks. As well, in human morality, societal structures, and the relationships of communities, insight can be gained in how the Greeks saw their world and themselves. Through the lens of *Harry Potter*, these discussions transcend the chronological divide and provide the same insight onto our world and ourselves.

READING 2.1   **Heaven, Hell, and Harry Potter**

Jerry L. Walls

The book that made Harry Potter famous comes to a climax in a deadly struggle for an extraordinary Stone with remarkable powers. Not only can this astonishing Stone turn any metal into gold, but it can also produce the Elixir of Life that will make the one who drinks it immortal. When the talented young wizard first learns about the amazing Sorcerer's Stone, his response is the same as one would expect from more ordinary beings: "A stone that makes gold and stops you from ever dying. ... *Anyone* would want it" (SS, p. 220).

As the story unfolds, it becomes apparent that one person who wants it very badly is the evil Voldemort. In the climactic chapter, Harry puts his life on the line to prevent Professor Quirrell, who has sold out to Voldemort, from capturing the Stone. Voldemort urges Quirrell to kill Harry, and if Dumbledore had not arrived in time to intervene, he might have succeeded. And the evil Voldemort would have secured the Stone and become immortal.

After this dramatic incident, Harry awakens in a hospital bed with Dumbledore standing over him and he immediately asks about the Stone, thinking Quirrell must have gotten it. He persists in this question until finally Dumbledore assures him that Quirrell did not in fact manage to steal it.

But then Dumbledore drops a bombshell on Harry. The Stone, he says, has been destroyed. Stunned, Harry then asks about Nicholas Flamel, Dumbledore's 665-year-old friend who created the Stone through alchemy and was its rightful owner. Does this mean that Nicholas and his 658-year-old wife will die? Indeed, Dumbledore informs Harry, they will. While they have enough elixir to set their affairs in order, Nicholas will apparently die before he is 666—a number that is infamous for suggesting evil.[1] When he sees the look of amazement on Harry's face, Dumbledore goes on to explain:

> To one as young as you, I'm sure it seems incredible, but to Nicholas and Perenelle, it really is like going to bed after a very, *very* long day. After all, to the well-organized mind, death is but the next great adventure. You know, the Stone was not really such a wonderful thing. As much money and life as you could want! The two things most human beings would choose above all—the trouble is, humans do have a knack of choosing precisely those things that are worst for them. (SS, p. 297)

These are striking thoughts indeed. No wonder the book goes on to tell us that Harry was "lost for words."

The significance of death is also an important theme in *Order of the Phoenix*. In another dramatic scene, Dumbledore confronts Voldemort but declines to kill him, remarking that taking his life would not satisfy him. As Voldemort sees it, there is nothing worse than death. In response to this, Dumbledore, sounding like Socrates, replies, "Indeed, your failure to understand that there are things much worse than death has always been your greatest weakness ..." (OP, p. 814).

Wise as he appears to be, is Dumbledore right about this? Are there things much worse than death? Is death really a great adventure? Are the things the Stone can offer really bad for us, despite the fact that what it can provide is what everyone seems to be looking for? There are several interesting and important questions here, so let us consider them.

---

1 This is the number of the anti-Christ in the Bible. See Revelation 13:18.

Are We Truly Happy?

Everyone, it seems, would like to have as much money and life as they could want. But death takes our life and taxes take our money. Death and taxes: no wonder they are the two things everyone would like to avoid!

But the fact that we want what we do not have is very telling. It reveals the sad fact that almost no one is truly and fully happy. That is why we want more money and more life. What we have just isn't enough to satisfy us. But if we had the magic Stone, just imagine the possibilities! For a start, I suspect my daughter would purchase her own personal health club, complete with beauty salon and every variety of makeup ever created. My son would purchase the latest BMW roadster, a house with a large music room, every cool CD ever made, a huge TV, and every video game system known to man and boy! Surely then boredom would be vanquished and happiness and joy would reign supreme. If not, well, there is always more stuff to buy if you had unlimited money and an endless life to enjoy it.

Notice Dumbledore's concern. Humans, he says, have a "knack of choosing precisely those things that are worst for them." As the wise old wizard sees it, then, the desire for unlimited money and endless life is deeply misguided. In fact, he suggests, getting these things is the worst thing that could happen to us.

At first glance, this is an odd claim. After all, a common conception of happiness is getting what we want. This was why the ancient Stoics counseled reducing our desires. Fewer and weaker desires clamoring for satisfaction are easier to fulfill. We are unhappy, we think, because our desires are unsatisfied. To put it another way, there is a huge gap between how things are and the way we wish them to be. If we could somehow close this gap, and satisfy all our desires, then we would be happy. And one crucial key to doing this is to have a lot of money, for this gives us the power to get what we want.

Dumbledore sharply challenges this common idea of happiness. His point is that if we desire the wrong things, it is not good for us to get what we want. True happiness is not only a matter of getting what you want, but also of wanting the right things. And that is where Muggles, not to mention young wizards, so often go astray. We don't just have a knack for *choosing* the wrong things, but for *wanting* the wrong things.

Now in one respect, this is conventional wisdom. It has been recognized for centuries that the desire for excessive wealth is a corrupting desire. As the old saying goes, the love of money is the root of all evil. Money is power, and some people will go to any length to get it. It drives people to lie, cheat, steal, and even kill. It can ruin friendships and other relationships. Dumbledore's warning about money is hardly surprising.

In another respect, however, Dumbledore's view appears to be far from conventional. At first glance, his words can be taken to suggest that the desire for unlimited life is also a corrupting desire, like the excessive love of money. Wanting to live forever, he implies, is also a form of greed that humans would be wise to reject. While we may desire immortality as naturally as we desire money, getting it would be a terrible thing for us. And if that is the case, then the love of immortality is also the root of all evil!

Is Death Really a Good Thing?

If we consult the worldview that has been dominant for most of western history and culture, including the British culture in which Rowling writes (namely, that of Christianity), the answer is a resounding *no*! And Christianity is hardly alone here. Many, if not most, other religions and philosophies before modern times not only believed in immortality, but also hoped for it. Indeed, many saw it as the ultimate meaning in life.

Life here in this world, on such a view, is in one sense only a preparation for the life of true happiness and joy that awaits us after death.

On this view, love of money is a root of evil because it can keep us focused on materialistic things and distract us from the greater goods, namely, the moral and spiritual truths that lead to eternal happiness. So love of money is an evil precisely because it keeps us from loving eternal things. It is a shortsighted outlook that blinds us to what is truly valuable and important.

What about worldviews other than Christianity? In this chapter we do not have the space to even name all the others that might be mentioned, but let us consider the worldview that has been the main alternative to Christianity in the West for several centuries now. I am referring to naturalism, the view, basically, that ultimate reality consists of matter, energy, laws of nature, and the like. According to this view, life evolved by chance over a period of billions of years. There is no God, so no one intended for us to be here or had a purpose in mind for our existence before we arrived on the scene. When we die, our lives are over for good. Our fate is the same as the universe at large in the long run. Eventually, all the stars will burn out, the energy will be gone, and all life will disappear as the universe goes on expanding forever. Bluntly put, naturalism tells us this is our fate:

You get old, go to pot;

You die, you rot.

You're soon forgot!

If this is the truth about ultimate reality, the right metaphysical view, then the widespread hope for immortality is completely groundless and futile. All those persons who yearn for it are unfortunate indeed, for their deepest desires are completely out of sync with reality. They want something that reality strictly forbids. E. O. Wilson, a prominent contemporary thinker who holds the naturalistic view, says this is humanity's big problem. He puts it like this: "The essence of humanity's spiritual dilemma is that we evolved genetically to accept one truth and discovered another."[2] What he means is that as human beings evolved they came to believe in God, in life after death, and objective morality. But eventually, in modern times, they came to discover that God does not exist, that morality is something we created for our own purposes, that there is no meaning beyond this life. Thus, our hearts lead us in one direction, but our heads lead another way altogether. If naturalism is true, this is our dilemma: we either have to sacrifice the deepest desires of our hearts or sacrifice intellectual honesty and integrity.

Now if this is our choice, an honest and realistic person might well opt to follow his intellect even if it means sacrificing his fondest wishes and dreams. And if this is the case, the desire for immortality could be seen as a wrongheaded desire that a well-ordered mind would reject. Clearheaded people need to come to terms with reality, even when it is harsh, and if death is the end of the line for all of us, then we need to face that fact and live our lives accordingly.

Indeed, on this view it makes sense to think that it would be self-centered to crave immortality. For the natural resources necessary for life are ultimately limited, a truth that becomes ever more apparent as the population on this little planet continues to grow. There is only so much matter to make up people and the resources they live on. If everybody lived forever, or even as long as Nicholas and Perenelle Flamel, then resources would

---

2   Edward O. Wilson, "The Biological Basis for Morality," *Atlantic Monthly* (April 1998), p. 70.

eventually run out. Given this outlook, it would indeed be greedy to want more life than nature grants to us. We should be grateful for the time we have, and then give our body back to Mother Earth to sustain the great "circle of life" in the generations to come. Nicholas and Perenelle, Harry Potter, and all the rest of us should resign ourselves to being "Happy Rotters"!

This is very idealistic, to put it mildly. Let's face it, naturalism at best is trying to put a positive spin on a bad situation. Here is the heart of the issue. Human beings, as rational creatures, are incurably inclined toward happiness. No rational being can deny the deep and constant desire to be happy. But as noted above, few people seem to be truly and deeply happy. It is an elusive goal we can never deny, but is seldom attained completely. Now then, if we die without experiencing it, we end our lives never having achieved what we most deeply and persistently want. Suppose we *did* find happiness. Surely we would not want to die if we were happy and deeply enjoying our life. Either way, death cannot be seen as anything other than a tragedy that brings whatever happiness we did experience to an unwelcome end.

This point is hardly novel in philosophical literature. Indeed, many leading philosophers have pointed out the ultimate futility of life within a naturalistic framework. For a particularly memorable instance of this consider the following passage from William James's famous work *The Varieties of Religious Experience*:

> For naturalism, fed on recent cosmological speculations, mankind is in a position similar to that of a set of people living on a frozen lake, surrounded by cliffs over which there is no escape, yet knowing that little by little the ice is melting, and the inevitable day drawing near when the last film of it will disappear, and to be drowned ignominiously will be the human creature's portion. The merrier the skating, the warmer and more sparkling the sun by day, and the ruddier the bonfires at night, the more poignant the sadness with which one must take in the meaning of the total situation.[3]

So Why Not Take the Money and Run?

Naturalism poses another glaring question that we cannot avoid. If ultimate reality is indeed matter, energy, and the like, then it is amoral. That is, it is morally indifferent since it is impersonal. Morality is a concern for persons and what is good for them, how they should live, and so on. If ultimate reality is impersonal, then morality is not a part of it. That is why Wilson, cited above, believes morality is a human creation and, as such, is open to our revision.

If naturalism is true, then it has great implications about what is worth valuing and what is of ultimate importance. If there is no life after death, if this life is the end, then it is not so clear why many traditional values are worth the cost. Think about self-sacrifice, for instance, an action that not only has great positive significance in traditional morality, but is also very highly valued in our story. For example, in the remarkable game of chess that Harry, Hermione, and Ron participate in while trying to get to the Stone, Ron is willing to sacrifice himself so Harry can get checkmate. When Harry and Hermione protest, Ron snaps at them, "You've got to make some sacrifices!" (SS, p. 283). And later, Dumbledore reveals to Harry the great significance of

---

3   William James, *The Varieties of Religious Experience* (New York: Modern Library, 1994), p. 159.

his mother's sacrifice in dying to save him when Voldemort tried to kill him as an infant. Such powerful love marked him with a sort of protection that would always be with him (SS, p. 299).

Dumbledore explains this more fully in *Order of the Phoenix* when he tells Harry why he arranged for him to be raised by his aunt and uncle.

> But I knew where Voldemort was weak. And so I made my decision. You would be protected by an ancient magic of which he knows, which he despises, and which he has always, therefore, underestimated—to his cost. I am speaking, of course, of the fact that your mother died to save you. She gave you a lingering protection he never expected, a protection that flows in your veins to this day. I put my trust, therefore, in your mother's blood. I delivered you to her sister, her only remaining relative. (OP, pp. 835–36)

Consider the very real sacrifices made by people in our world, such as the young soldiers who have given their lives in wars. If there is no life after death, then they have forfeited the only happiness available. Many people admire such sacrifice, but we cannot avoid asking why we should have this attitude. Or think about other smaller sacrifices that are made for the sake of living a moral life, like the choice not to have sex outside of marriage. The question is inevitable: if there is no life after death, is there any compelling reason to accept traditional morality, to live by honor, even if it may cost one certain very appealing pleasures, or more drastically, life itself?

A few years ago there was a beer commercial that summed up the issue very concisely, as beer commercials often do. It said, "you only go around once in life, so you've got to grab all the gusto you can."

If it really is true that we only go around once, then we die, we rot, and it's all forgot, then this view makes a good deal of sense. It does not make sense, however, given traditional moral assumptions. In particular, one fundamental assumption of traditional morality is that our ultimate happiness and well being is served, not by being selfish and immoral, but rather by being moral. This assumption makes sense if there is life after death and we are accountable for our actions in such a way that our eternal happiness depends on our doing the right thing and choosing what is truly good. But if there is no life after death and no final accountability, then the only goods that exist are the goods of this life. And if this is so, then some traditional moral requirements are harder to justify.

This is not to say that there is no reason to be moral if there is no life after death. Certainly naturalists have defended morality on their own principles and their arguments are not lightly to be dismissed. For instance, what is moral is often the smart thing to do, and serves our happiness and well being in the short run as well as the long run.

While this is undeniable and would be agreed upon by naturalists as well as theists, there is more to the story. Sometimes what is moral is not only inconvenient, it is also extremely costly and demanding. The more difficult question is whether there is any really good reason to be moral when that is the case. Even more to the point, is there any *obligation* to do what is moral?

Let us put the point in terms of a thought experiment. Suppose there is no life after death and one is given the choice of either 1) living a life of sacrifice to help others or 2) a life of wealth and pleasure, even if one has to cut a few moral corners. Which would be preferable? While some may choose the life of sacrifice because they would find it intrinsically satisfying, or they feel a duty to do so, is there really any convincing reason why one should not take the money and run if one is so inclined?

Magical Moral Obligations

This notion of moral obligation is key, and it is worthwhile to direct attention to it for a moment. It's not the only concern of ethics, but it's an important part. Do you think that Harry was morally obligated to risk himself in saving Dudley at the beginning of *Order of the Phoenix*? Despite Dudley's obvious character flaws, Harry probably was. If so, then we might wonder how moral obligations derive their binding power. Moral duties don't derive their force from serving self-interest, for sometimes they tell us to sacrifice self-interest. So where does their force come from? This is an ethical question that raises the deeper question of what kind of world we live in. If there really are moral obligations that tell us on occasion to sacrifice ourselves for the good of others, the natural question to ask is what sort of world would make best sense of this? It is exactly because moral obligations, if they existed, demand sacrifice of self-interest and feature other odd characteristics, that atheist J. L. Mackie was convinced that they wouldn't exist without an all-powerful God to create them.[4] Genuine moral duties that always trump other competing desires and concerns would be utterly odd entities in a purely natural world. Indeed, they would be practically magical! As an atheist, Mackie thus denied that there are any such obligations after all.

Mackie is not alone among atheists in recognizing that the denial of God's existence has serious moral repercussions. Another notable example is the atheistic existentialist Jean-Paul Sartre, one of the best-known philosophers of the twentieth century, who clearly saw that moral philosophy is profoundly affected if there is no God. He took strong issue with secular ethicists who confidently imagined that we can easily dispense with God while keeping morality pretty much the same as it has always been. He described their agenda as follows:

> Toward 1880, when the French professors endeavored to formulate a secular morality, they said something like this: God is a useless and costly hypothesis, so we will do without it. However, if we are to have morality, a society and a law-abiding world, it is essential that certain values should be taken seriously. ... It must be considered obligatory ... to be honest, not to lie, not to beat one's wife, to bring up children and so forth; so we are going to do a little work on this subject, which will enable us to show that these values exist all the same, inscribed in an intelligible heaven although, of course, there is no God. In other words ... nothing will be changed if God does not exist; we shall rediscover the same norms of honesty, progress and humanity, and we shall have disposed of God as an out-of-date hypothesis which will die away quietly of itself.[5]

Sartre remained unconvinced. He found it "extremely embarrassing that God does not exist, for there disappears with him all possibility of finding values in an intelligible heaven. ... It is nowhere written that 'the good' exists, that one must be honest or must not lie, since we are now upon the plane where there are only men."[6] In contrast, he took as his starting point Dostoevsky's claim that if God does not exist and this life is all there is, everything is permitted. Mackie and Sartre, although atheists, agreed that if God exists, this has enormous implications for morality.

This basic point was also recognized by theistic philosopher Immanuel Kant, who maintained that God's existence is essential for morality. He is well known for arguing that the moral enterprise needs the postulate

---

4   J. L. Mackie, *The Miracle of Theism* (Oxford: Oxford University Press, 1982), p. 115.

5   Jean-Paul Sartre, *Existentialism and Human Emotions*, translated by B. Frechtman (New York: Philosophical Library, 1957), pp. 21–22.

6   *Ibid.*

of a God who can, and will, make happiness correspond to virtue. As George Mavrodes writes, "I suspect that what we have in Kant is the recognition that there cannot be, in any 'reasonable' way, a moral demand upon me, unless reality itself is committed to morality in some deep way."[7] Again, then, we're reminded that the way the world is, the ultimate truth of the matter, has far-reaching implications for morality.

So let's raise the question again, is there any convincing reason why one shouldn't take the money and run if one is so inclined?

Some Damned Good Reasons

Let us return to Dumbledore's remarks cited above. Recall his claim that "to the well-organized mind, death is but the next great adventure." Does the great wizard believe in life after death after all? If so, his warning is not directed against desiring immortality itself, but rather against seeking to prolong *this* life indefinitely, no matter what we have to do to accomplish it.

But perhaps it is not up to us to prolong our lives at any cost. Perhaps immortality is a gift, but a gift to be received only under certain conditions. In this case, to the well-ordered mind, death could indeed be the next great adventure.

Just what this adventure is in Rowling's books remains unclear, at least through *Order of the Phoenix*. This is apparent in a conversation Harry has with Nearly Headless Nick the ghost after he lost Sirius. It is Harry's hope that Sirius will come back as a ghost so he can see him again. According to Nick, however, only wizards can come back, but most of them choose not to do so. Sirius, he says, will have "gone on." Harry presses the question: "Gone on where? Listen—what happens when you die, anyway? Where do you go? Why doesn't everyone come back?" Nick answers that he was afraid of death and that is why he himself remained behind. "I know nothing of the secrets of death, Harry, for I chose my feeble imitation of life instead" (OP, p. 861).

The life of a ghost, then, is "neither here nor there" as Nick puts it, and Harry is left with no answer to his urgent questions. The mystery of what happens when we die, unlike the Chamber of Secrets, remains closed.

By contrast, theism in general, and Christianity in particular, offer a more definite answer to Harry's questions. So let us briefly consider the Christian account of metaphysical reality and how it relates to morality and life after death. According to Christianity, ultimate reality is not matter, energy, and laws of nature. Rather, these are all things created by the ultimate reality, namely, God. The distinctively Christian view of God is striking indeed. According to it, the one God exists eternally as three persons, the Father, the Son, and the Holy Spirit. This is an admittedly mysterious idea, but what I want to emphasize is that it is the foundation for the well-known idea that God is love. C. S. Lewis, the noted Christian writer, pointed this out as follows.

> All sorts of people are fond of repeating the Christian statement that 'God is love'. But they seem not to notice that the words 'God is love' have no real meaning unless God contains at least two Persons. Love is something that one person has for another person. If God was a single person, then before the world was made, He was not love.[8]

---

7   George Mavrodes, "Religion and the Queerness of Morality" in Louis Pojman, *Ethical Theory: Classical and Contemporary Readings*, second edition (New York: Wadsworth, 1995), p. 585.
8   C. S. Lewis, *Mere Christianity* (New York: Macmillan, 1960), p. 151.

What this means is that the nature of ultimate reality, the fundamental metaphysical truth, is loving relationship. God from all eternity has existed as a loving relationship among three persons. Moreover, God loves all His creatures so deeply that He was willing to sacrifice himself to show how much He loves them and wants them to love Him in return. This is what is involved in the Christian belief that Jesus is the Son of God who willingly died for us on the cross to save us from our sins.

If this is true, the story about Harry Potter's mother and the power of her blood is a reflection of one of the deepest truths about reality, namely, that all of us are loved by One who was willing to spill his blood and die for us.[9] Furthermore, the love of Harry's mother is a picture of the fact that love is a greater and more powerful thing than evil and death. It was her sacrificial love that protected Harry when Voldemort and Quirrell tried to kill him. In the Christian story, the resurrection of Jesus shows that love is stronger than death. Jesus offers to share his life with all who believe in him, and this life gives those who receive it the power to live forever. So understood, Christianity is a great love story and it is based on the belief that love is the deepest reality and evil cannot defeat it.

As Dumbledore explains to Harry, the one thing Voldemort cannot understand is love (SS, p. 299). His way of life is the complete opposite of love. Rather than being willing to sacrifice himself for others, he is willing to sacrifice innocent beings for his own selfish purposes. This is shown in the fact that he was willing to perform the monstrous act of slaying a unicorn to keep himself alive. As Firenze, a Centaur, explains to Harry, the only sort of person who would do such a thing would be one "who has nothing to lose, and everything to gain." But to keep oneself alive in this manner is to have only a half-life, a cursed life. Harry's thought when he hears this is quite to the point: "If you're going to be cursed forever, death's better, isn't it?" (SS, p. 258).

It is because love is the deepest reality that it makes sense to do the right thing even if it requires sacrifice to do so. Since God is love, the irony is that when we show love to Him by doing the right thing, we are also acting in our own best self-interest, for He can be trusted to ensure our long-term well being. This is not the same as acting selfishly and it is very important to see the difference. To act selfishly is to promote one's own interest at the unfair advantage of others or even to be willing to do horrible things, like Voldemort, to serve one's own purposes.

The notion that being moral can be at odds with our true self-interest has been a major problem for modern and postmodern moral philosophy. It is a dilemma indeed if one must choose between being moral and acting in one's ultimate self-interest. And it is hard to see how one can reasonably be required to choose what is moral in such a case. And this dilemma arises easily for those with a naturalistic worldview. Prior to modern times, by contrast, moral philosophers generally agreed that there can be no conflict between being moral and our ultimate self-interest.

For the Christian worldview, this conflict simply does not arise. While I do not wish to suggest that there are no other possible answers to this conflict, I do want to emphasize that Christianity offers powerful resources to resolve it. I especially have in mind its account of life after death, particularly its beliefs about heaven and hell. In view of these beliefs, it is impossible to harm one's ultimate well being by doing what is right, even if doing what is right costs one's life. For the person who acts self-sacrificially in obedience to God is acting in accord with ultimate reality, which is the very love of God Himself. He has the gift of eternal life, and he will continue to live with God in heaven after he dies. Death cannot destroy him just as Voldemort could not kill Harry.

---

9   See for example Ephesians 1:7; Hebrews 9:14; I Peter 1:18–19. The strong reaction—both pro and con—to the Mel Gibson film on the passion of Christ is very suggestive in this regard.

Likewise, it is impossible to advance our ultimate well being by doing evil. While our short-term interests may be promoted by doing what is wrong, we are acting against the ultimate grain of reality and we will eventually have to account for our choices. To act immorally is to act against love and to cut ourselves off from God, whose very nature is love. This is hell. This is the cursed life of one like Voldemort who is willing to embrace evil to promote his own purposes.

The right metaphysical view of ultimate reality has huge implications for how we ought to live. On the Christian view, it is precisely because life is forever that there are powerfully good reasons to be moral and to choose the way of love rather than the way of getting as much money as we can for our own selfish purposes. Love is the deepest reality and, if we understand that, we can avoid the trap of choosing the very things that are worst for us. To understand the way of love is to have the sort of well-ordered mind that makes all of life, even death, a fabulous adventure![10]

---

10   To see a further developed version of some of the arguments of this chapter, see Jerry L. Walls, *Heaven: The Logic of Eternal Joy* (New York: Oxford University Press, 2002), pp. 161–200. I am thankful to Shawn Klein, Tracy Cooper, Tom Morris, and Phil Tallon for helpful comments on an earlier version of this essay. I am especially grateful to David Baggett for numerous helpful suggestions.

READING 2.2   Feminism and Equal Opportunity

Mimi R. Gladstein

Women in the enchanted and enchanting world of Harry Potter are anything but second-class citizens. J. K. Rowling depicts a world where equal opportunity among the sexes is a given. Unlike our Muggle world, equality is not something one needs to strive for; it is as natural a part of this world as flying on broomsticks and nearly headless ghosts. Rowling creates a world where what is and should be important is the "content of one's character" and the choices one makes. It is not through magic that the goal envisioned by classical liberal feminism is achieved at Hogwarts: equal rights for men *and* women. Rowling's world gives reality to John Stuart Mill's forward-looking words that the subordination of women should be replaced by a principle of "perfect equality, admitting no power or privilege on one side, nor disability on the other."[1]

While the history of Western philosophy is replete with instances of women being left out of the discussion or disregarded as worthy subjects of study, there is a tradition that sees women as equal moral and social agents. From Plato, up through several Enlightenment thinkers, and now contemporary feminists, philosophers have sought to treat women as the equals of men. This chapter will explore how Rowling's treatment of Hermione and the other important women in the wizarding world exemplifies this important tradition of equality, or at least more closely approximates it than our Muggle world does.

In the Image of Her Creator

Hermione Granger is by far the most important female character in the series, so it is not surprising to learn that she is based, in part, on her creator. Asked why she chose to make her main character a boy, Rowling explains that a heroine might have been nice, but that Harry was "almost fully formed" in her imagination when she began writing what she envisioned as the first of a series of seven books. That, she explains, is why her protagonist "isn't a Harriet instead of a Harry." Rowling adds that she created Hermione as a key figure in the series, "they couldn't do it without Hermione." Hermione is "a very strong character, but then she's based on me."[2] Rowling gave Harry some of her own characteristics—she wore thick glasses as a girl—but she says that she was perceived as being very bossy and often the brightest one in her class, and those traits she gave to Hermione.

Not Just One of the Guys

The close friendship of Harry, Hermione, and Ron is central to the series, projecting an image of equality among the sexes. The Three Musketeers, possibly the most famous trio of literature, are all male. Many other couples or trios in popular literature, such as The Hardy Boys, are also all male. Moreover, if the protagonist

---

1   John Stuart Mill, *On Liberty and On the Subjection of Women* (Ware: Wordsworth Classics, 1996), p. 117.
2   Linda Richards, "January Profile: J. K. Rowling" (January, 2003), p. 5. http://www.januarymagazine.com/profiles/jkrowling.html.

is male, often so is the sidekick as in Quixote and Sancho or the Lone Ranger and Tonto. While a female's presence in the key friendship of a novel is not unique, the ease with which the trio act towards each other highlights how natural equality is in Potter's world. No one thinks twice about this friendship. Hermione is not a lesser member of the group; she is not just a sidekick to Ron and Harry, but an equal and essential member.

While the efforts of early feminists were primarily to combat legal restrictions against women, many contemporary feminists focus on liberating women from psychological and emotional dependency on men. Feminists like Colette Dowling have argued that "the deep wish to be taken care of by others—is the chief force holding women down today."[3] We often see this embodied in the stereotypes that a woman must be saved by a man or that she must be taken care of by a man. Contrary to this stereotype, however, Hermione often acts to rescue Harry and Ron at crucial junctures in the plot. From the first book, where her magical ability saves the trio while they are hunting down the Sorcerer's Stone, to *Order of the Phoenix*, where Hermione saves them all from the tyranny of Professor Umbridge, Hermione's power is clear.

In *Sorcerer's Stone*, Harry, Ron, and Hermione attempt to sneak out of the Gryffindor dorm to find the Sorcerer's Stone. When fellow Gryffindor Neville Longbottom hopelessly attempts to prevent them from breaking any more rules, Harry says to Hermione: "*Do something*" (SS, p. 273). And Hermione does what neither Ron nor Harry can. She utters the charm, "*Petrificus Totalus!*" that immobilizes Neville. Later in that same chapter, Hermione saves both Ron and Harry from the Devil's Snare plant. In *Order of the Phoenix*, Hermione devises and executes a plan to trick the evil Professor Umbridge into her demise so that Harry, Hermione, and the others can get to the Ministry of Magic.

Further evidence that Hermione doesn't suffer from the kind of dependence on men that Dowling and other feminists are concerned about is that she is confident in her own intellect and ability. Hermione can take care of herself. She does not wait for her male friends to defend her when Malfoy insults her. Before the ball in *Goblet of Fire*, he expresses disbelief that anyone would ask her: "You're not telling me someone's asked *that* to the ball? Not the long-molared Mudblood?" (GF, p. 404). Rather than getting her feathers ruffled and retreating, Hermione frightens Malfoy into thinking that Mad-Eye Moody, who had previously turned Malfoy into a ferret, is right behind him. Hermione is not easily intimidated. When Ron warns her against taking on Rita Skeeter, who had caused both Harry and Hagrid such pain with her stories, Hermione refuses to back down.

Strength of Mind and Moral Virtue

Mary Wollstonecraft wrote in 1792 that "women are not allowed to have sufficient strength of mind to acquire what really deserves the name of virtue."[4] Her concern was that women were not being educated in a manner that would allow them to learn and practice virtue, thus preventing them from both becoming the equal of men and fulfilling their human nature. Such a problem is not apparent at Hogwarts. Hermione is able to excel not only in her magical education, but in her moral education as well. Her effectiveness is a product of her intellect, hard work, and persistence. She studies hard; she does her homework. In *Prisoner of Azkaban*, she even uses time travel to take several classes at the same exact time!

---

3   Colette Dowling, *The Cinderella Complex* (New York: Summit, 1981), p. 31.
4   Mary Wollstonecraft, *The Vindication of the Rights of Woman* (Peterborough, Ontario: Broadview Press, 1997), p. 126.

Hard work allows her to help Harry and Ron throughout the series. Harry comments after she had saved them from the Devil's Snare, "Lucky you pay attention in Herbology, Hermione" (SS, p. 278). In contrast, Harry is able to fly a broomstick with little effort and practice. A magic force that he is unaware of protects him, and as an infant, he passively defeats the powerful Lord Voldemort. Many of Harry's powers and abilities seem to come naturally to him, while Hermione's come from lots of hard work and practice. Harry struggles with his fame and identity as a great wizard, in part, because it comes so naturally to him. He wonders if he deserves the praise he receives. Hermione, however, never feels unworthy of her success precisely because it is something she has earned through her hard work.

Hermione's good study habits and subsequent strength of mind are a crucial part of her character. She excels in school throughout the series and her relentless reading often puts her in position to provide key pieces of information. In *Sorcerer's Stone*, she knows how to defeat the Devil's Snare from paying attention in class. In *Goblet of Fire*, she informs Harry and Ron about the reputation of the Durmstrang School of Wizardry. She knows from having read *An Appraisal of Magical Education in Europe* that Durmstrang has a bad reputation because of its emphasis on the Dark Arts. Having read *Hogwarts, A History*, Hermione knows that the school is hidden and disguised. If Muggles look at it, all they will see is an old ruin with a warning sign: Danger, Do Not Enter, Unsafe.

Harry often turns to Hermione for help because of her superior knowledge both in and out of the wizarding world. For example, when he is chosen one of the Hogwarts champions to compete in the Triwizard Tournament against the other magical schools, he goes to her for help on accomplishing the first task, getting past the dragon. He asks her to teach him the Summoning Charm and she even skips lunch to do so. Later, they continue working together until the early morning hours when she pronounces him ready. Harry doesn't seem able to keep up the work without her. When he keeps avoiding practicing for the second task, it is Hermione who is the voice of reason and responsibility, urging him to get on with it.

Throughout the series, Hermione develops her abilities as a witch, but her talents are not limited to magic. She is also good at logic and figuring out puzzles. When the group finds itself stymied by raging flames in *Sorcerer's Stone*, Hermione figures out the clues left on the paper by the seven bottles.[5] As she explains, "This isn't magic—it's logic—a puzzle. A lot of great wizards haven't got an ounce of logic, they'd be stuck in here forever" (SS, p. 285). Hermione also displays her logical abilities on the way to school in *Prisoner of Azkaban* when the trio runs into a sleeping stranger on the Hogwarts Express. While Ron and Harry wonder who this could be, Hermione observantly identifies him as Professor Lupin by looking at the name written on his suitcase. Hermione also quickly deduces what Professor Lupin will teach. "'That's obvious,' whispered Hermione. 'There's only one vacancy, isn't there? Defense Against the Dark Arts'" (PA, p. 75). Logic plays such an important role for philosophy that the influential Austrian philosopher, Ludwig Wittgenstein, thought that all philosophy was just the "logical clarification of thoughts."[6] Thus, in recognizing the importance of logic, Hermione may have the makings for a great philosopher as well as a great witch.

As the series progresses, Hermione adds to her admirable character traits a moral and psychological insight that both Harry and Ron seem to lack. When Harry is chosen to represent Hogwarts in the Triwizard Tournament in *Goblet of Fire*, Hermione explains Ron's jealousy to Harry. Patiently, she tells him, "Look, it's always

---

5   Roger Howe, "Hermione Granger's Solution," *Mathematics Teacher* 95, 2 (February 2002), pp. 86–89. In this article, Howe, who teaches mathematics at Yale University, works out Hermione's reasoning, which is not explained in the novel.
6   Ludwig Wittgenstein, *Tractatus Logico-Philosophicus* (London: Routledge, 1960), p. 77.

you who gets all the attention ..." (GF, p. 289). And when Harry avoids dealing with it himself and asks her to give Ron a message, she responds, "Tell him yourself. It's the only way to sort this out" (GF, p. 290).

As a sign of her moral maturity, Hermione shows concern not just with her own situation, but also for the freedom of others. Like the early nineteenth-century feminists who allied with abolitionists to free the slaves, Hermione is distraught about the plight of house-elves, telling Ron and Harry: "It's slavery, that's what it is!" (GF, p. 125). About Winky, Ron makes the predictable excuse: "that's what she likes, being bossed around ..." to which Hermione retorts, "It's people like *you* ... who prop up rotten and unjust systems, just because you are too lazy to—" (GF, p. 125). When she learns that house-elves have made the delicious meal at Hogwarts, she refuses to eat any more. Hermione takes up the cause of elf rights and works for their equality by creating S.P.E.W., the Society for the Promotion of Elfish Welfare, fighting first for short-term gains, such as fair wages and better working conditions. Eventually, she hopes to change the laws about wand use and achieve elf representation in the Department for the Regulation and Control of Magical Creatures.[7]

While Hermione has been bright, brave, perceptive, and crusading in the books leading up to *Order of the Phoenix*, it is in that work that she positively shines. As in the other books, Hermione keeps winning points for Gryffindor because she always knows the answers and is able to do the magic first. She is astute enough to understand the political implications of Professor Umbridge's first speech at Hogwarts; she understands that the Ministry is trying to interfere with the Hogwarts administration. In her role as prefect, she knows the right threat for the right occasion. When Fred and George's mischief goes awry and they challenge her to do something about it, she threatens them with their mother, which does the trick; they look thunderstruck. After the Cho-kissing incident, when Cho cries as she and Harry kiss, the boys are clueless on the causes of Cho's crying and Hermione has to explain to them what Cho is going through emotionally.

In something of a reversal of the popular stereotype that the male is rational and the female is emotional, Harry and Ron are sometimes masses of emotions, while Hermione is the calm voice of reason. Ever the good friend, she even gives up her Christmas ski holiday to help Harry through a difficult time. Hermione, Ron, and Ginny perform an intervention of sorts to bring Harry back to his senses. It is her idea to have Harry teach a select group secret Defense Against the Dark Arts classes to prepare them for the upcoming battles. When the group is caught in Umbridge's office, Hermione thinks of a plan to thwart her: first crying, then pretending to turn traitor, and finally leading Umbridge to the forest where Grawp, Hagrid's "little" brother, and the centaurs deal with her. This allows Neville, Ron, Ginny, and Luna to escape, leading to the climax of the novel.

The character of Hermione plays the important role of underlining and showing Rowling's vision of a world where what is important—regardless of sex—are people, their choices, and their actions. Hermione is not only just as good as one of the boys; she is often better than they. She excels in school but also in moral character, displaying the strength of mind and virtue that Wollstonecraft saw as essential. She plays key roles in the plot of all the novels, and without her friendship Harry would surely be lost.

Co-education at Hogwarts

More evidence of the high value of equal opportunity in Rowling's world is the co-educational student body at Hogwarts. Girls and boys alike get invitations to be part of each new class. When the prefects are announced,

---

7   For more on the plight of the house-elves, see Chapter 8 in this volume.

there is a boy and a girl chosen from each house, but it is not a matter of affirmative action or even commitment to diversity—it is a matter of merit. Illustrating Mill's "perfect equality," boys and girls are equally able to meet the same high standard to be a prefect.

A number of female students play minor, but key roles in the series. One important secondary character is the beautiful and popular Cho Chang, whom we first meet in *Prisoner of Azkaban* but who is more prominent in *Goblet of Fire* and *Order of the Phoenix*. She is Harry's first crush and a good Quidditch player to boot. Parvati and Padma are the girls Harry and Ron take to the Yule Ball in *Goblet of Fire*. While these dates don't go well for Ron or Harry, both Parvati and Padma join up with Dumbledore's Army in *Order of the Phoenix*. Then there is Luna Lovegood, nicknamed "Loony," who has a vague and distracted manner, but proves herself brave, sensitive, and a valuable ally. She first makes a connection with Harry when she is the only one of the group besides Harry who can see the thestrals (OP, p. 199).

Both at Hogwarts and in the greater wizarding world, women are not only represented in the traditional roles of schoolgirls, mothers, and teachers, but in the more nontraditional roles as sports heroes. Quidditch is the most popular sport in the wizarding world, and the fact that women play on the teams that are competing for the Quidditch World Cup is a major statement about equality. Rowling handles it artfully. In *Goblet of Fire*, at the big game, only the last names of the players are announced to the crowd. The reader does not know anything more about the individual players. We are privy to Harry's thinking as he marvels at the seamless and coordinated movements of Troy, Mullet, and Moran, the Irish Chasers. Not until several pages later do we learn that Mullet is female, when the narrator tells us "Mullet shot toward the goal posts yet again, clutching the Quaffle tightly under her arm ..." (GF, p. 109). When play resumes after a foul, Moran has the Quaffle. The reader learns that Moran is also female when Rowling uses the feminine pronoun to describe how Moran is almost knocked off her broom. The inclusion of female Quidditch players at the highest level of the sport is done without a trace of self-consciousness and their inclusion isn't an issue in the minds of the characters.

This natural participation and inclusion of girls in sports occurs not only in professional sports, but also at Hogwarts where they participate at a varsity level on co-educational teams. In *Sorcerer's Stone*, when team captain Oliver Wood addresses the team as "men," Angelina Johnson corrects him and adds "and women." Angelina is a Chaser for the team, as is Katie Bell. Angelina makes the first score for Gryffindor in the key game of *Sorcerer's Stone;* and eventually, she becomes captain. By *Prisoner of Azkaban*, all three Chasers from the Gryffindor team are girls. When Harry is prevented from playing on the Gryffindor team, Ginny Weasley replaces him as Seeker. Even the umpire, Madam Hooch, is female.

Elizabeth Bobrick, a feminist critic of the Potter series, complains that while the narrator describes the male professors as stately and serious, the female professors at Hogwarts are either fussy or ditzy.[8] A close reading of the texts proves that, on the contrary, Rowling, in her depiction of the professorial staff, is an equal opportunity author. There are the admirable and the questionable among both sexes. In the first place, Bobrick seemingly ignores the fact that under Dumbledore, the Headmaster of Hogwarts, Professor McGonagall is the second in command. Appropriately named Minerva—for the Roman goddess of wisdom—she is the Deputy Headmistress and Dumbledore's chief ally. She is uniformly imposing and admirable throughout the series. In all the books as well as in the movies, McGonagall is a responsible and positive figure. And, it is *she*, not a male professor, who is the faculty sponsor of Gryffindor, the house all the main characters inhabit. Professor

---

8   Elizabeth Bobrick, "Arrested Development," *Women's Review of Books* 20, p. 7 (8th April, 2003).

McGonagall is a teacher that everyone respects; she is "strict and clever." In *Order of the Phoenix*, McGonagall is the only teacher who effectively stands up to Professor Umbridge.

Besides McGonagall, a number of other women teach at Hogwarts. Professor Sprout is the suitably named Herbology teacher, who does her job effectively. When Hagrid goes missing, Professor Grubbly Plank temporarily and competently takes his place as instructor of the Care of Magical Creatures. Madam Pomfrey, the school nurse, runs the infirmary and mends many a victim of a magic experiment gone wrong. She and Professor Sprout heal all those petrified in *Chamber of Secrets*. After the great battle in the Ministry of Magic in *Order of the Phoenix*, Pomfrey restores Ginny, Ron, Hermione, and Neville to health. In addition, males and females author the texts that the students are required to study—for example, *The Standard Book of Spells* by Miranda Goshawk and *A History of Magic* by Bathilda Bagshott. Lastly, two of the four founders of Hogwarts are witches, Helga Hufflepuff and Rowena Ravenclaw.

Equal Opportunity Beyond Hogwarts

Outside of Hogwarts, the magic world is full of morally strong and interesting female characters. In *Order of the Phoenix,* we are introduced to Nymphadora Tonks, a Metamorphmagus—one who can change her appearance at will. She is described as young, with "a pale heart-shaped face, dark twinkling eyes, and short spiky hair that was a violent shade of violet" (OP, p. 47). She is part of the Order that is fighting the Death Eaters. Molly Weasley, who provides a warm and motherly presence in all the earlier works, takes a more active and assertive role at the Order Headquarters when the battle against Lord Voldemort becomes more overt.

Nothing depicts the equality that admits of "no power or privilege on one side, nor disability on the other" more than presenting women from the heights of heroism to the depths of villainy, and every variety of role in between. *Order of the Phoenix* introduces us to the scary and creepy Dolores Umbridge. Umbridge takes over Hogwarts, inspiring fear as she introduces rule after rule to control the student body and prevent the truth of Lord Voldemort's return from being fully recognized. Her punishment of Harry is a torture in which she seems to delight. She sends dementors after him and is prepared to perform the Cruciatus Curse to get him to reveal to her some information.

One of the most evil and capable warriors for the Death Eaters—Voldemort's followers—is Bellatrix Lestrange. It is she who tortured Neville's parents and in the final battle of *Order of the Phoenix*, she kills Sirius Black, Harry's godfather and her own cousin. After she finishes off Black, she wounds Kingsley and is even powerful enough to deflect Dumbledore's spell. She's the last Death Eater standing.

Not on the same level of villainy, but wonderfully smarmy in her own right, Rita Skeeter is introduced in *Goblet of Fire* and continues to practice her brand of yellow journalism in *Order of the Phoenix*. Her stories get Harry into all kinds of trouble and undermine his reputation at Hogwarts. There is also Professor Trelawney, the divinations teacher, who is constantly predicting the demise of Harry. As with most of her predictions, these never come to fruition. More flaky and incompetent than a fake or fraud, Trelawney does make a few predictions that come true. Let's not leave out Pansy Parkinson, a prefect in Slytherin, who is Draco Malfoy's date for the Yule Ball and shows her true colors when she assists Umbridge as part of the Inquisitorial Squad in *Order of the Phoenix.*

It is not just in the individual characters that we see the real equality between the sexes; it is in the action as well. In the big battle with the Death Eaters at the Ministry, the girls fight as hard as the boys, inflicting as much damage on the enemy and taking as much punishment. When they first engage, Hermione stupefies the Death Eater who grabs Harry and then seals a door for their escape by uttering *"Colloportus."* When Neville makes a big mistake by uttering a charm that causes Harry to lose his wand, Hermione repairs the damage by stupefying the Death Eater and getting Harry's wand back with an *Accio Wand* charm. When all seems lost and Harry is about to give the prophecy to Lucius Malfoy, Tonks sends a Stunning Spell at him and helps save the day.

Rowling creates male and female characters across the moral spectrum. We have the incompetent Trelawney and the fake Gilderoy Lockhart. We have Umbridge and Lestrange and Lord Voldemort as villains. And, of course, we have Dumbledore, McGonagall, Harry, and Hermione as heroes. In the world Rowling has created, sex is, as it should be, irrelevant to the question of one's moral fiber. It is never a big deal that women play Quidditch, are in the Triwizard Tournament, are great teachers and poor teachers, or are the heroes and the villains. Each character is judged individually by what kind of person he or she is, and each character is given the opportunity to be either good or evil. It is the individual characters' choices that make them what they are—not their gender. Such a world makes for a wonderful story, but it is one we Muggles should strive to make a reality as well.

READING 2.3   The Order of the Phoenix

Greg Garrett

> *"Harry had no one."*
> —Harry Potter and the Philosopher's Stone

> *"We're with you whatever happens," said Ron.*
> —Harry Potter and the Half-Blood Prince

Community and Compassion

I have never yet passed through King's Cross Station in London when I haven't seen people (often a great seething lump of humanity) gathered to get their pictures taken at Platform 9¾, where a luggage trolley (or, to be a prosaic Muggle, part of one) sticks out of a brick wall, something like the very brick we might imagine Harry and his Hogwarts colleagues passing through to board the Hogwarts Express. While I have not taken my turn trying to pass through the wall, I will confess that I have more than once wished that it were possible to cast a discreet jinx on someone or that I had access to a Time Turner to add just a few more hours to my next deadline. Although I think we've settled that magic in the Harry Potter books is not intended as an alternative belief system or the sign of a higher reality, magic is at the heart of the appeal to many readers of the saga—and likewise, as we've seen, at the heart of the fear of those who worry about their influence.

But whether Harry Potter rides a broom, drives a car, or steers a spaceship, his story is at its center about a boy who did not know where he came from and found home, a boy who so loved the community he became a part of that he willingly gave his life for it. The books bear only Harry Potter's name, and it is he, The Chosen One, The Boy Who Lived, whose life occupies the center of each of the novels. Each book bears the name of a different adventure—*The Prisoner of Azkaban, The Goblet of Fire*—but they are all part of one grand adventure, the adventure of a person finding home and entering community, of a person discovering where he belongs—and with whom. In this dramatic exploration of the importance of community in the novels, we find a subject ripe for our second level of reading, the allegorical, where we seek to find philosophical or spiritual meaning, wisdom with which to live our lives.

When our saga begins, Harry is an orphan who believes himself to be—and, for all intents and purposes, is—alone in the world. Is there a more heartbreaking line in modern fiction than the one from *Sorcerer's Stone* prompted by his first letter from Hogwarts: "No one, ever, in his whole life, had written to him"?[1] Harry is unloved by his nearest relatives, who shut him away in a cupboard under the stairs; he is friendless at school because his cousin Dudley and his gang despise him: "At school, Harry had no one. Everybody knew that Dudley's gang hated that odd Harry Potter in his baggy old clothes and broken glasses."[2] It's an aching loneliness, one that Harry feels will never lift. And yet, during the course of his story, he meets those who are his fellows, who become a new family to him, who shape him, who uphold him in all he does, and finally,

---

1   J. K. Rowling, *Harry Potter and the Sorcerer's Stone* (New York: Scholastic, 1998), 34.
2   Rowling, *Sorcerer's Stone*, 30.

who make it possible for him to do the great work to which he is called. Ultimately, Harry makes possible a world where old divisions are erased, old lines blurred, and a larger, more inclusive community can form—

And all of this has surprisingly little to do with magic. If Platform 9¾ is symbolic in some way, what is most important about it is not the idea of magic that draws people to gather there, but those people gathered, the Muggles like you and me in the station now—and the Hogwarts students and families in Harry's story. In one of the first serious discussions of the Potter books, Alan Jacobs wrote that the purpose of Hogwarts is not just to teach students how to use magic (the technical aspects of spell casting, potion-making, etc.), but to teach "the moral discernment necessary to avoid the continued reproduction" of dark wizards like Voldemort.[3]

We have already seen Dumbledore speak of how he hoped that Hogwarts would shape Tom Riddle, not simply how he would be taught to use magic; a primary purpose of communities like Hogwarts School of Witchcraft and Wizardry is to develop character. In reading the books, we follow Harry through seven years of education and formation, both formal and informal. It is for this reason that Harry's story is sometimes referred to by literary critics as a *Bildungsroman*, the traditional literary term for a story about the education of a young person. "It is Harry's journey," Rowling says of the saga she wrote, and what matters most in the course of the story is how Harry learns from encounters, people, and his own successes and failures to become a worthy person—a person capable of doing what is right.[4] Much of that moral discernment comes in response to those in Harry's life—family, friends, and the communities to which he belongs, either by accident or by choice.

Love, friendship, tolerance, and family are all central themes of the Harry Potter story, and all revolve around our relationships with others. Rowling clearly thinks these are vital; not only did she foreground these thematic elements in the Potter tale, but in her commencement address at Harvard, Rowling discussed imagination (in the sense of empathy and compassion with others) and friendship as the two pieces of wisdom she wished to pass on to those best and brightest. The focus on friendship, compassion, and empathy supports a powerful wisdom reading of the Potter novels, for one of the great spiritual truths is that we must recognize the importance and validity of others.

Compassion and concern for one's fellow human beings seem to be universally extolled among the great wisdom traditions. In Buddhism, this understanding is found in the centrality of compassion for all life; four of the Five Noble Precepts of Buddhism revolve around respectful relationship with others (and the fifth, which is to avoid intoxication, could also be interpreted in light of our treatment of others). One of the Five Pillars of Islam is *Jakat*: all good Muslims are called to share of their possessions with those who are in need, and this act of turning toward another is considered to be as important as the action of turning toward Mecca in daily prayer. Within the Jewish tradition, the Rabbi Hillel, a contemporary of Jesus, told a seeker who wanted a summary of the Jewish Law, "What is hateful to yourself, do not do to your fellow man. That is the whole of the Torah and the remainder is but commentary." Hillel's version of what we now call the Golden Rule—treat others as you yourself wish to be treated—is one of many such formulations from many different cultures. Charles Kimball suggests that this clear requirement is at the heart of all

---

3   Alan Jacobs, "Harry Potter's Magic," *First Things* 99 (January 2000): 35–38, http://www.firstthings.com/article/2007/01 /harry-potters-magic-28.

4   "J. K. Rowling at the Royal Albert Hall, 26 June 2003," *Accio Quote!* http://www.accio-quote.org/articles/2003/0626 -alberthall-fry.htm.

wisdom traditions that are "authentic, healthy, life-sustaining."[5] Other versions, spoken by Jesus, Confucius, or Socrates, to name a few, show us that compassion and empathy are at the heart of any transformational spiritual understanding.

Rowling herself has talked about how empathy is essential for human beings on a journey, and we see it expressed dramatically in her stories. Hermione, particularly, is a person capable of seeing and feeling the suffering of others. When at the beginning of *Order of the Phoenix* Harry has, by Dumbledore's orders, been left alone with the Dursleys all one miserable summer and angrily takes his friends to task when he sees them again, his angry resentment and bitter speech would call up defensiveness and indignation in many of us. But Hermione listens to him rant and then responds, "'Harry, we're really sorry!' ... 'You're absolutely right, Harry—I'd be furious if it was me!'"[6] It is Hermione who recognizes that "Professor Moody's" demonstration of the Cruciatus Curse on the spider is disturbing Neville (whose parents, we later learn, were tortured by the self-same spell) and who—fine student though she is—actually interrupts the lesson:

> "Stop it!" Hermione said shrilly.
>
> Harry looked around at her. She was looking, not at the spider, but at Neville, and Harry, following her gaze, saw that Neville's hands were clenched upon the desk in front of him, his knuckles white, his eyes wide and horrified.[7]

Hermione later rushes Ron and Harry out of the class, not to go to the library, as Ron suspects, but to check on Neville, who they find standing frozen in the middle of the hallway, "staring at the stone wall opposite him with the same horrified, wide-eyed look he had worn when Moody had demonstrated the Cruciatus Curse."[8] Although Hermione speaks gently to him, he's clearly strongly affected by what he has witnessed—emotions to which Harry and Ron have been oblivious.

And in contrast to almost all the other characters, who respond with revulsion and disgust to Kreacher, Hermione joins Dumbledore in showing sympathy to the ancient house elf who has imbibed the vile blood theories and evil of the House of Black. Even though Kreacher reviles her as "Mudblood" and recoils from her touch, Hermione can imagine his lot and his life, even understanding why he might have betrayed his master Sirius Black to Sirius' cousins Narcissa Malfoy and Bellatrix Lestrange:

> "Harry, Kreacher doesn't think like that," said Hermione, wiping her eyes on the back of her hand. "He's a slave; house-elves are used to bad, even brutal treatment. ... He's loyal to people who are kind to him, and Mrs. Black must have been, and Regulus certainly was, so he served them willingly and parroted their beliefs. ... Sirius was horrible to Kreacher, Harry ... Kreacher had been alone for a long time when Sirius came to live here, and he was probably starving for a bit of affection. I'm sure 'Miss Cissy' and 'Miss Bella' were perfectly lovely to Kreacher when he turned up, so he did them a favor and told them everything they wanted to know."[9]

---

5   Charles Kimball, *When Religion Becomes Evil* (New York: Harper-SanFrancisco, 2002), 39.

6   J. K. Rowling, *Harry Potter and the Order of the Phoenix* (New York: Scholastic, 2003), 66.

7   J. K. Rowling, *Harry Potter and the Goblet of Fire* (New York: Scholastic, 2000), 214–15.

8   Rowling, *Goblet of Fire*, 218.

9   J. K. Rowling, *Harry Potter and the Deathly Hallows* (New York: Scholastic, 2007), 198.

Hermione is one of Rowling's characters who displays the compassion and empathy that truly good people are supposed to demonstrate; Dumbledore is another. More centrally, of course, Harry learns these qualities, embraces them, and becomes a sacrificial hero who gives his life for the people he loves. Voldemort doesn't have these qualities and, what's more, doesn't ever want them, and he is destroyed—physically and spiritually—because he fails to see the importance of communion. But other villains besides Voldemort result from the human failure to see our common humanity; there are also real world villains, as J. K. Rowling knows better than most of us. During her time working at Amnesty International, she encountered the broken victims of power-hungry people, but she also saw the power of human good: "The power of human empathy, leading to collective action, saves lives and frees prisoners. ... Unlike any other creature on this planet, humans can learn and understand, without having experiences," she said in her speech at Harvard. This ability to empathize, she went on, was more than just a gift; it was a responsibility. Refusing to empathize with others might not mean that the person cutting her- or himself off would personally become a monster, she noted, but it certainly made the actions of actual monsters possible.[10] The failure of people of good will to understand the needs of those who suffer ultimately leads to as much damage as the active evil of those who exploit them, for without that empathy, how can anyone be engaged to care?

Compassion means more than simply kindness to the weak and downtrodden, however, although in almost all wisdom traditions it certainly means that. It also means loving and attempting to understand those who oppose us, those who share our humanity if not our opinions. This is a countercultural and perhaps even a counterintuitive action, but it is at the heart of compassion teachings. In surprising ways, the Potter novels also show us unaccountable mercies rendered to others—even to those we might think of as aliens or enemies. Dumbledore's willingness to offer people a second chance (one of his defining characteristics, according to Hagrid), Hermione's concern for all creatures including goblins and house elves, Harry's mercy extended to Peter Pettigrew when Sirius and Lupin intend to kill him in *Prisoner of Azkaban*, Harry's rescue of his longtime enemy Draco Malfoy from the blazing Room of Missing Things in *Deathly Hallows*, and even Harry's concern for the mewling naked fetus that is the remnant of Voldemort's soul in the ethereal King's Cross Station at the end of *Deathly Hallows* are strong reminders that we are called to be in relationship with others, to recognize the needs of others, and to forgive others, even when they are different or difficult.

Rowling has said, in fact, that one of Harry's defining characteristics is that he is a person who rescues others, even when it is inconvenient or dangerous or even—as in the case with Voldemort's maimed soul—counterproductive. "Harry's impulse, to the point of utter wrongheadedness," Rowling said, "is to save. His deepest nature is to try and save, even when he's wrong to do so, when he's led into traps ... now he goes off and tries to save as many people as he can."[11] Harry even offers Voldemort one last chance to repent—to feel remorse—although the Dark Lord disdainfully refuses it, and goes on to his own doom:

> "I'd advise you to think about what you've done. ... Think, and try for some remorse, Riddle. ..."
> ... "It's your one last chance," said Harry. "It's all you've got left. ... I've seen what you'll become otherwise. ... Be a man ... try ... Try for some remorse. ..."[12]

---

10   J. K. Rowling, "The Fringe Benefits of Failure, and the Importance of Imagination," *Harvard Magazine*, June 5, 2008, http://harvardmagazine.com/commencement/the-fringe-benefits-failure-the-importance-imagination.

11   "Rowling Answers 10 Questions About Harry," *Time*, http://www.time.com/time/specials/2007/personoftheyear/article/0,28804,1690753_1695388_1695569,00.html.

12   Rowling, *Deathly Hallows*, 741.

By "be a man," Harry means that Voldemort should put away his notions of being more than human, as he had told the Muggle caretaker, and to embrace his humanity, with all the responsibility that comes with it. To be truly human is to be a person who cares for others, although this is unfortunately something Voldemort will never do, and it is the end of him. Being unable to imagine and care about the lives of others not only leaves him spiritually void, it also leaves him blinded to the way others think, feel, and react—and results in his physical death as well.

Community and Formation

But being in community is about more than what we are able to do for others; we are also formed in community, educated and supported and challenged to reach our fullest potential as human beings. Dumbledore had hoped that Tom Riddle might find himself transformed from a selfish and dangerous boy into a more responsible man by the Hogwarts experience; certainly this is what happens to Harry Potter, another orphan who comes to Hogwarts. Harry fulfills his destiny only through his interactions within that community, and he is ultimately pointed toward and strengthened to become his best and most noble self in and through others. He learns formally from his teachers, even those he hates, like Snape (perhaps especially from Snape, by the time the series is concluded); he learns informally from Ron, Hermione, Neville, and Luna. When we consider the Harry Potter story start to finish, we discover that it is the story of how an orphan finds a family; how a boy alone winds up surrounded by people who love, support, and follow him; and how a group of people comes together to become a community with sufficient virtue to stand up for the truth even when it means facing death. These are powerful truths worth carrying into our own lives.

Since we are made for community, it is with great sadness that we recognize that when we first meet him, Harry Potter's essential condition is that of isolation, a condition that recurs with some frequency throughout Harry's story. Although he discovers friends and a sort of family in the Wizarding world, Harry is also, by virtue of who he is and what he is called to do, lonely for much of his life. We see this isolation most strongly in *Order of the Phoenix*. When Dumbledore pulls away from Harry for fear of inducing Voldemort to exploit the connection between himself and the boy, when most people in the Wizarding world refuse to believe Harry's version of his encounter with Voldemort and Cedric Diggory's death at the conclusion of *Goblet of Fire*, and when even close friends such as his roommate Seamus pull away from him or question his veracity, Harry is left in a fearful state of solitude. The film version of *Order of the Phoenix* finds a wonderful way to express this theme visually in shots of Harry alone, and in a new scene between Harry and Luna Lovegood placed early in the film:

> **Luna Lovegood:** [about her father] We believe you, by the way. That He-Who-Must-Not-Be-Named is back, and you fought him, and the Ministry and the Prophet are conspiring against you and Dumbledore.
>
> **Harry Potter:** Thanks. Seems you're about the only ones that do.
>
> **Luna Lovegood:** I don't think that's true. But I suppose that's how he wants you to feel.
>
> **Harry Potter:** What do you mean?
>
> **Luna Lovegood:** Well if I were You-Know-Who, I'd want you to feel cut off from everyone else. Because if it's just you alone you're not as much of a threat.

There are many times in the novels when Harry feels completely alone, abandoned, misunderstood. In *Order of the Phoenix*, he lashes out at his friends after being left alone all summer, and after Sirius' death at the Ministry of Magic, Harry pushes back even against Dumbledore. The headmaster, who loved Sirius and Harry alike, and who has lost more than a few people he loved to death, tells Harry that he knows how he must be feeling, but Harry cannot see beyond his own intense pain: "'YOU DON'T KNOW HOW I FEEL!'" Harry roared. "'YOU—STANDING THERE—YOU—'"[13] In that moment, Harry again feels as though he is alone in the universe. Through the love and patience of Dumbledore, Hermione and Ron, and Hagrid, however, he is reminded that he is part of a community, but he still cannot help but feel separate in some ways, particularly after he hears about the prophecy from Dumbledore:

> Perhaps the reason he wanted to be alone was because he had felt isolated from everybody since his talk with Dumbledore. An invisible barrier separated him from the rest of the world. He was—he had always been—a marked man. ... It was sunny, and the grounds around him were full of laughing people, and even though he felt as distant from them as though he belonged to a different race, it was still very hard to believe. ...[14]

When we study Harry's loneliness and the importance of community in relieving it, we also gain new understanding of the Dark Lord's brokenness. Voldemort's essential state of solitude is self-chosen; to love others or to be part of a larger community are the furthest things from his mind. The closest he will ever come to community is to create Horcruxes, fragments of his own self, a horrid parody of community that Voldemort hopes will spare him from the fate of all humankind—and from any need for it. Like Jean Paul Sartre, perhaps, Voldemort would opine that Hell is other people.

C. S. Lewis explores this idea in his novel *The Great Divorce*, where he actually depicts Hell as a great gray city, its interior largely depopulated. Its inhabitants have all moved out farther and farther into the suburbs because they can't bear to be in contact with anyone. "They've been moving on and on," a character on the bus tells the novel's narrator. "Getting farther apart. They're so far off by now that they could never think of coming to the bus stop at all. ... Millions of miles from us and from one another. Every now and then they move further."[15] Voldemort would perhaps be happy out in the suburbs of Hell, if only because he would have no need for or contact with others, but for those of us who are called to community, distance and nonengagement are not options.

Voldemort does not understand—in fact, denigrates—love, but Dumbledore has long recognized that strength is to be found only in that deeper magic. It is Dumbledore who forms the two iterations of the Order of the Phoenix; it is in his honor that his students name their student magic class Dumbledore's Army; and it is the headmaster who constantly insists that Harry include his bosom friends Ron and Hermione in the difficult and dangerous adventures thrust upon him, as in the beginning of *Half-Blood Prince*, when Harry admits he has not told anyone about the contents of the prophecy about him. Dumbledore approves his reticence, but then urges him to relax his discipline "in favor of your friends":

> "I think they ought to know. You do them a disservice by not confiding something this important to them."

---

13 Rowling, *Order of the Phoenix*, 824.
14 Rowling, *Order of the Phoenix*, 855–56.
15 C. S. Lewis, *The Great Divorce* (New York: Macmillan, 1946), 19.

"I didn't want—"

"—to worry or frighten them?" said Dumbledore, surveying Harry over the top of his half-moon spectacles. "Or perhaps, to confess that you yourself are worried and frightened? You need your friends, Harry. As you so rightly said, Sirius would not have wanted you to shut yourself away."[16]

Sirius, who loved and needed his friends, is a good model for Harry, for when Sirius disregarded his friends and struck out on his own, disaster often followed.

We need others, as we are reminded throughout the Potter series, although our tendency often is to draw away from others or, even worse, to voluntarily divide ourselves. Witness the song of the Sorting Hat in *Order of the Phoenix*, the beginning of the first Hogwarts year following Voldemort's return. After noting the historic conflict between the Hogwarts founders and the departure of Slytherin, the Sorting Hat goes on to sing,

> And never since the founders four
>
> Were whittled down to three
>
> Have the Houses been united
>
> As they once were meant to be.
>
> And now the Sorting Hat is here
>
> And you all know the score:
>
> I sort you into houses
>
> Because this is what I'm for,
>
> But this year I'll go further,
>
> Listen closely to my song:
>
> Though condemned I am to split you
>
> Still I worry that it's wrong, ...
>
> Still I wonder whether sorting
>
> May not bring the end I fear.[17]

By setting ourselves apart, whether it is in failing to confide in others or segregating ourselves from others, we make hells for ourselves—and cut ourselves off from becoming who we are supposed to be.

It is within family that we first hope to encounter community, and it is there that we hope to have our emotional and formational needs met. When families work right, we find a soothing similarity—Leo Tolstoy began the novel *Anna Karenina* by saying that "Happy families are all alike." But, as in Harry Potter's story, family can and sometimes does fall short of acting as a loving and supportive community. Henri Nouwen

---

16   J. K. Rowling, *Harry Potter and the Half-Blood Prince* (New York: Scholastic, 2005), 78.

17   Rowling, *Order of the Phoenix*, 206.

noted that in many families, "love comes in a very broken and limited way. It can be tainted by power plays, jealousy, resentment, vindictiveness, and even abuse. ... Sometimes human love is so imperfect that we can hardly recognize it as love," which seems an apt description of life at 4 Privet Drive.[18]

One would hardly recognize what the Dursleys have given Harry as "love." Dumbledore sums up Harry's existence with Uncle Vernon and Aunt Petunia in Book 6:

> "You have never treated Harry as a son. He has known nothing but neglect and often cruelty at your hands. The best that can be said is that he has at least escaped the appalling damage you have inflicted upon the unfortunate boy sitting between you [Dudley]. ... However miserable [Harry] has been here, however unwelcome, however badly treated, you have at least, grudgingly, allowed him houseroom."[19]

Although the Dursleys are related to Harry by blood, they have failed him, and Barbara Brown Taylor observes that, unfortunately, "Many families do not work right. They are not schools in forbearance and forgiveness but reformatories where rules are more important than people and where the first rule is silence."[20] For Harry, imprisoned at first under the Dursleys' stairs and later forced to tell people that he is a student at St. Brutus' Secure Center for Criminally Incurable Boys, "reformatory" seems an apt metaphor. In Book 3, we read that "For years Aunt Petunia and Uncle Vernon had hoped that if they kept Harry as downtrodden as possible, they would be able to squash the magic out of him," and perhaps they think that all of this is for his own good.[21] It is certainly for theirs.

Families are our first community, but Harry, in time-honored literary fashion, is an orphan, cut off from loving parents and forced into the care of strangers, these Dursleys. Another notable orphan is Tom Riddle, whose upbringing at the orphanage we observe in Dumbledore's memories in *Half-Blood Prince* suggests that his emotional needs were quite as badly ignored as were Harry's. Throughout, Rowling draws parallels between the two, the Dark Lord and The Chosen One, yet one boy becomes a hero, the other a villain; one tries to reclaim family, one rejects it.

Harry is constantly filled with desire for communion with the family he lost. In his first adventure, when Harry discovers the Mirror of Erised and sees his mother and father within it, he becomes so taken with the images that he loses interest in all other activities—until Dumbledore discovers what he is doing. Dumbledore cautions Harry against the Mirror, for "It shows us nothing more or less than the deepest, most desperate desire of our hearts. You, who have never known your family, see them standing around you ... It does not do to dwell on dreams and forget to live, remember that."[22] Dumbledore, who according to Rowling would have seen his own mangled family whole and alive in the Mirror (not, as he tells Harry, a warm pair of thick woolen socks), knows whereof he speaks.[23] Harry's desire for attachment to the parents he has never known can never be realized, and so could paralyze him in the present—or could it be realized? For Harry's family continues

---

18   Henri Nouwen, "June 13," in *Bread for the Journey: A Daybook of Wisdom and Faith* (San Francisco: HarperSanFrancisco, 1997), n.p.

19   Rowling, *Half-Blood Prince*, 55.

20   Barbara Brown Taylor, *The Seeds of Heaven: Sermons on the Gospel of Matthew* (Louisville: Westminster John Knox, 2004), 85.

21   J. K. Rowling, *Harry Potter and the Prisoner of Azkaban* (New York: Scholastic, 1999), 2.

22   Rowling, *Sorcerer's Stone*, 213–14.

23   "Rowling Answers 10 Questions About Harry," *Time*.

to pop up during his adventures. In *Prisoner of Azkaban*, he believes that he and Sirius have been saved from Dementors by his father's Petronus charm—although Harry later discovers that it was he himself, traveling back in time, who cast that spell. In *Half-Blood Prince*, Harry imagines that the marvelous potion-maker who had used his potions text before him was actually his father, although there is little real evidence of that.

Harry learns early that it is impossible for magic to truly raise the dead, but it must be difficult indeed not to seek communion with your family when you live in a world in which magic like the Mirror of Erised can dredge their memories up for you again, willingly or unwillingly. At the end of *Philosopher's Stone*, Hagrid gives Harry a photo album full of magically moving wizard pictures of his parents; in *Prisoner of Azkaban*, the foul magic of the Dementors forces Harry to relive the deaths of his parents when he was an infant, sounds that would otherwise have been unavailable to him; in various memories of Snape's and Dumbledore's, Harry witnesses his parents as children and Hogwarts students; in the collision of his wand with Voldemort's at the end of *Order of the Phoenix*, Harry's parents are brought back to a sort of life, as they are by the Resurrection Stone shortly before Harry offers his own life in Book 7.

Forging Families—and Character

These are mere simulacra of family, however; for real relationship, Harry requires flesh and blood, and this is what he discovers at Hogwarts. As he and the other first years wait nervously to enter the hall, Professor McGonagall says, "Before you take your seats in the Great Hall, you will be sorted into your houses. The Sorting is a very important ceremony because, while you are here, your house will be something like your family within Hogwarts. You will have classes with the rest of your house, sleep in your house dormitory, and spend free time in your house common room."[24] The boy who has never been a part of a family before is now going to be launched into the midst of community.

Through his relationships with Hermione and Ron and in his time with the Weasleys (Harry's favorite family), who begin hosting Harry for portions of holidays starting in Book 2, Harry learns about the unqualified acceptance of family. When Harry goes to be with the Weasleys, what he finds most different from his time with the Dursleys is not the clanking of pipes from the ghoul or the random explosions from Fred and George's room; it is the strange and unaccountable "fact that everybody there seemed to like him."[25] They do more than like him, of course; Hermione and all of the Weasleys—even the ambitious Percy, who for several novels is on the outs with his family—will love, support, sacrifice for, and fight on Harry's behalf, and before the saga is complete, some will be badly wounded or even killed in the struggle against Voldemort.

Later in his education, Harry will meet his godfather, Sirius Black, another orphan who found a family at Hogwarts that shaped his life and gave it meaning, although their time together proves too brief. Harry grieves in *Half-Blood Prince*, since "the fact that he had had someone outside Hogwarts who cared what happened to him, almost like a parent, had been one of the best things about discovering his godfather. ... and now the post owls would never bring him that comfort again."[26] Although someday Harry will form his own family with Ginny Weasley and, it appears, give his children the stable and loving home he never had, in the present action

---

24 Rowling, *Sorcerer's Stone*, 114.
25 J. K. Rowling, *Harry Potter and the Chamber of Secrets* (New York: Scholastic, 1999), 42.
26 Rowling, *Half-Blood Prince*, 77.

of the novel Harry experiences little of real community through those to whom he is related; but since we are made to be in community, he seeks it elsewhere. His realization in Book 4 "that he would rather be here [at Hogwarts] and facing a dragon than back on Privet Drive with Dudley" marks the contrast between the two places.[27] One of them is a home in name only; the other has become Harry's home in fact.

For Harry, Hogwarts is indeed the community within which his moral formation takes place, an extended family with a father figure (Dumbledore), brother and sister (Ron and Hermione), spinster aunt (Professor McGonagall), and eccentric uncle (Hagrid), as well as the home he never expected to find. It also reveals some essential facts about community—those wildly diverse "family members" are actually a central part of his formation. Hogwarts exemplifies this regard for unity amidst difference from its very formation; the four founders of Hogwarts (Helga Hufflepuff, Rowena Ravenclaw, Godric Gryffindor, and Salazar Slytherin), different though they each were, believed that their differences could create a formative experience for the students of the larger school. As the Sorting Hat sings at the beginning of term in *Goblet of Fire*,

> They shared a wish, a hope, a dream,
>
> They hatched a daring plan
>
> To educate young sorcerers
>
> Thus Hogwarts School began.
>
> Now each of these four founders
>
> Formed their own house, for each
>
> Did value different virtues
>
> In the ones they had to teach.[28]

Rowling says that she designed the four houses at Hogwarts to conform to the four elements, all of which are necessary to form the universe (Hufflepuff, earth; Ravenclaw, air; Gryffindor, fire; Slytherin, water): "It was this idea of harmony and balance, that you had four necessary components and by integrating them you would make a very strong place."[29] Moreover, it would make for a strong and balanced community. Hogwarts is a vision of a body with many members in which not all have the same function. Rowling herself spoke of the need to have four different houses by saying, "You have to embrace all of a person, you have to take them with their flaws and everyone's got them. It's the same way with a student body. If only they could achieve perfect unity, you would have an absolutely unstoppable force, and I suppose it's that craving for unity and wholeness that means that they keep the quarter of the school that maybe does not encapsulate the most generous and noble qualities ... in the very Dumbledore-esque hope that they will achieve union, and they will achieve harmony."[30]

---

27 Rowling, *Goblet of Fire*, 339.

28 Rowling, *Goblet of Fire*, 177.

29 Melissa Anelli and Emerson Spartz, "The Leaky Cauldron and Mugglenet Interview: Joanne Kathleen Rowling: Part Three," *The Leaky Cauldron*, July 16, 2005, http://www.the-leaky-cauldron.org/features/interviews/jkr3.

30 Anelli and Spartz, "The Leaky Cauldron."

The ideal community recognizes that not everyone shares the same function, yet all are essential to the operation of the whole. So it is that each house represents a cardinal virtue: Students sorted into Gryffindor tend to be courageous, Hufflepuffs hardworking, Slytherins ambitious, Ravenclaws intellectual. And even within houses there is diversity of gifts. Within Gryffindor, renowned for bravery, we nonetheless find diverse wizards: Harry is brilliant at defense against the dark arts; Neville is a gifted herbologist; Fred and George Weasley create complicated gag gifts; Pavarti Patil is drawn to divination; Hermione excels at transfiguration.

It is true that members of houses compete for things like the Quidditch team and dates to the Yule Ball and that the four houses are pitted against each other in formal competition, more "us" versus "them" differentiation. The House Cup is a primary plot element of the first three Potter novels, but it becomes clear as the stakes become higher in the later books that this competition is not nearly so important as it at first seemed. In fact, as the dangers mount and the challenges come hard and fast, what matters is people coming together to confront a common problem. At the conclusion of *Goblet of Fire*, Dumbledore addresses the assembled students—including those from the rival wizarding schools Durmstrang and Beauxbatons—about the necessity of their coming together to face difficult times: "The Triwizard Tournament's aim was to further and promote magical understanding. In the light of what has happened—of Lord Voldemort's return—such ties are more important than ever before. ... we are only as strong as we are united, as weak as we are divided." Although Voldemort was uniquely skilled in creating discord and pushing people apart, Dumbledore said this did not have to be the case; wizards could fight the malice of He-Who-Must-Not-Be-Named "by showing an equally strong bond of friendship and trust."[31]

This trust between houses does seem to grow in the course of the books, so that when we reach the end of the story in Book 7, when Slytherin Pansy Parkinson suggests to the assembled houses in the Great Hall that they grab Harry and turn him over to Voldemort, the response from all but the Slytherins is immediate and unanimous: Gryffindors, Hufflepuffs, and Ravenclaws stand to their feet and draw their wands, forming a barrier between Harry and any who might hurt him, all of them united around their belief in him and in each other.[32]

This solidarity is not singular; by this time, Gryffindors, Hufflepuffs, and Ravenclaws have been united before, as we shall see, in the student organization known as Dumbledore's Army, formed in *The Order of the Phoenix*, and in the actual Order of the Phoenix as well. But what of the House of Slytherin? Are they, as Pansy's outburst and the house's subsequent slinking away from the forthcoming battle in *Deathly Hallows* suggest, simply outsiders, the "them" to be expelled, at best, and destroyed at worst? By no means. Professor Horace Slughorn, the Head of Slytherin, is roused to fight back against Voldemort and the Death Eaters in the final battle, and he himself duels the Dark Lord, alongside McGonagall and Kingsley Shacklebolt; Regulus Black, younger brother of Sirius, turns against the Dark Lord and steals one of Voldemort's Horcruxes at the cost of his own life; and Severus Snape spends his entire life watching over Harry, a child he loathes, to atone for the wrong he did as a young man in allowing Lily Potter to be killed. At the conclusion of Book 7, the old Slytherin headmaster, Phineas Nigellus Black, joins the portraits of all the former Hogwarts headmasters in applauding the victorious Harry, Ron, and Hermione, and he calls out, "And let it be noted that Slytherin House played its part! Let our contribution not be forgotten!"[33]

---

31 Rowling, *Goblet of Fire*, 723.
32 Rowling, *Deathly Hallows*, 610.
33 Rowling, *Deathly Hallows*, 749.

Rowling is clear that while the vast majority of dark wizards may emerge from Slytherin, the Noble House of Slytherin is also necessary for the health of the Hogwarts body. Our experience in these books is somewhat lopsided, she suggests, because it is almost entirely from the perspectives of Malfoy, Crabbe, and Goyle, Harry's nemeses. "You are seeing Slytherin house always from the perspectives of Death Eaters' children. They are a small fraction of the total Slytherin population. I'm not saying all the other Slytherins are adorable, but they're certainly not Draco."[34] Ambition, the cardinal virtue of Slytherins, can lead some to explore dark magic, but it is also a prerequisite for greatness, perhaps one of the reasons the Sorting Hat originally suggested that Harry might do well in Slytherin:

> "Not Slytherin, eh?" said the small voice. "Are you sure? You could be great, you know, it's all here in your head, and Slytherin will help you on the way to greatness, no doubt about that—no? Well, if you're sure—better be GRYFFINDOR!"[35]

Ambition unchecked can lead to danger, but in truth, the defining qualities of any of the houses could be a bad thing if overemphasized or left unchecked—too much book learning, or resolute hard work, or bravery would also unbalance a life and perhaps damage a person and those around him.

One must have, at the very least, tolerance if diverse people are going to live and work together, because this diversity is, as the founders of Hogwarts—and later Albus Dumbledore—knew, necessary for the development of the whole. The Slytherins may be difficult, but nonetheless, they are part of the community, a valuable part, to be forgiven as many times as necessary to keep them within the family. It may not be possible for members of this artificial family to be close; sometimes, as seems to be the case with the Malfoys, tolerance seems to be as far as anyone can possibly go. At the conclusion of the Battle of Hogwarts, when fifty of Harry's friends and followers lie dead, the Malfoys sit, unmolested, in the Great Hall of Hogwarts as mourning goes on around them; they are not welcomed with open arms, but in the general joy, as everywhere Harry looks he sees families reunited, they share that joy of reunion, and, perhaps, they begin to repent for the things they have done to those around them in the name of the Dark Lord they served so unwisely.[36]

Harry and his friends save Draco's life—twice!—in *Deathly Hallows*, yet in the final chapter, set nineteen years after the climactic Battle of Hogwarts, Draco's son Scorpius (like Harry's Albus Severus) is headed to his first year at Hogwarts, but Draco still stands apart from the other parents on Platform 9¾: "Draco caught sight of Harry, Ron, Hermione, and Ginny staring at him, nodded curtly, and turned away again."[37] Rowling, likewise, suggested in an interview that while Draco and Harry might have "a kind of rapprochement, in that Harry knows Draco hated being a Death Eater ... [and] Draco would feel a grudging gratitude toward Harry for saving his life ... Real friendship would be out of the question ... Too much had happened prior to the final battle."[38] Perhaps Harry and Draco will never be friends. But still, there they both stand, two fathers, both seeing their beloved children off to Hogwarts.

Draco is gathered into the light, albeit somewhat unwillingly and tentatively; so too are some who are no longer with us, such as Severus Snape, one-time Head of Slytherin. When in the final chapter of the saga

---

34   Anelli and Spartz, "The Leaky Cauldron."

35   Rowling, *Sorcerer's Stone*, 120.

36   Rowling, *Deathly Hallows*, 745–46.

37   Rowling, *Deathly Hallows*, 756.

38   "J. K. Rowling Web Chat Transcript," *The Leaky Cauldron*, July 30, 2007, http://www.the-leaky-cauldron.org/2007/7/30/j-k-rowling-web-chat-transcript.

Harry's son Albus Severus tells his father that he fears the Sorting Hat will place him into Slytherin, Harry reminds him that he was named for two headmasters of Hogwarts, one of whom was a Slytherin. If the Sorting Hat puts him into Slytherin, "then Slytherin House will have gained an excellent student, won't it? It doesn't matter to us, Al."[39] The important thing about this sorting, as Harry has long known, is that choice enters into it. Who you are is less a matter of what someone else decrees about you and, as Dumbledore had told Harry at the end of *Chamber of Secrets*, more about what you choose. Similarly, Dumbledore tells Cornelius Fudge in *Goblet of Fire*, "it matters not what someone is born, but what they grow to be!"[40] Choice is an essential element in moral formation.

We cannot choose our families (although we can choose our relation to them), but in the communities Harry does choose there is much we can learn. During his time at Hogwarts, Harry chooses friendships, chooses to lead the student organization called Dumbledore's Army, and chooses to affiliate himself with the anti-Voldemort group called the Order of the Phoenix. These choices reveal much about what we are called to be and do.

Members and Friends

With the help of Hermione and Ron, Harry is involved in the creation of a diverse group of students seeking to learn Defense Against the Dark Arts in contravention of Dolores Umbridge's teaching—and policies. They gather specifically in response to Harry's news about Voldemort's return: "I want to be properly trained in Defense [Against the Dark Arts] because," Hermione tells the assembled group, "Lord Voldemort's back."[41]

The students take the name "Dumbledore's Army" in response to Umbridge's ridiculous fears that if the students learn real magic they'll form a militia Dumbledore can lead against the Ministry of Magic. Under Harry's tutelage, they train assiduously for their real purpose—confronting dark magic. In their time together, this group forms attachments to each other and to the cause they fight for. They support each other, with Harry teaching them and the others reinforcing his teaching. They communicate with each other—Hermione enchants fake Galleons they can use as magical pagers. And they stand up for each other—in Umbridge's office, when Umbridge is about to torture Harry for information about who he has been communicating with, Hermione, obeyer of rules and respecter of authority, comes up with a devious plan to get her and Harry out of that office—a plan that ultimately gets Umbridge carried off by centaurs into the Forbidden Forest. Then when Harry heads to the Department of Mysteries thinking he is going to save Sirius, he is convinced to let Neville, Ginny, and Luna come along with him, Ron, and Hermione:

> "We were all in the D.A. together," said Neville quietly. "It was all supposed to be about fighting You-Know-Who, wasn't it? And this is the first chance we've had to do something real—or was that all a game or something?"
>
> "No—of course it wasn't—" said Harry impatiently.
>
> "Then we should come too," said Neville simply. "We want to help."[42]

---

39 Rowling, *Deathly Hallows*, 758.
40 Rowling, *Goblet of Fire*, 708.
41 Rowling, *Order of the Phoenix*, 340.
42 Rowling, *Order of the Phoenix*, 761.

When Ginny, Neville, and Luna join Harry, Hermione, and Ron in invading the Ministry of Magic's Department of Mysteries to keep Voldemort from gaining the prophecy he seeks, the notion of community takes its most substantial shape and begins to show its function. This is, as Harry notes, not the group he would have put together; "he would not have picked Ginny, Neville, or Luna."[43] But they pull together, they fight together, and as Hauerwas said, they help each other become who they are supposed to be.

We have said that Harry is formed by others, but this same type of formation is true of many within the Hogwarts community. We can see radical change most clearly in the person of Neville Longbottom, son of members of the first Order of the Phoenix who were tortured into insanity; as Dumbledore later relates, both Harry and Neville were born at the right time to fulfill the prophecy that a child would destroy Voldemort, so Neville could just as easily have been Voldemort's target instead of Harry. During the first books, Neville seems to be a bumbling incompetent as unlikely to live up to his grandmother's grandiose hopes for him as he is to be the prophesied One who will defeat the Dark Lord. However, by the time Book 7 has ended, we can see that Neville has been transformed by his time among friends who support and encourage him. Neville becomes the focal point for anti-Voldemort activity at Hogwarts when Harry, Ron, and Hermione do not return to school for their final year, and he leads a guerilla war against new headmaster Severus Snape and the other Death Eaters on his faculty. Neville actually keeps hope alive at Hogwarts until Harry and the others arrive, and we can see how different he seems now compared to the boy who could do nothing right; thanks to his experiences with Harry, in the D.A., and in the Ministry, Neville has become a hero as well. When he welcomes Harry, Ron, and Hermione to the Room of Requirement toward the end of *Deathly Hallows*, he explains a little of what has gone on in their absence:

> "Alecto, Amycus's sister, teaches Muggle Studies, which is compulsory for everyone. We've all got to listen to her explain how Muggles are like animals, stupid and dirty, and how they drove wizards into hiding by being vicious toward them ... I got this one," he indicated another slash to his face, "for asking her how much Muggle blood she and her brother have got."
>
> "Blimey, Neville," said Ron, "there's a time and a place for getting a smart mouth."
>
> "You didn't hear her," said Neville. "You wouldn't have stood it either. The thing is, it helps when people stand up to them, it gives everyone hope. I used to notice that when you did it, Harry."[44]

In the end, Neville proves that Professor Trelawney's long-ago prophecy was valid, no matter which boy it referred to; while Harry's willing sacrifice is the most important element in the defeat of Lord Voldemort, it is Neville who produces the Sword of Gryffindor—which can only be drawn by a worthy Gryffindor—and slays the serpent Nagini. By the conclusion of the saga, Neville has grown into the man—and the wizard—he is supposed to be, the ultimate goal for any of us, and his friendships and membership in Dumbledore's Army are at the heart of his transformation.

This is likewise the way the organization known as the Order of the Phoenix functions: as a supportive community that forms around a set of beliefs and actions. During the First Wizarding War, this group assembles around Dumbledore and includes many younger wizards, including James and Lily Potter, Sirius Black, and Remus Lupin. The group re-forms when Voldemort returns at the end of *Goblet of Fire*, at the beginning of the Second Wizarding War.

---

43   Rowling, *Order of the Phoenix*, 761.
44   Rowling, *Deathly Hallows*, 574.

Harry Potter meets all sorts of people: some who want to know him because he is famous, some who hate him because he is famous, some who look to him to be a leader, some who oppose him because of what he represents. But Harry is fortunate that in his life he finds a series of true friends who love and encourage him—and challenge him—to become the person he is meant to be. Among the most important of them is Dumbledore. Albus Dumbledore was a friend to James and Lily Potter, a member with them in the first Order of the Phoenix, and it is Dumbledore we assume to have taken charge of details when the Potters were killed. He sets up Harry's stay with the Dursleys, and he seems to be responsible for the burial of the Potters and the setting up of their grave marker. And then, when Harry comes to Hogwarts, Dumbledore takes a special interest in him, looking after him, encouraging him, challenging him. Theirs is a relationship that marks Dumbledore as Harry's mentor and true friend.

We have observed that friendship is valuable and beautiful. But what, exactly, is a friend? The ancient world gave serious thought to this relationship. In Bronze Age epics, warriors are often depicted as brothers, their friendships sometimes closer even than sexual relationships. Xenophon, a student of Socrates, wrote a dialogue between his teacher and Critobulus on the topic of friendship. After discussing the sorts of self-serving and self-centered people one would not desire as a friend, Socrates turned to the question of whom to choose for true friendship: "I should say he must be just the converse of the above: he has control over the pleasures of the body, he is kindly disposed, upright in all his dealings, very zealous is he not to be outdone in kindness by his benefactors, if only his friends may derive some profit from his acquaintance."

When Critobulus asked how we might test those qualities before seeking friendship, Socrates answered, "How do we test the merits of a sculptor? Not by inferences drawn from the talk of the artist merely. No, we look to what he has already achieved. These former statues of his were nobly executed, and we trust he will do equally well with the rest." So a person who has been kind to his friends may be trusted, as Critobulus concludes from their discussion, to treat the newer friend as amiably.[45]

In these understandings, a true friend is a person whose works are unselfish, true, and beautiful, and whose earlier kindnesses to friends are well known. Dumbledore would certainly fit this description. Although Dumbledore seems to show up at important moments in Harry's life and always to be present at adventure's end to explain what has happened and what might happen next, it is not until *Order of the Phoenix* that we realize the degree to which Dumbledore has watched over Harry. At the end of *Order of the Phoenix*, he tells Harry how he has followed all that has happened to him over the years: "I defy anyone who has watched you as I have—and I have watched you more closely than you can have imagined—not to want to save you more pain than you had already suffered."[46] Surely this is what a friend does—watches, loves, tries to spare one from pain—but also calls a friend to her or his best self. As Rowling pointed out, "Dumbledore is a very wise man who knows that Harry is going to have to learn a few hard lessons to prepare him for what may be coming in his life. He allows Harry to get into what he wouldn't allow another pupil to do and he also unwillingly permits Harry to confront things he'd rather protect him from."[47]

In the Celtic tradition, people speak of the *anam cara*, the soul friend, and surely that is what Ron, Harry, and Hermione are to each other. Without an *anam cara*, we are lost, for we have no one with whom to share our truest selves, and it is here, of course, that Voldemort is most destitute. In response to an interview question

---

45   Xenophon, *The Memorabilia*, II.vi.
46   Rowling, *Order of the Phoenix*, 838–39.
47   "J. K. Rowling at the Royal Albert Hall," *Accio Quote!*

about whether Voldemort had ever loved, Rowling responded, "No, he loved only power, and himself. He valued people whom he could use to advance his own objectives."[48] But nothing more. As Dumbledore told Harry after sharing with him his first memory of encountering the future Lord Voldemort, even as a boy, Tom Riddle did not want to be like anyone else or considered ordinary, and he certainly did not wish companions:

> I trust that you also noticed that Tom Riddle was already highly self-sufficient, secretive, and, apparently, friendless? ... The adult Voldemort is the same. You will hear many of his Death Eaters claiming that they are in his confidence, that they alone are close to him, even understand him. They are deluded. Lord Voldemort has never had a friend, nor do I believe that he has ever wanted one.[49]

Many believe that they are Voldemort's *anam cara*; all are deluded, mere tools for him to use, and that is both their—and his—loss.

In this chapter we've explored the power of community in the Potter novels and in the world, and we'll close by considering the purposes of community. Like the new families formed in Harry Potter, like the communities coming together around a common mission, like the Order of the Phoenix, organizing as a force for justice and good, a true community gathers diverse people, begins the task of transforming them, and through them, begins to transform the world as well. The harmful values of society and the painful mistakes of individuals can begin to be corrected through this faithful, if imperfect, community—and it is to that act of transformation of a world gone dangerously wrong, to the heroic acts of sacrifice and good, that we turn now.

What is wrong with the world? How can we hope to fix it? What values will be life-giving, and how can we have the courage to champion them? Harry, Hermione, Ron, and their friends and family show us that we must learn to choose between what is right and what is easy, as well as how to recognize those things so that we can choose wisely.

---

48   "J. K. Rowling Web Chat Transcript," *The Leaky Cauldron.*
49   Rowling, *Half-Blood Prince*, 277.

Comprehension

Directions: Refer to the readings to respond correctly to the questions below.

1. How do theists and naturalists ultimately consolidate moral living in their differing views of reality? Where do the humanistic views of the Greek philosophers fit in?
2. Review the many ways Rowling makes gender "irrelevant" to her stories.
3. Who were the most influential friends to Harry Potter, and how did their compassion and friendship influence him?

Critical Thinking

Directions: Think about the ideas presented in the readings as you form your own answers to the questions below. When possible, use these ideas to support your answer.

1. Compare and contrast the modern (theism and *Harry Potter*) and ancient (Greek mythology) takes on love. Having an inherently better understanding of modern love (in all its forms), what are your views of the ancient Greeks and their uses of love in their lives?
2. While considering the *Harry Potter* stories, in what ways can strong female characters be found in Greek mythology? How are their actions reflections of their society (i.e., what makes them strong)?

How might the path of Harry Potter been altered had he not met Hermione and Ron on the way to Hogwarts? Do you feel the same result would have transpired?

UNIT III

. . . .

Heroes

While the gods were credited for the world in which the Greeks lived and the societal rules and morals they must follow, it is the heroes that served as role models for how to do so successfully. Whether of direct (Achilles, Hercules) or indirect (Odysseus) divine lineage, what made the Greek heroes heroic often boiled down not to their godly abilities but rather actions and attitudes when faced with mortal dilemmas. The previous readings have focused on dramas and comedies of the gods in which there are no real dangers for the divine and humans are subjugated to supporting roles. This unit shifts the spotlight onto the mortals who inhabited the Greek world, playing out their own dramas with death an ever-present danger, while the gods reveled in their roles as puppet masters. This dichotomy underscores the tragedy of mortality and enhances the magnificence of heroes. Included in this unit are modern summaries of the *Iliad*, *Odyssey*, and Heracles in which the author, David Mulroy, eliminates the superfluous in favor of not just the important plot points but also central moments that define the heroes.

In the first line of the *Iliad*, Homer distinguishes the story as one of the anger of Achilles. While reading Reading 3.1, "The Anger of Achilles (Homer's *Iliad*)," recognize the ways that Achilles changes the tide of the Trojan War. Keep in mind that the story takes place ten years into a war in which both sides have seen the darkest depths of humanity as each seeks the utter destruction of the other. Such a trying decade has inevitably left the main cast of characters struggling, with the daily threat of death affecting them in different ways. Agamemnon, king of the Greeks, striving to keep his army motivated to win a personal vendetta. Odysseus and Diomedes fighting with their strength, intelligence, and divine help. Priam, king of the Trojans, fearing the end of his kingdom and family at the hands of an army knocking on his palace gates. Hector, greatest warrior of Troy, forced to bravely defend his city, in which lay his wife and newborn son, owing to the indiscretion of his brother, Paris. Helen, queen of Sparta and now princess of Troy, regretting her choice of love with Paris over her duty as wife to Menelaus. While the drama plays out among the mortals, behind the scenes the gods have chosen sides in the war. In the end, the will of the gods, chief among them the anger of Hera at Troy and the reluctant loyalty of Zeus to his wife, determines the fate of man.

In "Homer and the *Iliad*: Necessity and Grace" (Reading 3.2), Ilham Dilman confronts the power war demands, leading those enthralled within it to single-mindedly follow its rule: kill or be killed. The civility of mankind is thus lost except in the fleeting moments during temporary peace and only to, almost begrudgingly, escape us once more at the beginning of the next battle. These fleeting, but important moments, do not just endear the characters a semblance of humanity among the inhumane but also highlight the brutality of war, the highs and lows of the story. Think about how Homer's *Iliad* affords us the insight into the necessity and grace of war. Further, it is important to appreciate that Homer's view of the *Iliad* does not lend the reader or listener to favor one side or the other. In fact, there are points in which both sides look to be both the hero and the villain. The Trojan Paris instigated the war, but his brother Hector fights admirably to protect his home and family. Agamemnon and Achilles fall prey to their base desires of glory and hubris yet return to humility and acceptance of their fate. Both sides display heroic bravery and despicable cruelty during the war, in large part because they are staring at their own mortality in the faces of the opposing armies hell-bent on their destruction.

Taking place a decade after the Trojan war, the *Odyssey* (Reading 3.3), "The Return of Odysseus (Homer's *Odyssey*)," serves as a sequel of sorts for the *Iliad*, shifting the heroic focus onto Odysseus. We learn the fates of many of the Greek leaders on their homebound voyages, with everyone but the titular character having arrived or perished along the way. As Odysseus recounts his journey home, compare the ways in which he overcomes the constant obstacles he encounters with his actions in the war. At Ithaca, Penelope and Telemachus, wife and son of Odysseus, are still playing host to the suitors who arrived twenty years earlier, looking to take Odysseus's place as king and all the while eating and drinking their way through the kingdom's stores. The suitors represent the penultimate problem for our hero, with his wife as the final barrier, keeping Odysseus from a reunion with his family. While not lacking in bravery, leadership, or courage, the defining characteristic of Odysseus's heroism is his intelligence. Even as he is given divine help, reflect upon the nonviolent solutions to his problems that characterize his position as a Greek hero. Recognize as well that throughout both of Homer's epics, Odysseus's actions as champion, leader of men, husband, and father optimized what it was to be Greek.

The greatest, or at least most revered, of the Greek heroes was Heracles (Latin: Hercules). Even though a son of Zeus, his life (Reading 3.4, "The Life of Hercules") was filled with trials and tribulations that often beset mortals, albeit to a far more dramatic degree. While reading Mulroy's summary, piece together the character of Heracles as portrayed in the myths. Observe both the superhuman and fallible aspects of the man and how these attributes led to his heroic deeds as well as ultimate downfall. Many of the misfortunes that befall Hercules arise as consequences of the wrath of Hera and her jealousy of Zeus's philandering. The queen of the gods manipulates the births of Eurystheus and Heracles to ensure Zeus's prophecy does not grant the latter the kingdom of Mycenae. Additionally, the labors of Hercules represent not-so-subtle attempts by Hera to lead the hero to his death. Heracles represents perhaps the gravest example of humankind's subjection to the wills of the gods. Yet, in the end, having overcome the worst Mount Olympus and the Greek world can throw at him, Heracles's ascent to divinity is the only fitting reward.

Reading through the heroic exploits of Achilles, Odysseus, and Heracles (among others) results in many of the defining characteristics of a Greek hero becoming evident, such as bravery, intelligence, and strength. In Rowling's Wizarding World, on the other hand, Harry Potter personifies more classical virtues throughout his adventures, namely courage. Tom Morris ("The Courageous Harry Potter," Reading 3.5) outlines the strategies Harry followed to gather his courage: preparation, support, dialogue, focus, and action. When reading, think upon the circumstances in which Rowling places Harry that elicit courage. Compare them to the typical heroic situations of Greek myth—for instance in Achilles at the battle of Troy, Odysseus on his journey home, and Heracles in completing his tasks. Reflect on these comparisons and recognize the parallels between the stories of Rowling and the Greeks. Whereas Harry Potter's courage being different from the Greeks can often be rooted in the modern settings of the tale (i.e., a school), recognizing that facing difficult circumstances is an inherent part of life and one that can separate heroes of a story from its supporting characters is also true.

Heroic myths were intrinsically more relatable to the Greeks. The main characters, albeit often divinely blessed, faced physical and mental obstacles that were not entirely unlike that of the real world. The same can be said of Harry Potter and his adventures in the Wizarding World of J. K. Rowling. To the Greeks millennia ago, hearing Achilles face his inevitable death, Odysseus outwit his enemies, and Heracles complete each impossible task gave guidance to overcoming their own mortal difficulties. Almost three thousand years later, Harry Potter can be just as much of a role model. To a generation of modern readers, the adventures in which Rowling places Harry are enveloped by magic but require very muggle attributes to conquer. Perhaps it is exactly that aspect, Harry's triumphs through courage instead of magic, that makes him a greater hero than the Greeks ever were.

READING 3.1   The Anger of Achilles

David Mulroy

The Greek army is assembled on the shore of Troy, where it has been waging war for ten years. An elderly man with a cart full of treasure approaches. He holds a golden staff festooned with ribbons. He is Chryses, priest of Apollo. The Greeks took his daughter, Chryseis, captive when they raided his city. She is now the slave of Agamemnon, king of Mycenae and the Greeks' supreme commander. Chryses wishes the Greeks well and asks them to exchange his daughter for the gifts he has brought. The other Greeks shout approval, but Agamemnon rejects the offer, saying that Chryseis will grow old in his service, weaving and keeping him company in bed. If he sees Chryses in camp again, his sacred staff will not protect him.

Terrified, Chryses goes back along the shore, praying to Apollo to punish the Greeks. Apollo hears the prayer and rushes toward the Greek camp with his quiver clanging. Kneeling nearby, he unleashes his arrows, which cause a deadly plague. First mules and dogs die, then soldiers, and the camp is filled with funeral pyres.

After nine days, Achilles calls an assembly. He wants to ask some holy man why Apollo has sent a plague. The Greeks' priest, Calchas, says that he is willing to speak but asks Achilles for a promise of protection since his words may anger a great king. Achilles promises.

Calchas says that the Greeks have to free Chryses' daughter without a ransom to end the plague. This irks Agamemnon, who says that Calchas's prophesies are never beneficial for him. He wanted to keep Chryseis, because he prefers her to his own wife, Clytemnestra. He will give her up to save the army, but he demands to be compensated with a new prize.

Achilles objects, calling Agamemnon the greediest of men. He points out that the Greeks have no spare prizes. They have distributed all the booty that they have won. After they conquer Troy, he says, they will repay Agamemnon for the loss of Chyrseis.

Agamemnon rejects that suggestion. He says that he will not go without a prize. Either the Greeks will give him one, or he will just take one—from anyone he chooses, including Achilles.

This outrages Achilles. He has no personal grievance against the Trojans, he says. He fights only as a favor to Agamemnon and his brother Menelaus. He does more than his share of the work while Agamemnon gets the biggest gifts. He is going home.

Agamemnon tells him to go. Meanwhile, however, he will take Achilles' prize, the slave girl Briseis, as compensation for Chryseis. Hearing this, Achilles reaches for his sword. He is on the verge of killing Agamemnon, but before he does it, Athena appears to him alone. She grabs the hair on the back of his head and tells him to put back his sword. He will be repaid for this insult in the future.

Achilles obeys. Calling Agamemnon a "wineskin with the eyes of a dog and the heart of a deer," he swears a formal oath that Greeks will look for him in vain someday, when they are being slaughtered by the Trojan Hector.

After the elderly King Nestor fails to reconcile Agamemnon and Achilles, the assembly breaks up. Odysseus escorts Chryseis back to her father. Agamemnon sends heralds to Achilles' tent to take Briseis. Achilles receives them courteously and has his comrade, Patroclus, bring the girl to them.

Achilles goes to a lonely spot on the beach, weeps, and calls to his mother, the sea goddess Thetis. When she arrives, Achilles describes what has happened. He reminds her that she claims to have influence with

Zeus. Supposedly, Thetis once saved him from a rebellion by Hera, Poseidon, and Athena by bringing him a hundred-armed giant to be a bodyguard. Would she now ask Zeus to punish the Greeks in battle, to teach Agamemnon a lesson? Thetis agrees to do so—in 12 days, when Zeus returns from Ethiopia, where he is attending a feast.

Twelve days later, Thetis flies to Olympus, finds Zeus alone on the mountain's highest peak, and explains what she wants. Zeus lets her know that her favor is not easy since his wife Hera already complains that he helps the Trojans too much. Nevertheless, he assents. Olympus shakes when he nods his head.

During the night, Zeus sends a deceptive dream to Agamemnon, promising him that Troy will fall if he leads the army into battle that morning. Agamemnon rises, shares his dream with the other generals, and assembles the entire host, though Achilles and his men stay in their tents.

At the assembly, Agamemnon tests his troops' morale by pretending to be discouraged, suggesting that they all go home. At once, the assembly breaks up, and the soldiers run for the ships. All that prevents the war from ending at this point is that Hera sends Athena to the scene. She goes to Odysseus and tells him to talk the men into coming back. Odysseus chases down the retreating soldiers, reasoning with kings and abusing common men. The army flows back into the assembly.

Now, a man named Thersites addresses the soldiers. Bowlegged and lame, he is the ugliest man in the army, has round shoulders, a hollow chest, and a bald, pointed head, and loves to criticize his leaders. He urges the Greeks to give up and go home. Agamemnon, he says, is too greedy and has now offended the army's best warrior. Odysseus rises to silence Thersites. He says that the has no right to criticize superior warriors, and if he ever speaks again, Odysseus will strip him naked and flog him. Then, to the cheers of the other soldiers, Odysseus hits Thersites across the back with the scepter that he holds, driving him away in tears.

Odysseus next reminds the army of a sign that they saw when leaving for Troy. A snake climbed a tree, devoured a mother sparrow and eight chicks, and was then changed to stone by the gods. At that time, Calchas predicted that Troy would hold out for nine years and fall in the tenth. And this is the tenth year.

The Greeks disperse for breakfast, then assemble in battle formation, representing the various tribes of Greece. Ajax the Lesser leads the Locrians. He is small and dresses in linen but is a good spearman. Ajax the Greater leads a small fleet from the island of Salamis. Diomedes leads a great fleet from Argos and Tiryns. Agamemnon, the greatest king of all, leads the largest fleet from Mycenae. His brother, Menelaus, leads the men of Sparta. He is eager to avenge the loss of Helen. The elderly Nestor leads the men of Pylos. Odysseus leads a small fleet from Ithaca and other nearby islands. Idomeneus leads the men of Crete. Achilles leads the men of Phthia and nearby regions. They are known as the Myrmidons. They stay in their tents because of Achilles' anger. The others march into the plain.

In Troy, old king Priam is holding an assembly, when the goddess Iris, disguised as a young Trojan lookout, announces that the Greeks are marching toward the city. The Trojans march out to meet them. They are led by Priam's son, Hector. Other Trojan leaders are Aeneas, son of Aphrodite and Anchises, and the archer Pandaros. Foreign allies swell the Trojan army. These include Sarpedon of Lycia and his comrade Glaucus.

As the armies approach each other, Hector's brother Paris sees Menelaus and shrinks back behind the front lines. Hector scolds him for stealing Menelaus's wife but not being man enough to stand up to him in battle—where good looks don't help. Paris acknowledges the justice of Hector's words and volunteers to fight Menelaus in a single combat to end the war. Hector strides between the armies and gets everybody on both sides to sit down so that arrangements can be made for a truce and the single combat. Soldiers on both sides are very happy.

Soon, the fight is underway. After the warriors exchange spear casts, Menelaus charges Paris with a drawn sword, which he shatters on Paris' helmet. Frustrated, he grabs the helmet by hand, spins Paris around, and drags him toward the Greek lines—and certain death. Aphrodite, however, breaks the helmet's chin strap so that it comes off in Menelaus's hand. As Menelaus turns back, Aphrodite wraps Paris in a dark mist, picks him up, and sets him down in his bedroom. Then, disguised as an old seamstress, she finds Helen and tells her to visit Paris in their bedroom. She says that he looks like he has just come from a dance, not a battle. Helen recognizes Aphrodite through her disguise and refuses to go, because of what the Trojan women will say. This draws an angry rebuke from Aphrodite, who threatens to abandon Helen to the hatred of Greeks and Trojans alike. Helen is frightened and obeys.

In the bedroom, Helen scolds Paris for having boasted that he was a better warrior than Menelaus. Paris says that Menelaus just happened to have the gods on his side. They will fight again in the future. For the present, they should go to bed together. He has never desired her more, not even when they made love the first time on the island of Cranae as they were sailing away from Sparta. Helen gives in.

Outside the city walls, Menelaus is storming up and down, looking for Paris. Agamemnon announces that his brother won and that the war should end on the Greeks' terms. Zeus, however, sends Athena to the battlefield to restart the war. She crosses the sky in the form of a comet and then appears on the plain disguised as a young Trojan noble. She sidles up to Pandaros, the archer, and tells him to take a shot at Menelaus. Paris, she says, will give him a huge reward for killing him. Persuaded, Pandaros shoots but only grazes Menelaus's waist. Seeing the blood flow down his leg—like red dye on ivory—Agamemnon fears the worst and summons physicians, who quickly mend the wound. Meanwhile, the two sides put their armor back on and resume their march toward each other. The Greeks advance in silence; the Trojans bleating like sheep. Soon the battle rages, with countless deaths on both sides.

The Greek Diomedes is wounded in the foot by Pandaros. Then, revived by Athena, he goes on a rampage. One of the first to fall to him is Pandaros himself. Diomedes' spear enters Pandaros's face beside the eye, severs his tongue, and comes out the bottom of his jaw. When Aphrodite carries the wounded Aeneas out of harm's way, Diomedes even wounds her in the wrist. Later, with Athena's help, he strikes Ares himself in the belly and forces him to withdraw from battle.

Diomedes finally slows down when he is about to fight the Trojan ally, Glaucus. He asks Glaucus whether he is a god or a mortal man, since he does not want to do battle against the gods. Glaucus responds,

> "High-spirited son of Tydeus, why ask about my origins.
>
> Generations of men are like generations of leaves.
>
> Some leaves are flung down to the earth by the breeze, while others
>
> Burst to life in the woods when the season of spring arrives.
>
> Just so a generation of men is born; another passes."

Glaucus goes on to explain that he is the grandson of a great hero, Bellerophon. Hearing this, Diomedes exclaims that his own grandfather, Oeneus, was a friend to Bellerophon. Hence, he and Glaucus have an ancient connection. Instead of fighting, therefore, the two heroes exchange gifts and agree to avoid each other in battle. Glaucus loses out in the exchange of gifts, giving Diomedes golden armor in return for bronze.

Since the Trojans are losing, Hector goes into the city to ask the Trojan women to say special prayers to Athena for help. Before he returns to battle, Hector stops by Paris's bedroom. Paris says that he is just getting ready to fight.

Hector also seeks out his wife, Andromache. She has gone to the city walls with their infant son to watch the battle. Seeing Hector, she tells him that it is cruel of him to risk his life. She was born in a nearby town that was stormed by the Greeks. Achilles killed her father and seven brothers in one day. Her mother then died of an illness. Hector is all she has left. Instead of fighting in the plain, he should adopt a defensive strategy by strengthening the weak spots in the wall.

Hector replies that his pride will not let him act like a coward. He knows that Troy will fall. The worst part is that Andromache will be taken into slavery by the Greeks. Hector says he wants to be dead before that happens.

Hector extends his arms to pick up his baby son. The child cries, frightened by his father's war helmet. Hector and Andromache laugh. Hector takes off his helmet, picks up the boy, and prays that he grow up to be a mighty warrior and bring home bloody spoil to delight his mother's heart.

Turning to Andromache, Hector tells her not to grieve. He will not die before his fated time. She should go back to her work at the loom. War, he says, is the business of men, especially him. As Hector runs back into the battlefield, he is joined by an enthusiastic Paris, who is heading in the same direction.

After more fighting, the gods inspire a Trojan prophet to suggest a single combat to bring the battle to an end for the day. He passes the suggestion on to Hector, who separates the armies, and challenges any Greek to fight him one on one. After a long silence, Menelaus reluctantly volunteers, but he is immediately overridden by Agamemnon, who tells him that he would have no chance against Hector. Nestor then criticizes the Greeks for their fear of Hector and wishes he was young again like the time he killed a giant in single combat. Stung by his words, all the Greeks volunteer—except Menelaus. One is chosen by lot. It turns out to be their best warrior, Ajax the Greater. He and Hector fight. Ajax is dominant, but darkness falls and heralds part them. They exchange gifts, and the two armies retire for the night. There is a truce, during which both sides bury their dead and the Greeks build a defensive wall and trench in front of their camp.

On the next day of battle, the Trojans, aided by Zeus and Achilles' absence, gain the upper hand, driving the Greeks back within their wall. When night falls, the jubilant Trojans pitch camp on the plain.

Meeting with the other kings, Agamemnon is despondent, and regrets offending Achilles. He sends three ambassadors—Odysseus, Ajax the Greater, and Phoenix, Achilles' elderly tutor—to ask him to return to battle. If Achilles agrees, Agamemnon promises to give him seven tripods, ten talents of gold, 20 bronze cauldrons, 12 horses, and seven slave girls from Lesbos, and to return Briseis untouched. After the war, Achilles can have 20 Trojan women of his choice, any one of Agamemnon's three daughters in marriage, and seven of Agamemnon's cities. The ambassadors report Agamemnon's offer in long speeches, but Achilles rejects it. He is considering going home. His mother has told him, he says, that he will die if he stays in Troy, although he will win everlasting glory. If he goes home, he will have a long life but lose his glory. In any event, Agamemnon's gifts mean nothing to him. He cannot forgive his insults.

Later that same night, Diomedes and Odysseus sneak into the Trojan camp, kill a Thracian king who has just arrived to help Troy, and steal his magnificent, snowy white horses.

A new battle begins. The Greeks are being worn down. Agamemnon, Diomedes, and Odysseus are wounded and withdraw from battle. Then the Greek physician himself, Machaon, is wounded and taken back to the camp by Nestor. Watching the battle from the prow of his ship, Achilles notices this, and sends Patroclus to ask Nestor if the wounded soldier is indeed Machaon. Nestor confirms the fact and detains Patroclus, telling him how desperate the Greeks situation is. He suggests that Patroclus borrow Achilles' armor—to frighten the Trojans—and lead the Myrmidons into battle, just to keep the Trojans from destroying the Greek fleet. Patroclus leaves to ask Achilles about this, but he must stop on the way to bandage the wounds of a comrade.

Sarpedon and Hector lead an attack against the Greek wall. Finally, Hector breaks through the gate with a huge boulder, and the Trojans pour inside the Greek camp, where the Greeks rally and the battle rages. The best Greek warriors still fighting are the two Ajaxes, Idomeneus of Crete, Menelaus, and Nestor's young son, Antilochus.

The Greeks are given some encouragement by Poseidon, but he does not help them openly, because Zeus has forbidden the gods to interfere in battle and is watching the scene from the top of Mount Ida, south of Troy. Understanding this, Hera decides to put Zeus to sleep. Bathing and dressing, she asks Aphrodite to lend her loveliness and desirability. Hera claims that she is on her way to patch up a quarrel between their parents, Oceanus and Tethys. Aphrodite removes a richly embroidered undergarment, and tells Hera to place it in her bosom. She is sure to get her wish.

Hera next visits the god of Sleep, to ask him to descend on Zeus after she has lain with him. At first, Sleep refuses from fear of Zeus, but Hera wins him over by offering to let him marry Pasithea, one of the younger Graces, whom he has always loved.

While Sleep watches in the form of a bird on the branch of a pine, Hera walks by Zeus. She again claims to be on her way to Oceanus and Tethys. Zeus asks her to lie with him instead. He declares that he has never desired any woman or goddess more—not when he fathered Pirithous on Ixion's wife, Perseus on Danae, Minos on Europa, Dionysus on Semele, or Heracles on Alcmene, not when he made love to Demeter or to Leto—or to Hera herself. Hera objects that somebody might see them if they make love outdoors. Zeus takes care of that by enclosing them in a golden cloud. As they lie down, grass, clover, and hyacinth and crocus blossoms instantly grow out of the ground to cushion them. Soon, Zeus is unconscious.

Sleep rushes to the plain to tell Poseidon to help the Greeks as openly as he wants. Poseidon rouses the two Ajaxes to lead a great rally. Soon, the Trojans are running out of the camp. Ajax knocks Hector out with a boulder. Then, Zeus wakes up and figures out what is going on. He sends Iris to order Poseidon out of the battle and Apollo to revive Hector. Roused by Apollo, Hector leads the Trojans back into the Greek camp, all the way to the ships.

As Ajax the Greater leads a desperate defense of the ships, barely preventing Hector from setting them on fire, Patroclus comes to Achilles in tears, asking him to let him save the ships. Achilles ridicules him, saying that he looks like a baby girl running to her mother, but agrees to his request. The Myrmidons prepare for battle. As they do, Hector finally drives Ajax back and sets fire to the first ship.

Patroclus and the Myrmidons rush into battle. The tide turns. Soon, the Trojans are retreating over the plain. Despite Achilles' command and his own promise, Patroclus does not turn back. He continues his rampage, hoping that Troy will fall that very day. Among the soldiers he kills is Sarpedon, Zeus's son and the best of Troy's allies. Zeus considers saving Sarpedon from his fate but is talked out of it by Hera. When Sarpedon falls, Zeus cries tears of blood and sends Sleep and Death to convey Sarpedon's body back to his homeland of Lycia.

Patroclus reaches the walls of Troy. Troy is not fated to fall at this point, however. To save it, Apollo sneaks up behind Patroclus and slaps him on the back, knocking off his armor, splintering his spear, and dazing him. A Trojan named Euphorbas sticks him in the back with his javelin and runs away. Finally, Hector steps up and drives his sword into his belly, killing him.

Hector recovers the armor of Achilles, which Patroclus had been wearing, but a great battle ensues over the corpse of Patroclus. Antilochus is sent to the camp to tell Achilles that Patroclus is dead. Achilles rolls in the dirt, weeping. His mother hears and arrives with a group of sea goddesses to comfort him. He says that he must avenge Patroclus's death by killing Hector. She points out that he is fated to die soon after Hector does, but that does not shake his resolution. He would like to enter the battle immediately. She tells him to wait until she brings him new armor made by Hephaestus.

Meanwhile, the two Ajaxes and Menelaus are laboring to bring Patroclus's body off the battlefield, barely fending off Hector. Unarmed, Achilles goes to the ditch. Thanks to Athena, a great flame shoots from his head. He lets out a battle cry that panics the Trojans. They retreat in such disorder that 12 of them are killed by their own chariots and spears. The Greeks easily bring Patroclus the rest of the way into the camp.

Thetis arrives at Hephaestus's home, and asks him to make new armor for Achilles. He is happy to comply. The most spectacular piece is a huge shield, in which numerous scenes of war and peace, farming, and herding are depicted in gold, silver, and bronze. The figures on the shield move. The earth turns black beneath the farmers' plows in one scene, while a battle rages in another; a marriage is celebrated in a third scene.

The next morning, Thetis delivers the armor, which is so beautiful that it terrifies the Myrmidons. Agamemnon arrives. He and Achilles announce the end of their quarrel. Achilles says that it was foolish to let a girl cause so much suffering and wishes that Briseis had died on the day she was captured. Agamemnon attributes his behavior to a goddess, Atē (Blindness), a daughter of Zeus. He delivers the gifts he promised, including Briseis, and swears that he never slept with her. Achilles would like to go into battle immediately, but Odysseus convinces him that the other soldiers need to eat first. As Achilles prepares for battle, he bitterly tells the horses that pull his chariot to take better care of him than they did of Patroclus. The lead horse, Xanthos (Goldie), is given the power of speech by Hera. He says that it was not their fault that Patroclus died; he was killed by Apollo, and there was nothing they could have done to save him. They will bring Achilles back today, but he is fated to die soon anyway, and they cannot prevent that either.

Achilles leads the Greeks into battle and slaughters the Trojans. Many flee into a river, the Scamander, which is clogged with the corpses of Trojans killed by Achilles. The river itself comes to life and asks Achilles to stop polluting his waters. When Achilles refuses, the river attacks him, pummeling him with waves. Achilles gets extra strength from Poseidon and Athena, but the Scamander is also reinforced by his tributaries. Finally, Hera has Hephaestus ignite fire all around the river, so that the water starts boiling. The river meekly settles down, begging for mercy.

To enable the Trojans to escape Achilles' attack, Apollo disguises himself as a Trojan and draws Achilles away from the city by taunting him and running away. By the time Apollo reveals himself, they are some distance away, and most of the Trojans are safely within the city gates. Hector, however, stays outside.

On the walls of Troy, Hector's father and mother beg Hector to preserve his own life and Troy's chances of survival by coming inside. Otherwise, Priam foresees that he will be slain by the Greeks, and his own dogs will eat his corpse, mutilating his gray head and beard and private parts. Hector's mother, Hecuba, bares her breasts and holds one out in her hand, asking Hector to have pity on her if she nursed him when he was a baby.

Despite their pleas, Hector stays. He converses with his own spirit. It would be shameful to retreat now, he thinks. Perhaps he should take off his armor and negotiate with Achilles. He could promise to give back Helen and her treasure and let the Greeks have all of Troy's wealth. And yet Achilles might kill him like a woman if he approached him unarmed. He decides that there is no way to avoid fighting him.

As Achilles approaches, however, Hector suddenly panics and flees. Achilles chases him around the walls of Troy three times. Each time, they pass the two springs, one hot and one cold, where the Trojan women wash clothes in times of peace. As they approach the springs the fourth time, Athena draws alongside Hector. She is disguised as his brother, Deiphobos, and volunteers to help him fight Achilles.

Hector turns to face his enemy with the help of "Deiphobos." They exchange spear casts, but neither draws blood. Hector asks the fake Deiphobos for another spear, but no one is there. He realizes what is happening and speaks to his own spirit again. "That was not Deiphobos," he says, "but Athena tricking me. The gods are summoning me to death. That must have been Zeus's plan all along. I will, however, not die without a glorious struggle." With this, Hector draws his sword and charges. Achilles sees a vulnerable spot in Hector's armor at the base of his neck and drives his spear into it. He wounds him fatally but does not sever Hector's windpipe. With his dying breath, Hector asks Achilles to let his parents have his corpse for burial. Achilles says that he would not return Hector's corpse for its weight in gold. He makes holes by the tendons between Hector's heels and his ankles. Inserting leather straps, he ties Hector to his chariot, and drags him around Troy.

On the wall, the Trojans lament. Andromache has been preparing a warm bath for Hector. She hears the cries, runs to the walls, and sees Hector being dragged. At first, she faints. Then she recovers and joins in the lamentation. Now that Hector's son is fatherless, she says, his playmates will treat him with contempt, hitting him and throwing him out of their banquets.

Achilles returns to camp with Hector's body, which he drags in front of Patroclus's bier, then leaves it, exposed for dogs to mangle. Apollo and Aphrodite, however, protect the body from damage. That night, the ghost of Patroclus appears to Achilles in a dream and asks that his body be cremated, since he will not be permitted to cross the river to Hades' house until that happens. The next day, Patroclus is cremated on a great pyre, a hundred feet square. Cattle and sheep are sacrificed. Achilles cuts the throats of four horses, two dogs, and 12 young Trojan prisoners, and burns them on the pyre too. Then he organizes funeral games with lavish prizes to honor Patroclus. Diomedes wins the chariot race when the favorite crashes. Odysseus upsets Ajax the Lesser in the footrace, when the latter slips and falls face-first in dung left behind by sacrificial oxen.

After the funeral, Achilles is still sad about Patroclus. He spends time crying. Occasionally, he drags Hector's body with his chariot. The gods are angered by this behavior. Thetis goes to Achilles at Zeus's command, and tells him that Zeus wants him to accept ransom for the body. Achilles consents. Meanwhile, Iris appears to Priam, who is in deep mourning, and tells him that he can ransom Hector's body from Achilles. Hermes will escort him safely to the Greek camp.

Priam loads a donkey cart with treasures, and sets out across the plain at dusk. He is met by Hermes disguised as a young Myrmidon. With Hermes' help, Priam comes to Achilles' shelter and bursts in on him just as he finishes eating dinner. He asks Achilles for mercy. He once had 50 sons, he says, 19 by one mother. Now, most of them are dead, including the best one, and he has done something unheard of: kissed the hands of the man who killed his children.

The appeal moves Achilles to tears as he thinks of his own father. He tells Priam that Zeus has two urns beside his throne, one with blessings, the other with evils, and he scatters them indiscriminately. Then when Priam asks if he may have Hector's body immediately, Achilles flares up at him. He says that he will give up the body because his mother brought him a message from Zeus telling him to. He is also aware that Priam must have had divine help getting into his shelter. Achilles then leaves to have servants unload Priam's ransom, wash and anoint Hector's body, and load it on the wagon. Afterward, he and Priam share a meal, and Priam is given a place to sleep. In the middle of the night, Hermes wakes Priam, and tells him to leave before he is discovered by the other Greeks. As the sun rises, Priam's daughter, Cassandra, standing atop the Trojan citadel, sees him returning to the city, and summons the people of Troy. Andromache, Hecuba, and Helen mourn for Hector. Helen has the last word, saying that Hector never let the other Trojans speak harshly to her. Priam announces that Achilles has granted a 12-day truce to the Trojans. During this time, they bury Hector, tamer of horses.

READING 3.2   **Homer and the *Iliad*: Necessity and Grace**

Ilham Dilman

War: Its Hazards and Necessities

Early Greek thinkers, whether they be poets, dramatists or philosophers, had a tragic perception of the subjection of human beings to what they themselves initiate. But they thought of it as subject to their own character and of that, in turn, as subject to something in them all, something which belongs to 'human nature'. Some represented this as a subjection to a destiny with which the exceptional individual is in struggle, though as helpless in the face of it as the rest. They thought further that the direction in which he was moving inexorably and where he would end up was accessible to a certain kind of perception or insight, given often to those lacking physical sight—*viz* Teiresias in *Oedipus Rex*—and so not distracted by interests rooted in its vision—*viz* the importance of detachment for the possibility of knowledge in the *Phaedo*.

In Homer's poem the *Iliad* human beings initiate the Trojan war. The poem represents the men fighting on both sides as caught up in and enslaved by it. It is they who wage the war, but they become what the war makes of them. Yet it is because they are human that they become what the war makes of them. They are transformed by their pursuit of victory: both by the nearness of victory before it eludes them and by the nearness of death when victory slips from them. On the crest of its wave they are oblivious of their own vulnerability and are hard with and merciless towards those on the brink of defeat. In this blindness to themselves and to others, in the arrogance which hides their kinship to those at their mercy and makes them indifferent to their plight, they are puppets whose strings are pulled by their fortune in the war. They are not its architect. It is their fortune which makes them arrogant, and that fortune in turn is subject to chance and so open to change. The arrogance which it engenders is thus an empty bubble sustained temporarily by a lie about the human condition.

When it is their turn to be in the trough of the wave they come to know what it is to be at the mercy of others who are as hard with them as they themselves were with others. They come to see that their previous good fortune was not something they could have relied on and that it was not their due or desert. In the face of defeat they experience their impotence and the illusory character of the power they had. It was not really theirs. They and the power they exercised were not one but two, and when it was not theirs to exercise because they came face to face with somebody stronger or suffered a chance set back they were left exposed to the same power in the hands of others. That power was not theirs since it was now wielded by others and they were its object. This is not a grammatical platitude about the way power is individuated. It is a truth to which those who wield power and are drunk with it are blind: while they wield it they really think they are invulnerable and immortal.

Thus power, the poem shows, while it is something which many, perhaps most people, find desirable and seek, is not something anyone can appropriate or make his own. Those who have it are deceived by the idea it gives them that they can overcome any obstacle that stands in the way of what they want and that they are safe against any predatory attack. No one can be that. They are deceived equally by the idea it gives them that it is there to stay with them, that it is something they hold and so something they can keep. In reality not only is it by chance that they are able to exercise the power they exercise, but they are also its slave. It determines their conduct and they do not know how to get on without it.

At home, before the expedition, the Greeks each had their own individual life and character. They had their family, wife and children, and the different preoccupations that filled their lives. On the battleground all this is a memory, almost unreal. The Trojans are, of course, on their home ground, exerting themselves to defend it. But it was they who brought the Greeks to their doorstep. It was Paris, their king Priam's son, who kidnapped Menelaus' beautiful wife Helen. The Greeks are there to reclaim her and avenge the kidnapping. But if that is what leads the Greeks to mount the Trojan expedition, once the catch has been released, the spring which is set free has an inertia all its own. It drags all concerned into a milieu in which they are no longer in control over their actions.

While they act in character, they are cut off from the things that are of importance and interest to them in the life in which they have up to now been themselves. Being in exile from that life their life has been arrested and they have been taken over by the desire to crush the enemy and to defend themselves. It is only in short intervals, during lulls in the fighting, when they can remember and mourn, that their humanity is restored, only to be lost again. Within their one-dimensional life on the battlefield, they have no choice but to obey what takes them over: they have to prevail over the enemy, teach them a lesson, avenge their dead. As the scores to settle mount each side is further and further anchored in their determination to prevail, to avenge, to destroy. That is how they are locked in an endless cycle of reaction and counterreaction, each side bent on destroying the other, whatever it takes to do so, that is at whatever cost to themselves.

In such a scene their physical strength and prowess is the only thing they can count on; it is the only thing on which their sense of self, of being someone to be reckoned with, depends. It is the other side of despair; for without it they have nothing, they are nothing, and they are at the mercy of those who know no mercy. They cling to it and it turns them into things.

This is a powerful picture of human subjection, of the slavery of individuals to a cycle of reactions that are natural but mindless—mindless because in his uprooted state the individual has very little to mind: to care, to respect, to take into consideration. With the rupture inherent in such uprootedness, the natural reactions that take over are those of self-assertion and retaliation to any threats to such assertion, taken as insult to the self, and self-preservation. The reactions of self-assertion are ruthlessly aggressive, while those of self-preservation have their source in near-animal fears. Both sets of reactions are human, but at source they are entangled with the activation of the capacity to survive that is part of all biological life.

When I spoke of 'rupture' just now I meant from the many-dimensionality of human life. A human being is free who can move within these many dimensions and choose within their framework. Anything that severs the individual from access to what is part of his life enslaves him. Thus, an individual who is unable to take into consideration any of it in his actions because it has lost its reality for him, temporarily or permanently, is someone driven to what he does.

Simone Weil on the Iliad: Necessity and Grace

Simone Weil who has written a very searching and thoughtful essay on the *Iliad* takes a deeper view of what the poem portrays and expresses. She characterizes it as 'le poem de la force'; she says that force is its real subject. It changes, she says, all those it touches, all those who are subject to it, into things: its victims, the weak, as well as those who wield it, the strong—like Achilles. In those it crushes it wipes out all inner life. Those who have been crushed by it, in their affliction, cannot think of either the past or the future, they cannot compare their present state with anything, they cannot rebel or make plans for the future. As she puts it:

> At first war is easy and is loved basely. The day comes when fear, defeat and the death of comrades bring the soul of the warrior to its knees before *necessity*. War then stops being a game or a dream; the warrior comes to see that it is real, that it contains death. Death changes from being a limit imposed in advance on the future to being the future itself. Then one cannot think of anything in the future without passing through the idea, the image of death. Thus war erases all idea of an end—of something to aim at—even the aims of the war. ... Those who are there do nothing that will bring it to an end. Intolerable afflictions of this kind last on account of their own weight ... because they take away the resources necessary for coming out of them.

> (Weil 1963, p. 29 my translation)

Force petrifies, she argues, differently but equally, the souls of all those who are its victims and those who manipulate it (p. 32). Those who manipulate it become drunk with it. We shall see how this connects with Plato's claim that those into whose souls evil has entered no longer know what they are doing and have lost all mastery over themselves. Those who wield force walk in a medium which offers no resistance to their progress, since brute force eliminates obstacles. They do not, therefore, feel the need to plan, consider how to realize their intentions, to attend, give thought to and negotiate difficulties. They become, as we say, 'too big for their boots', contemptuous of what stands in their way and careless. 'They ignore the fact that their power is limited and finally they find that things no longer obey them' (p. 21).

Thus the attraction of power, once one gives in to it, sets off an automatic chain of reactions: drunkenness with power generates 'hubris', an arrogant self-confidence, which regards all obstacles and difficulties with contempt. That leads one to ignore the limits of one's power. Sooner or later one exceeds these limits and is delivered to fate: one passes to the other side and becomes the victim of force. The same fate awaits those into whose hands force now passes and the cycle goes on indefinitely. Men are thus not the initiators of the events depicted in the *Iliad*; they are the passive or inert vehicles through which these events take place. They are the cogs in a mechanism of nature which, in tune with the early Greeks, Simone Weil calls *necessity*. The battles, she says, are not decided by men who calculate, enter into deals, take resolutions and execute them, but by men who have become bereft of their faculties, transformed into the grade of inert matter, which is nothing but passivity, and so by blind forces (p. 32).

The *Iliad*, she says, gives us a just representation of the empire of force and, therefore, of the rule of necessity in human life. Men are its slaves. She further believes that force occupies the centre stage in human affairs: it is at the centre of all human history (p. 11). It forms part of what elsewhere she called 'moral gravity', a counterpart in the human world of Newton's gravity which operates in the physical world (Weil 1948). She compares the way it erases inner life with the way nature does, when vital needs such as hunger come into play, say, with starvation. That too erases all inner life, even the pain of a mother—the way Niobé, when she is tired of tears, thinks of eating, or the way sleep overtakes those crying at the death of their comrades.

But although necessity thus rules in the human world, the early Greeks had a conception of something with which they contrasted the determinism to which they gave prominence in their literature and philosophy with something else. Simone Weil calls it *grace*:

> The lightness of those who manipulate without respect and without taking any thought the men and things they have or think they have at their mercy, the despair which forces the soldier to

destroy, the way the slave and the defeated are crushed, the massacres, all contribute to making a scene of undiluted horror. Force is its sole hero. The result would have been a gloomy monotony, had there not been, scattered here and there, some luminous moments, moments brief and divine in which men have a soul. The soul which thus awakes, for a moment, to be lost soon after because of the empire of force over the souls of men, is awakened pure and intact. In such moments there appears no ambiguous, complicated or troubled sentiment; only courage and love illuminate such sentiments. Sometimes a man thus finds his soul in self-deliberation, such as when Hector in front of Troy, without any help from God or man, tries on his own to stand and face his destiny. The other moments when men find their souls are those in which they love. Almost none of the pure forms of love between human beings is absent in the *Iliad* (p. 33).

'These moments of grace are rare in the *Iliad*,' she says, 'but they suffice to make us feel with extreme regret what violence destroys and will destroy' (p. 35). She then points out the 'accent of inconsolable bitterness which continually makes itself felt' in the poem, a 'bitterness which proceeds from tenderness, one which extends to all human beings equally like the clarity of the sun', one which, however, 'never lowers itself into complaint'.

Justice and love, which can never have a place in this scene of extreme and unjust acts of violence, bathe them with their light, without ever becoming visible other than by the accent of the verse. Nothing precious, destined or not to destruction, is despised, the misery of all concerned is exposed without dissimulation or disdain, no man is put above or below the condition that is common to all men, everything that is destroyed is regretted. The victors and the vanquished are equally close to the author and the audience and made of the same clay as them (pp. 35–6).

She talks of this as the just expression of affliction (p. 40). For 'the cold brutality of the facts of war are not disguised by anything, since neither victors nor the vanquished are admired, but not despised or hated either'. They are both represented as the victims of force; it is the gods who decide the changing fate of the combatants. They are like the particles of water that are one moment on the crest of a wave, the next moment at the trough. This is an image Simone Weil uses elsewhere. It is a just expression because it comes from the perspective of love and justice: 'the idea of justice illuminates it without ever intervening in what is depicted' (p. 38). She means that there is no suggestion of any compensation of the injustices depicted, no suggestion that there will be any time when the wrongs that are depicted will be righted or compensated. The poem offers no such consolation.

Homer's Objectivity: Love and Detachment

Alexander Pope wrote that 'Nature and Homer were the same' (*Essays on Criticism*, p. 124). In an essay on *Anna Karenina* Lionel Trilling compares Pope on Homer and Matthew Arnold who said something similar about Tolstoy to the effect that *Anna Karenina* is not a work of art but a piece of life. He comments that the 'objectivity' which Arnold finds in Tolstoy's novel and Pope in Homer's poem is an illusion:

Homer gives us, we are told, the object itself without interposing his personality between it and us. He gives us the person or thing or event without judging it, as Nature itself gives it to us. And to the extent that this is true of Homer, it is true of Tolstoy. But again we are dealing with a manner of speaking. Homer and Nature are of course not the same, and Tolstoy and Nature are not the same. Indeed, what is called the objectivity of Homer or of Tolstoy is not objectivity at all. Quite to the contrary it is the most lavish and prodigal subjectivity possible, for every object in the *Iliad* or in *Anna Karenina* exist in the medium of what we must call the author's love. But this love is so pervasive, it is so constant, and it is so equitable, that it creates the illusion of objectivity ... For Tolstoy everyone and everything has a saving grace. Like Homer, he scarcely permits us to choose between antagonists'.

(Trilling 1955, p. 68–9)

Others, such as Kierkegaard, have pointed out that in the kind of judgement that is in question here truth is subjectivity. In other words here we are in the sphere of the personal, and where the person making a judgement does not or cannot speak for himself he has nothing to say at all. But that does not mean that no distinction can be made between different judgements that belong to the personal. Thus Trilling contrasts Tolstoy's 'objectivity' with Flaubert's:

> Flaubert's objectivity is charged with irritability and Tolstoy's with affection ... it is when a novelist really loves his characters that he can show them in their completeness and contradiction, in their failures as well as in their great moments, in their triviality as well as in their charm ... What we call Tolstoy's objectivity is simply the power of his love to suffer no abatement from the notice and account it takes of the fact that life usually falls below its ideal of itself (p. 69).

Simone Weil shows the same to be true of Homer. Here what is in question is not so much a case of life falling below its ideal of itself, as life in the raw, in its naked reality, undiluted by any comforting fiction and unsoftened by any consolation. But what makes that possible is the *personal* perspective of Homer's *impersonal* love—'personal' in the way that Homer stands to it and 'impersonal' in that it makes no distinction between the strong and the weak, the victor and the vanquished, between Greeks and Trojans. As Simone Weil puts it: one can hardly tell that the poet is Greek and not a Trojan (p. 38).

Thus, Simone Weil argues, in the *Iliad* what is presented belongs to the mode and spirit of its presentation: it allows nothing to creep in that will disguise the truth about the empire of force over the human soul. What would disguise it are pride, humilation, hatred, contempt, indifference, the desire to ignore or forget it. For all this anchors one to a point of view on things from their midst. To be able to see the reality about force in the way the *Iliad* does, one needs to ascend to a detached point of view, which is not indifference, not the detachment of an outsider, nor that of scientific objectivity. It is the detachment of a love which takes no sides in human affairs, without condoning evil, one that recognizes the helplessness and vulnerability of all human beings instead of blaming them. It sees those who perpetrate evil deeds, as Plato did, as acting in slavery to evil, and—to use Simone Weil's comparison—as 'tiles blown off a roof by the wind and falling at random' (Weil 1968, p. 177). It is thus, as we shall see Spinoza also emphasized, detached from all such reactive and retaliatory attitudes which pin one down to the world on which the author of the *Iliad* holds a magnifying glass in its presentation of the Trojan War. One cannot, however, achieve such a love or compassion and detachment, such justice in one's feelings and apprehension, 'unless one knows the empire of force (as Simone Weil puts it in her essay on the *Iliad*) and learns not to respect it' (p. 40).

Simone Weil speaks of such a perspective, 'the light of justice', as not belonging to the world depicted in the *Iliad*. She points out that in the scenes depicted in the poem love and justice appear only in rare moments of grace; they are more conspicuous by their absence. What is for the most part absent in what the poem contemplates, however, appears in the manner in which it is contemplated. It appears in the tone of the poem, in the bitterness and regret in that tone—a bitterness at the way men are transformed by force and the pained love of everything that is lost in the process. Without *that* what is depicted in the poem could not have come to view at all; for it constitutes the perspective from which what is depicted comes to view.

Simone Weil, following Plato, characterizes what is depicted in the *Iliad* as what belongs to 'the social' in the affairs of men, the world of Plato's 'great beast'. What cannot be directly described without mislocating it and so diluting what is described, so that it no longer speaks the truth, lies outside that world. It lies 'outside' in the sense that it cannot be seen or found without detachment from the world of human affairs and so without taking a point of view from outside it—not an outsider's point of view, but that of someone who feels at one with the actions without, however, sharing their tunnel vision.

The World of Human Bondage and the Possibility of Freedom

In the world depicted by Homer thus it is *necessity* that rules, and this is not meant to be just the case in the kind of extreme situation depicted in the *Iliad*. Homer is certainly writing about the Trojan war. But the way human beings are transformed in that war makes us see the vulnerability of human beings and what they are vulnerable to. That is not confined to the war depicted but pervades the whole of human affairs and human relations. Thus elsewhere Simone Weil writes:

> The reality of this world is necessity. The part of man which is in this world is the part which is in bondage to necessity and subject to the misery of need.
>
> (Weil 1962, p. 221)

This is a form of determinism of which the early Greeks had a very strong sense and which we, in our obsession with scientific determinism, seem to have lost:

> The recognition of might [or force] as an absolutely sovereign thing in all of nature, including the natural part of the human soul, with all the thoughts and all the feelings the soul contains, and at the same time as an absolutely detestable thing; this is the innate grandeur of Greece. Today one sees many people who honour might above all, whether they give it that name or other names possessed of a more agreeable sound ... For to know, not abstractly but with the whole soul, that all in nature, including psychological nature, is under the dominance of a force as brutal, as pitilessly directed downwards as gravity, such a knowledge glues, so to speak, the soul to prayer like a prisoner who, when he is able, remains glued to the window of his cell, or like a fly stays stuck to the bottom of a bottle by the force of its urge towards light.
>
> (*Intimations of Christianity*, p. 116)

The light that Simone Weil speaks of is what would deliver the individual from such necessity to freedom—not to a freedom to do what he wants or as he pleases, but to freedom from the endless cycle of reaction and counterreaction to which he is a slave.

I believe that it was largely the same determinism which Spinoza articulated in his *Ethics*. But the early Greeks believed, as Spinoza did, that such a determinism does not absolve men from responsibility for the way they live nor, as I said, does it exclude the possibility of freedom of choice. Men may be vulnerable to natural needs and, in extreme cases where they are deprived of all possibility of meeting those needs, all other considerations may lose their hold on them in their lives. There, except for the exceptional individual, we cannot speak of freedom of choice, since none is left. An individual who has grown dependent on some such natural need may be in a similar plight even when he is not deprived of the possibility of meeting it. But here the situation is very different since his dependency is an individual matter and he need not be dependent.

It is the same with power. In the kind of extreme situation portrayed by Homer, only the exceptional individual can renounce power and, if he survives, break the cycle in which he turns into a thing continually tossed up and down while his life lasts. But men are often caught up in the same cycle in their professional and personal lives and then are tossed up and down in a similar way. Without minimizing the difficulties in most such cases, it could still be said that the cycle can be broken.

Simone Weil says that 'the reality of this world is necessity' and I go along with her in that this is a thought we find among the great thinkers of early Greece. She continues: 'The part of man which is in this world is the part which is in bondage to necessity.' But she believes there is a part of man which is not in this world, not of this world, though it may be lost to the individual. She makes it quite clear that Homer was well aware of it and of its preciousness and fragility. She speaks of those rare moments of grace in the *Iliad* when it appears and of the way the poem mourns its destruction. As she puts it:

> Everything which, in the interior of the soul and in human relations, which escapes the empire of force is loved, but loved with a pain, on account of the danger of destruction continually threatening it (p. 39).

She attributes this to 'the spirit of the only true epic which the West possesses'. It portrays the *necessity* which rules in '*this* world'; the world depicted in the *Iliad*, the world in which we live and cannot escape so long as we deny that there is a part of the soul whose life belongs to 'another world'. If we can find it and keep it alive we shall be free, while we continue to take part in the practices of the world, the social world. Even then we shall remain vulnerable to the needs on which that world threatens to make us dependent. We shall be free though in that our relation to it will have changed.

Our relation to it, however, is not one we can change *at will*. What being able to change it calls for is not the assertion of our will, but faith, trust, attention and patience. That involves, among other things, forgiving those who offend against us which sets us free from the need to retaliate. It involves gratitude for any good that comes out of doing so and humility before it: not 'I did it' but 'it was mercifully granted me'. It is precisely all that is contained in these three words 'I did it' which, Simone Weil holds, ties us into the cycle which the early Greeks spoke of as *necessity*. In the attitude which she contrasts with it and which, if we are lucky, would give us freedom in a world of necessity through our changed relation to it, such a change is attributed to *grace*. We have here a conception of the way that good comes about through an attitude of faith or trust and patience. Such an attitude is the antithesis of 'willing'. In it a person actively gives himself to what he has faith in and trusts, and in that trust he finds the confidence to wait unconditionally. This is the capacity for patience which takes the good it receives as a gift of grace.

READING 3.3 The Return of Odysseus

David Mulroy

The Trojan War is over. All the survivors have made their way home, except for Odysseus. He has been captured on an island by the goddess Calypso. She wants to marry Odysseus.

In his palace, Zeus complains that mortal men blame the gods unfairly for suffering beyond their lot, but they cause their own problems by their foolishness. For example, the gods warned Aegisthus not to kill Agamemnon and court his wife. Aegisthus ignored the advice. Now Agamemnon's son, Orestes, has killed him.

Athena asks why the gods are punishing Odysseus. Zeus explains that Poseidon is angry at Odysseus for blinding his son Polyphemus, but that it is time to arrange for Odysseus's homecoming. Athena suggests that Hermes go tell Calypso to release Odysseus. She herself will go to Ithaca and inspire Odysseus's son, Telemachus, to denounce his mother's suitors, who are slaughtering his sheep and cattle, and to look for his father in mainland Greece.

Athena goes to Ithaca, disguised as a foreign friend of Odysseus. She finds Telemachus brooding in the midst of Penelope's suitors, who are gambling, listening to music, drinking wine, and getting ready for a feast. Athena tells him to hold an assembly to denounce the suitors and then to sail to the mainland looking for news of Odysseus. Then she disappears into the air like a bird. Telemachus suspects that he has been visited by a god.

The next day, Telemachus holds an assembly to denounce the suitors and request a ship. He breaks down crying as he describes his plight. Antinous, the leading suitor, says that the problem is Penelope's indecisiveness. She sends encouraging notes to individual suitors. A few years ago, she announced that she would select a new husband when she finished weaving a burial sheet for her father-in-law, Laertes, Odysseus's father. She wove during the day but undid her weaving in secret at night. In the fourth year, the women servants revealed the trick to the suitors, and Penelope had to finish the job—but still she delays.

The assembly does nothing to help Telemachus with the suitors, since opinions are angrily divided on that issue, but friends will help him sail to the mainland. Telemachus sails to Pylos, keeping his journey a secret from Penelope. King Nestor receives him hospitably and describes the Greeks' departure from Troy. Athena was angry at the army. In a drunken assembly, opinion was divided on whether to stay and make a sacrifice to her or to sail home at once. Half the army stayed at Troy with Agamemnon. Nestor, Odysseus, and Diomedes joined Menelaus in sailing at once, but Odysseus soon changed his mind and went back. Nestor and Diomedes had smooth sailing all the way home. Menelaus was delayed by the death of his pilot and then blown off course to Egypt. He returned seven years later, on the same day that Orestes killed Aegisthus.

Nestor recommends that Telemachus visit Menelaus himself to see if he knows anything about Odysseus. He provides a chariot and his young son, Pisistratus, as a traveling companion. Menelaus receives the boy's hospitably a day later. He invites them to join an ongoing feast even before he learns their identities. Telemachus, however, gives himself away by crying when Menelaus mentions how much he misses his wartime comrades, especially Odysseus. Helen joins the conversation. To prevent it from being too maudlin, she slips some nepenthe into the wine. This is a potion that she acquired in Egypt. It is so powerful that a person who takes it would not be saddened by seeing his parents, brother, or child put to the sword.

Early the next morning, Menelaus tells Telemachus what he knows about his father. Menelaus was stuck with no winds on the island of Pharos, off the Egyptian shore. Walking along the shore, he met a goddess named

Eidothea, who told him that her father could help him. He was Proteus, the old man of the sea. If Menelaus caught him while he napped on the sand with his herd of seals—and held onto him while he changed his shape—Proteus would eventually resume his original form and answer all questions. With Eidothea's help, Menelaus and selected crew members ambushed Proteus by hiding under seal skins. In Menelaus's grasp, Proteus changed into a lion, a serpent, a panther, a boar, water, and a tree. Then, as an old man again, he told Menelaus that he had to return to Egypt and offer sacrifice to Zeus to get home safely. In addition, Proteus revealed that Ajax the Lesser had been lost at sea going home, that Agamemnon had been murdered, and that Odysseus was a prisoner on Calypso's island. Proteus's final piece of information was that Menelaus would not die but be sent by the gods to the Elysian plain because he was the son-in-law of Zeus.

Meanwhile, back in Ithaca, the suitors learn about Telemachus's journey. Antinous dispatches a ship with 20 crewmen to ambush Telemachus on his way back.

Hermes makes the long flight to Calypso's island. She welcomes him into her cave but is resentful when she learns that she has to let Odysseus go. She says that the gods are always jealous when goddesses take mortal men as lovers. Nevertheless, she will obey. Odysseus has been spending his days weeping on the shore, his nights sleeping with Calypso against his will. She finds him on the shore, and tells him that she will help him make a raft and head for home. Odysseus makes her swear that she is not playing a trick on him. Back in the cave, Calypso asks Odysseus over dinner if he is sure that he prefers a long, difficult journey to staying with her and being immortal. He says that Penelope cannot be compared to a goddess, but his only desire is to go home. That night, they make love inside the cave. The next morning, Odysseus starts to work on a raft. Five days later, he puts out to sea.

After 18 days without sleep, Odysseus spies the island of Phaeacia. Poseidon happens to be in the area, returning from an Ethiopian festival, notices Odysseus, and unleashes a violent storm. Odysseus's raft is demolished. He ends up swimming for three days and then nearly being killed by the surf on Phaeacia's rocky coast before he gains the shore at the mouth of a river and falls asleep naked in a pile of leaves.

That night, Athena appears to the Phaeacian princess Nausicaa in a dream, and suggests she wash her family's laundry at the river when she wakes up. Nausicaa has many suitors, she says, and will soon need clean clothes for her wedding day. In the morning, Nausicaa and some girl servants load clothes in a mule wagon and make their way to the mouth of the river at the seashore. While the clothes are drying, the girls play with a ball. Nausicaa is the tallest and loveliest. When they are ready to leave, she throws the ball too hard, and it goes in the river. The girls scream, waking up Odysseus. He emerges from the bushes, breaking off a branch to cover his genitals. The girls all scatter except Nausicaa. Keeping his distance, Odysseus asks if she is a goddess or a mortal girl. If a goddess, he says, she must be Artemis. He goes on to ask for a rag to wear and directions into town. Nausicaa provides clothing and directions to the palace. After Odysseus is bathed, dressed, and magically beautified by Athena, Nausicaa confides to the serving girls that he is just the kind of man she would like to marry.

Nausicaa's parents are King Alcinoos and Queen Arete. They live in a palace made of bronze, gold, and silver, and are surrounded by a garden whose trees bear fruit all year round. The Phaeacian men excel all others in sailing, the women in weaving.

Odysseus enters the palace at the end of a feast, calls down blessings on the Phaeacians, and says that he seeks a convoy to his native land. He then assumes the position of a suppliant in the hearth. The eldest Phaeacian noble suggests that they give the stranger some food. Alcinoos agrees and announces that tomorrow they will invite more nobles to the palace, welcome the stranger properly with a new feast, and arrange a convoy.

At an assembly the next morning, Alcinoos commands that a ship with a crew of 52 be prepared to take the stranger home. Meanwhile, he decrees, they will entertain him. All the kings of Phaeacia must come to Alcinoos's palace. When they assemble, a blind bard named Demodocus sings about a quarrel between Odysseus and Achilles. Odysseus weeps quietly. Only Alcinoos notices.

Alcinoos suggests that they go outside for the athletic contests. After several competitions, Alcinoos's son invites Odysseus to compete. When Odysseus declines, a young Phaeacian says that he looks more like a merchant than an athlete. Enraged, Odysseus takes one of the weights that the Phaeacians are throwing and tosses it well past the farthest marks. Alcinoos apologizes for the youngster's insult and has Demodocus sing the story of the love of Ares and Aphrodite.

Demodocus tells how Hephaestus's wife, Aphrodite, was making love secretly to Ares, using her own marriage bed when Hephaestus was not at home. Helius saw this and told Hephaestus. Hephaestus spread subtle metal bonds above the bed, like a spiderweb, and pretended to go to the island of Lemnos. Ares saw him leave, went to the house immediately, and took Aphrodite into the bed. As they slept, the bonds fell on them so that they could not get away. Hephaestus doubled back, opened his door, and shouted for Zeus and the other gods to come and see how Aphrodite was dishonoring him. Though the goddesses avoided the scene, the male gods came and laughed uncontrollably. Apollo asked Hermes how he would like to be in Ares' position. Hermes said that he would be glad to lie next to golden Aphrodite, even with three times as many bonds and all the gods and goddesses watching.

After the song, all return to the palace for another meal. Odysseus happens to see Nausicaa standing beside a pillar. She says she hopes that he will remember her when he gets home. Odysseus says that he will pray to her as to a goddess for the rest of his days, since she saved his life.

At dinner, Odysseus asks Demodocus to sing about the Trojan horse. When he begins, Odysseus weeps. Alcinoos stops the music and asks that Odysseus state his name and explain why he weeps whenever he hears about the Trojan War. Odysseus identifies himself and volunteers to tell the assembly about his difficult journey homeward from Troy.

This is the story that Odysseus tells:

Soon after leaving Troy, he sacked the city of the Cicones, killing the men and capturing their wives and many possessions. He ordered his men to flee at once, but they refused and stayed on the shore, feasting. The Cicones and their neighbors launched a counterattack the next morning. Odysseus lost six men from each of his ships.

The fleet then survived a storm but was driven off course rounding the southern tip of Greece. Ten days later, it washed ashore in the land of the Lotus Eaters. Odysseus's scouts mingled with the Lotus Eaters. They were harmless, but the men who ate the sweet lotus blossoms lost all desire to return home. Odysseus had to force them back to the ship.

Next, the fleet landed on a goat-infested island, opposite the harbor of the lawless Cyclopes. Odysseus took one ship and 12 crewmen to the mainland. He also brought some very potent wine. This was a gift from Maron, a priest of Apollo, whose household the Greeks spared when they attacked the Cicones.

Odysseus and his companions entered a cave belonging to a giant shepherd, who was out tending his flocks. The cave was full of lambs and kids. Odysseus's companions wanted to steal them and leave, but Odysseus insisted on staying to ask for gifts from the cave's owner.

The owner, a Cyclops, returned. He shut the doorway with a boulder so large that 22 wagons could not have budged it. Fixing a meal and tending to his chores, he noticed Odysseus and his companions and asked where they came from. Odysseus said that they were Greeks from Troy and asked for a gift in the name of Zeus. The Cyclops said that he had no respect for Zeus. He leapt up, seized two of Odysseus's men, dashed their brains out on the ground, and ate them. He then drank some milk, lay down, and slept. Odysseus would have killed him with his sword, but he and his men all would have died in the cave with no one to move the boulder.

The next morning, the Cyclops rose, built a fire, ate two more men, let his flock out to graze, replaced the boulder, and walked away whistling. In the cave, Odysseus found a stick the size of a ship's mast. He sharpened its point, hid it under manure, and chose four companions by lot to help him use it. The Cyclops returned, took care of his chores, seized two men, and ate them. Odysseus then offered him some wine. Trying it, the Cyclops was pleased, took some more, and asked Odysseus to tell him his name so that he could give him a gift. Odysseus replied that his name was Noman. The Cyclops said that his gift would be that he would eat Noman last. He then fell asleep, belching up wine and pieces of flesh. Odysseus and his companions retrieved the sharpened stick and heated it in the fire until it glowed. Then they plunged it into the eye of the Cyclops, and twisted it like a drill. His eye sizzled and popped. He let out a great roar. Other Cyclopes gathered around outside the cave, and calling him by his name, Polyphemus, asked what the trouble was. Polyphemus replied that "Noman" was murdering him. They replied that if no man was hurting him, his pain must come from Zeus, and left.

Odysseus tied his companions underneath some sheep. He himself clung to the belly of the lead ram. In the morning, Polyphemus sat by the door of the cave, examining the sheep as they went out to graze but not feeling the men underneath them. The ram came out last. Polyphemus stopped him and asked why he was lagging behind, since he was usually the first to leave. He then decided that the ram must be grieving for his eye and let him pass, with Odysseus hanging on below.

When Odysseus and his companions reached their ship, Odysseus shouted to Polyphemus that Zeus had punished him. Polyphemus broke off part of a mountain peak and threw it at the ship. It landed in front and drove the ship back to mainland. Odysseus's crew tried to silence him, but he shouted again. "If anyone asks the name of the man who blinded you," he screamed, "it is Odysseus of Ithaca!" Hearing this, Polyphemus prayed to his father, Poseidon, that Odysseus of Ithaca would never get home—or at least that he would get home late, with no companions, and face further troubles when he did. He then hurled another boulder that drove the ship forward across the harbor to the island where the rest of the fleet was anchored.

The fleet made its way to the kingdom of Aeolus. King Aeolus lived in a wealthy palace with six sons and six daughters, who were married to each other. After entertaining Odysseus for a month, he gave him a leather bag with a silver cord, containing all the unfavorable winds, since Zeus had placed him in charge of the winds. Wafted by a west wind, Odysseus's fleet drew within sight of Ithaca in ten days. At this point, Odysseus fell asleep. His companions thought that the bag contained gold or silver from Aeolus. They opened it. Instantly, the bad winds blew the ships back into the midst of the sea. The fleet headed back to Aeolus's kingdom. Odysseus asked him for more help, but Aeolus refused. He said that it would be unlawful to help a man who was evidently hated by the gods.

Another week of sailing brought the fleet to the land of the Laestrygonians. This contained a sheltered harbor with calm water, where the other ships came to rest. Odysseus himself dropped anchor on the rocky coast outside the harbor. Three of his men went ashore to investigate. They met the king's daughter at a spring and followed her into a palace. There they saw her mother, a disgusting giantess. She, in turn, summoned her husband. Also a giant, he immediately snatched one of the men and ate him. Then he raised a shout, and thousands of Laestrygonians poured out of their houses. They attacked the fleet in the harbor, crushing the ships with boulders and spearing the men like fish. Odysseus ran to his ship, cut his anchor line with his sword, and got away.

Reduced to one ship, Odysseus landed on Aeaea, the home of the goddess Circe. Hunting for food, Odysseus saw smoke rising in the middle of the island. He divided the crew into two groups of 23, one led by him, the other by the crewman Eurylochus. By lot, Eurylochus's group was chosen to investigate the smoke.

Outside Circe's house, wolves and lions fawned on Eurylochus and the others like friendly dogs. Circe was heard singing inside. She invited them in. All except Eurylochus entered. She served them a mixture of cheese, barley, honey, wine, and magic drugs. Then by striking them with a wand, she changed their bodies into those of pigs, although their minds were unaltered. She drove them into her pig sties and tossed them some acorns.

Outside, Eurylochus panicked, even though he did not know what was happening in Circe's house, and ran back to Odysseus, begging him to leave the island. Odysseus, however, went to investigate. On his way, he met Hermes, who told him all about Circe, and said he would give him a drug to ward off her magic. When her magic fails, he said, she will suggest that they go to bed together. Before agreeing, Odysseus should have her swear not to make him unmanly when he is naked. He then gave Odysseus a plant, moly, that was an antidote to Circe's drugs.

Odysseus entered Circe's house and events fell out as foretold. When Circe swore not to make Odysseus unmanly, they went to bed together. Afterward, Circe prepared a meal, but Odysseus would not eat until his companions were restored to human form. The men looked better than ever, but they wept loudly over their ordeal. Circe became a hospitable hostess, entertaining Odysseus and his men for a full year. Then his men suggested that it was time to leave. That night Odysseus brought up the subject in bed with Circe. She told him that to get home safely, he would have to consult the seer, Tiresias, in Hades' kingdom, and she provided directions. Odysseus's ships would be blown by the North Wind to the shores of Oceanus. There, Odysseus should dig a trench and fill it with honey, wine, water, and barley. Then he should slay a ram and a black sheep, letting the blood spill into the trench. This would attract the ghosts. When they drank the blood, they would talk to him. Odysseus should hold the others back and speak with Tiresias first.

At dawn, Odysseus set sail. In departing, he lost a young crewman without realizing it. Young Elpenor had slept on Circe's roof for coolness after drinking a lot of wine. When the sounds of departure woke him up, he forget where he was, slipped, fell, and broke his neck.

Circe provided a fair wind that brought Odysseus's ship to a land always covered by mist on the shores of Oceanus. Odysseus followed Circe's instructions, and soon ghosts gathered around him and the trench. First came Elpenor. Odysseus asked him how he had gotten to the land of the dead so quickly. Elpenor described his accident and begged Odysseus to find his body and bury it when he returned to Aeaea.

Odysseus then recognized the ghost of his mother, Anticleia. He wept since he had left her alive in Ithaca. But he did not let her spirit approach the trench before he talked to Tiresias. The prophet appeared next and told Odysseus his future. Odysseus would encounter the herds of the Sun, grazing on the island of Thrinacria. If he did not hurt them, he might get home. If he did hurt them, he might still get home, but late and without companions—and he would find trouble waiting for him. Once at home, he had to travel inland, carrying a ship's oar. When another traveler referred to the oar as a "winnowing fan," he should fix it in the earth and offer sacrifice to Poseidon. Death would come to him gently from the sea in old age.

Next, Anticleia's ghost drank the dark blood and spoke, asking why Odysseus had come, and describing the situation at Ithaca. Penelope longed for Odysseus's return, Telemachus was treated respectfully in the neighborhood, Odysseus's father, Laertes, was deeply depressed because of Odysseus's long absence, and Anticleia herself had died from longing to see him. Odysseus tried to embrace her three times, but she vanished in his arms. She explained that once mortals die, they no longer have bones or flesh. Anticleia's spirit was followed by those of a number of famous ladies: Oedipus's mother, Epicaste; Nestor's mother, Chloris; Leda; and others.

Odysseus interrupts his own tale at this point to say that it is time to go to bed. Alcinoos and the others ask him to continue. Alcinoos wants to know if he saw any comrades from Troy in the underworld. Odysseus says that the next soul he saw was Agamemnon's.

Agamemnon drank the blood, and wept at seeing Odysseus. He was lamenting his own murder by Aegisthus and Clytemnestra. They ambushed him at a feast. The last thing he heard was Cassandra's piteous cries. Clytemnestra did not even bother to close his eyes and mouth for him when he died. Agamemnon advised Odysseus to return home secretly to avoid a similar fate.

Achilles approached in a group of great warriors. Odysseus said that the Greeks honored Achilles more than anyone when he was alive and that he was very powerful among the dead. Therefore, he should not lament his death. Achilles replied:

> Do not make light of my death, noble Odysseus.
>
> I'd rather dwell on earth and serve another,
>
> a landless man who is barely getting by,
>
> than be the lord of all the withered dead.

Achilles also asked about his father and son. Odysseus had no news of Peleus, but described Neoptolemus as an outstanding young warrior. Cheered, Achilles walked across the fields of asphodel with lengthened strides.

The soul of Ajax the Greater did not speak to Odysseus. He was still grieving over the judgment by which Achilles' armor was awarded to Odysseus. Odysseus felt that he could have gotten him to talk eventually, but he wished to see other spirits. He watched Minos making judgments among the dead, Orion hunting, and Tityos, Tantalus, and Sisyphus being punished for their sins. Finally, he saw a phantom of Heracles. (Heracles himself lived with the gods.) The phantom greeted Odysseus as a fellow long-suffering hero. Finally, Odysseus grew afraid of all the ghosts and returned to his ship.

Back on Circe's island, Elpenor was buried. The men feasted on food provided by Circe. At night she lay with Odysseus, telling him about forthcoming dangers. He would come to the Sirens, who fatally enchanted men with their song. They lived in a meadow surrounded by corpses. If Odysseus wanted to hear them, he should tie himself to the ship's mast and put wax in his men's ears. After that, one way led to the Wandering Rocks, which nothing could pass through—although Hera did enable Jason and the Argonauts to do so. The other way led between two crags. Scylla, a six-headed monster, lived in one. She devoured six sailors from every ship that passed. On the other side, Charybdis sucked the water down three times a day and spat it out. It would be better, Circe said, to sacrifice six sailors to Scylla than risk the whole ship by sailing over Charybdis. Odysseus would then come to Thrinacria, where the sheep and cattle of the Sun grazed. If he hurt these, his ship and companions would be lost, and his own return delayed.

The next day, the ship approached the island of the Sirens in a dead calm. Odysseus had himself tied to the mast and put wax in his men's ears. When Odysseus heard the Sirens claiming to know all about Troy and everything else, he wanted to be freed to listen and signaled to his men with his eyebrows, but they ignored him.

The straits were now near. Odysseus directed the crew to row quickly past Scylla's crag. On the other side of the channel, Charybdis sucked the water down. When Odysseus tore his eyes away from that spectacle, he saw six of his crew being hoisted through the air toward Scylla's mouths. The men shrieked and stretched their hands to him for help as she ate them.

Soon, the ship was passing Thrinacria. Odysseus urged the crew to keep going, but Eurylochus argued that it was dangerous to sail at night. Odysseus gave in, urging the men not to harm the herds on the island. As they slept, Zeus sent a great storm, which made it impossible to leave the island. The storm winds blew steadily for a month. Supplies ran out. They had to live by fishing and killing birds. Hunger became a problem. One day, Odysseus went off by himself to pray; he fell asleep. While he was gone, Eurylochus persuaded the rest of the crew to slaughter some of the cattle. They could appease Helius later by building a temple in Ithaca. Besides, he argued, any form of death was preferable to starvation. As soon as they slaughtered the cattle, one of the goddesses guarding them reported the fact to Helius. He instantly went to Zeus to demand revenge. Otherwise, he said, he would go shine in Hades. Zeus promised to blast the crew's ship. (Odysseus learned about this from Calypso, who heard it from Hermes.) Back on the island, Odysseus was horrified, but the deed was done. The crew feasted for six days on the cattle, whose hides crawled and flesh mooed. On the seventh day, the storm winds stopped blowing. Odysseus and his men set sail. As soon as they were out of sight of land, Zeus destroyed the ship in a sudden thunderstorm. All members of the crew drowned. As the ship disintegrated, Odysseus strapped the mast and keel together and rode out the storm. By dawn the following day, he found himself back at the straits of Scylla and Charybdis. As he drifted over Charybdis, she sucked the water down. Stretching, Odysseus caught the branch of an overhanging fig tree and clung to it like a bat until Charybdis vomited up the mast and keel many hours later. Odysseus plopped down beside them and rode them for nine days. On the tenth, he landed on Ogygia, Calypso's island.

Here Odysseus ends his tale, since he has already told Alcinoos about Calypso. Alcinoos decrees that more gifts should be given to Odysseus, and all retire for the night. The next day is taken up with another feast at the palace. When the sun finally sets, Odysseus is given a royal escort to the ship. He falls into a sound sleep on the deck. The ship races over the waves, arriving at Ithaca as the morning star appears in the sky. The Phaeacian crew lays the sleeping Odysseus on the shore and piles his gifts under a nearby olive tree. Learning of Odysseus's safe return, Poseidon is annoyed. When the Phaeacian ship comes back within sight of its home port, Poseidon turns it to stone. Seeing this, Alcinoos remembers an ancient prophecy that Poseidon would eventually petrify one of their ships and then hide the Phaeacian city with a mountain. The Phaeacians pray and offer sacrifice to Poseidon to prevent the rest of the prophecy from coming true.

When Odysseus wakes up, he does not know where he is because Athena has covered the land in mist. When she approaches disguised as a shepherd, Odysseus asks the name of the land. Though inwardly delighted to hear her say Ithaca, he tells an elaborate lie, claiming to be a Cretan veteran of Troy trying to get to Pylos. Amused, Athena identifies herself and assures Odysseus that he really is home. They hide his gifts in a cave. Athena says that they must plan an attack on the suitors who have taken over Odysseus's palace for the last three years. She tells him to go first, disguised as a beggar, to the hut of his swineherd. Meanwhile, she will see to it that Telemachus returns from Sparta. She strikes Odysseus with a wand, transforming him into a pathetic beggar in appearance.

Eumaeus, the swineherd, receives the "beggar" with outstanding hospitality. After they dine on young porkers, a stormy night descends. The "beggar" sleeps snug in an extra blanket that he wheedles from Eumaeus, but the swineherd spends the night outdoors, keeping watch over his pigs.

On the same night, Athena appears to Telemachus in a dream, telling him that it is time to go home. She warns him about the suitors' ambush and tells him to stop first at Eumaeus's shelter when he gets back to Ithaca.

Back in Eumaeus's shelter, the beggar is eager to go to the palace to beg and observe the suitors, but Eumaeus persuades him to wait for Telemachus there in the shelter.

Telemachus arrives at Eumaeus's hut as he and the beggar prepare breakfast. Telemachus sends Eumaeus to the palace to tell Penelope that he is safe. When he is gone, Athena appears outside the door of the shelter, making herself visible just to Odysseus, and signals to him with her eyebrows to come outside. When he does, she tells him to reveal his identity to his son and transforms him back to his regal, robust appearance. Telemachus is startled by the transformation. At first he thinks that some god is tricking him, but when Odysseus insists that he is telling the truth, they embrace and weep noisily, like grief-stricken vultures. Then they discuss the suitors. Telemachus does not see how it will be possible to attack them, since there are a hundred and eight of them, but Odysseus says that they will be helped by Athena and Zeus. He gives Telemachus the job of putting the suitors' weapons away in a storeroom at an appropriate time.

In Ithaca, Eumaeus arrives at the palace at the same time as a sailor from Telemachus's ship. Both have the job of reporting Telemachus's safe return to Penelope and do so. Antinous, the leading suitor, is upset that Telemachus has eluded the ambush, and wants to lay another plan to kill him. Another suitor named Amphinomus objects, saying that it is dreadful to kill a member of a royal family. He would approve only if they had clear signs of divine favor from Zeus. The other suitors go along with this point of view. Eumaeus returns to his shelter. Just before he enters, Athena transforms Odysseus into the beggar again.

At dawn, Telemachus leaves for the palace. He is followed somewhat later by Eumaeus and the beggar. En route, they meet Melanthius, a goatherd who has befriended the suitors. He insults the beggar and kicks him in the thigh. Inwardly, Odysseus considers killing Melanthius but decides to restrain himself. Outside the palace, Odysseus sees his former hunting dog, Argus, who is now suffering from old age and neglect. Lying on a pile of manure, infested by fleas, the dog recognizes Odysseus, lifts his head, wags his tail, and dies.

Inside the palace, the beggar asks the feasting suitors for food. All give him something, except for their leader, Antinous, who refuses—and ends up hitting the beggar with a footstool to get rid of him. The other suitors disapprove of this action, saying that the beggar might be a god in disguise. Penelope is also offended by Antinous's action and says that she would like to talk to the beggar to see if he has any news of Odysseus. At the beggar's suggestion, however, the interview is postponed until the end of the evening.

A real beggar arrives at the palace. He is an oversized glutton whom the suitors call Irus because he carries messages for them.[1] Antinous insists that the two beggars have a boxing match. The prize is a grilled goat's stomach full of fat and blood and the exclusive right to beg at the palace. Inwardly, Odysseus decides just to knock Irus out, not kill him. He strikes him in the neck, below the ear, crushing several bones, and drags him outside, unconscious. When Odysseus returns, Antinous gives him his goat's stomach, and Amphinomus brings him bread. The beggar tells Amphinomus that disaster often catches human beings by surprise and that he should leave the palace while he still can. Amphinomus knows that he is right, but just walks away, shaking his head, since he has been doomed by Athena to be killed by Telemachus.

---

1 Iris was the lovely goddess of the rainbow, and one of the gods' messengers. *Irus* is the masculine form of the name. The name, "Rainbow," was a comical one for this character.

Beautified by Athena, Penelope appears to the suitors. She says that the time for her to select a husband is drawing near, but complains that rival suitors in the past brought gifts. The suitors dispatch heralds, who quickly return with a large number of valuable gifts, mostly jewelry.

Of the maids who are sleeping with the suitors, the prettiest is Melantho. Her lover is Eurymachos, the most influential suitor after Antinous. Later in the evening, the beggar starts a quarrel with Melantho by volunteering to take care of the torches so that the maids can go to bed early. Eurymachos gets involved and ends up throwing a footstool at the beggar. Amphinomus, however, restores order, and persuades everyone to retire for the night.

Now the beggar joins Penelope. He claims to be a Cretan and to have met Odysseus when he was on his way to Troy. He says that he is sure that Odysseus is on his way home. Penelope is skeptical, but has the oldest, most loyal of the maids, Euryclea, bring a basin to wash the beggar's feet. As she begins to do so, the disguised Odysseus is suddenly panic-stricken. He has a scar on his knee that Euryclea will certainly recognize. He got it as a youth on a boar hunt when he visited his maternal grandfather, Autolycus, a famous trickster. (Autolycus gave Odysseus his name as a way of commemorating the fact that he [Autolycus] had often been "angered" [*odyssamenos*]. So that is how Odysseus came to have that name.) Euryclea recognizes the scar, drops Odysseus's foot so that it knocks over the basin, and starts to cry out to Penelope, but Penelope is momentarily distracted by Athena. Odysseus grabs Euryclea by the throat and tells her to keep his secret. Euryclea is happy to cooperate.

When they resume their talk, Penelope asks the beggar to evaluate a dream. She has 20 pet geese. In her dream, they were all killed by an eagle, and she was grief-stricken. The eagle then perched on a rafter and announced that the dream was a vision of the future. The geese, he continued, represented the suitors and he, the eagle, was really Odysseus. The beggar says that the dream is a sure sign of the suitors' forthcoming destruction. Penelope, however, argues that some dreams come from the underworld through a gateway of horn and are true, but others come through a gateway of ivory and are deceptive. In any event, she plans to have a contest the following day. She will marry the suitor who can string Odysseus's old bow and shoot an arrow through 12 axes. The beggar encourages her to hold the contest. Odysseus will be back, he says, before any of them can string his bow.

In the morning, the household prepares for another feast. Eumaeus arrives with three pigs, Melanthius with goats, and a certain Philoetius, a loyal cowherd, with a heifer. Outside, the suitors discuss making another attempt on Telemachus's life, but an eagle clutching a dove appears on their left. Amphinomus announces that their plot would not succeed. They agree, and turn toward the palace. Inside, Athena inspires the suitors to act badly in order to anger Odysseus. One of them throws an ox's foot at the beggar as a "gift." Telemachus rebukes him sternly, and Athena stirs hysterical laughing in the suitors. A wandering prophet, who has joined the feasting, rises amid the laughter to leave the palace, saying that he sees darkness enveloping the suitors, blood on the walls, and ghosts in the courtyard. This makes the suitors laugh even harder.

Penelope fetches the bow from a storeroom, enters the dining hall with it, and announces the contest. Telemachus quickly sets up the target of 12 axes. He laughs as he does so and apologizes, saying that he has no reason to laugh on such an occasion. When the target is ready, he tests the bow himself. He is about to string it when the beggar catches his eye and shakes his head.

When the first suitor fails to string the bow, Antinous has the goatherd, Melanthius, heat the bow and grease it. When others fail to string it, Antinous says that they cannot succeed because it is a feast day of the archer Apollo. They will try again tomorrow. The beggar asks if he can try. Antinous and Eurymachos oppose the idea, but they are overruled by Penelope and Telemachus. Eumaeus gives the beggar the bow. He strings it effortlessly, like a musician with a lyre. Thunder sounds. He shoots an arrow through the axes. Then he tells Telemachus that the time has come for a banquet with music and dancing.

Throwing off his rags, the beggar leaps onto the steps leading to the main doorway. "Now," he says, "I will hit another target that no man has ever hit." With this, he shoots Antinous in the throat with an arrow, just as the suitor is about to take a drink of wine from a golden goblet. His wine and his blood mix on the floor as he falls.

The other suitors assume that this is an accident and warn the beggar of the dire consequences, but then he reveals his identity, saying, "Dogs! You thought that I would never return."

The suitors are terrified. Eurymachos says that Antinous was responsible for the suitors' crimes and offers to pay Odysseus back for all damages. Odysseus rejects the offer. Eurymachos then urges the suitors to charge Odysseus in a mass. Odysseus shoots Eurymachos down with an arrow that strikes his chest beside a nipple and lodges in his liver. Amphinomus draws his sword and tries to push his way past Odysseus, but Telemachus spears him in the back.

Odysseus continues to drop suitors with arrows, while Telemachus brings armor and weapons out of the storeroom. Noticing this, the suitors send Melanthius to the storeroom to get weapons for themselves. After three trips, he is caught in the act by Telemachus and Eumaeus. They tie him up and hang him to a rafter.

The battle rages. Though outnumbered, Odysseus and friends are aided by the gods. Their spears never miss; the suitors' always do. Soon, all the suitors lie in the dining hall like dead fish. Odysseus has Telemachus and the herdsmen take the corpses outside, while the 12 disloyal maids are made to clean up the blood. When they are finished, Odysseus tells Telemachus to take them outside and strike them down with swords "until they forget Aphrodite." Telemachus takes them outside, but decides against killing them with a "pure" death. Instead, he hangs them all in nooses attached to a single cable. They struggle briefly with their dangling feet. Melanthius is then brought into the courtyard where his nose, ears, genitals, hands, and feet are cut off and fed to the dogs.

An elderly maid wakes Penelope out of a sound sleep to tell her the news. When Penelope comes down stairs, she refuses to believe in Odysseus's identity. They sit on separate sides of the dining hall for some time, eyeing each other. Finally, Penelope asks a maid to move the bed that Odysseus made for them into the corridor. Odysseus immediately flares up. He says that it is not possible to move the bed, since he carved it out of a giant olive tree still rooted in the ground. This knowledge is the proof that Penelope was hoping for. Now they embrace. She feels like a sailor who barely reaches land after nearly drowning at sea. Odysseus and Penelope go to bed, make love, and exchange stories. Athena delays sunrise so that they have plenty of time.

Hermes leads the souls of the suitors into the land of the dead, where the ghosts of Agamemnon and Achilles are conversing. Agamemnon recalls Achilles' funeral. Achilles' body was recovered from the Trojans after a huge battle. He was mourned for 18 days by Thetis and the other goddesses of the sea. The nine Muses sang a dirge. His bones were placed in a golden urn with the bones of Patroclus and buried in a mound that is visible for miles around. Funeral games were held, for which Thetis provided divinely manufactured prizes. In contrast, Agamemnon says, he himself had no funeral after being murdered by his wife.

Seeing the suitors' souls, Agamemnon asks what caused the death of so many youths. One suitor summarizes the whole story, emphasizing Penelope's claim that she had to weave a burial sheet for Laertes. He also assumes that the archery contest was Odysseus's idea. Agamemnon praises Penelope as being the opposite in character from his wife, whose treachery has given all women a bad name.

In the morning, Odysseus and his comrades go to a farmhouse that is part of the royal estate. Odysseus finds his father, Laertes, pulling up weeds in the vineyard. He is dressed in a dirty, patched tunic, with leather gloves and leggings for protection against thorns. Odysseus pretends to think that he is a slave and jokes that he takes better care of the vineyard than his masters do of him. Odysseus claims to be Eperitus from Alybas ("Man of Strife from Wanderville") and to be looking for Odysseus, who visited him five years ago. He says that they parted in friendship and were looking forward to seeing each other again. At this, Laertes breaks down crying. Odysseus then reveals his true identity, proving it with his scar and detailed knowledge of the trees in the vineyard.

After a joyous reunion, father and son return to the farmhouse to deal with the threat posed by the relatives of the suitors, who will probably be looking for revenge. In town, Antinous's father, Eupeithes, urges an assembly to attack Odysseus, who is responsible for the loss of the entire fleet, as well as the murders that he has just committed. Others speak in Odysseus's defense, but over half follow Eupeithes. Odysseus and friends arm and march forth to meet them. They are joined by Athena, disguised as Mentor. Odysseus urges Telemachus not to be a disgrace to his family's name in battle. Telemachus says that he certainly will not be. "Dear gods, what a day!" exclaims Laertes. "My son and my grandson competing over courage!"

"Mentor" tells Laertes to say a prayer to Athena and hurl his spear. Laertes is filled with power, hurls his weapon, and hits Eupeithes in the face, killing him. The two sides clash. Athena lets out a great shout that causes panic among the Ithacans, who retreat headlong. Then Zeus stops the battle with a thunderbolt. Disguised as Mentor, Athena administers oaths to both sides, establishing peace.

READING 3.4   The Life of Heracles

David Mulroy

Electryon became king of Mycenae after the death of Perseus. He was supported by his nephew, Amphitryon, to whom he betrothed his daughter, Alcmene. A rival branch of the family had settled on the Taphian Islands off the west coast of Greece. They raided Electryon's cattle, killing several of his sons in the process. Amphitryon recovered the cattle, but as he was bringing them back into the city, a cow started to run away. Amphitryon threw his club at her. The club bounced off the cow's horns and struck Electryon, killing him. Therefore, Amphitryon and his fiancée, Alcmene, had to go into exile. They settled in Thebes. Another one of Perseus's sons, Sthenelus, took over Mycenae.

In Thebes, Alcmene said that she would not sleep with Amphitryon until he avenged her brothers' deaths. Amphitryon asked Creon, king of Thebes, to let him lead the Theban army against the Taphians. Creon agreed to do so if Amphitryon would first rid Thebes of a monstrous fox, which was fated never to be caught. Amphitryon went to Athens, where he borrowed the king's magical hound, which was fated to catch everything it chased. When the dog set off after the fox, Zeus turned them both to stone.

Now, Amphitryon led the Theban army against the Taphian islanders, conquered them, and hastened back to Thebes and his loving wife. Before he got there, however, Zeus assumed his likeness and lay with Alcmene, making the night three times as long as usual to extend his enjoyment. Amphitryon returned the next day and was surprised to learn that Alcmene thought she had slept with him the night before. The prophet Tiresias then explained what had happened. In due course, Alcmene bore two sons—Heracles, son of Zeus; and Iphicles, who was sired by Amphitryon one night later.

When Heracles was eight months old, Hera sent two huge serpents into his crib. Alcmene called for help from Amphitryon, but baby Heracles strangled the serpents with his bare hands.

As a boy, Heracles was given lyre lessons by Linus, Orpheus's brother. When Linus struck him for misbehaving, Heracles flew into a rage and killed him. He was tried for murder and acquitted on a plea of self-defense. For the rest of his childhood, however, Amphitryon had him raised on a cattle farm.

At age 18, Heracles killed a lion that had become a problem for herdsmen in the vicinity of Thebes. During the hunt, he stayed for 50 days with King Thespius of the nearby town of Thespiae. This king had 50 daughters. Wanting grandchildren by Heracles, he had a different one sleep with Heracles each night, though Heracles thought it was the same girl every night. He finally killed the lion and wore its skin and scalp ever after.

Soon afterward, Heracles led the Thebans to a victory over the neighboring Minyans, who had been exacting an annual tribute from Thebes, as a result of an earlier war. As a reward, King Creon had Heracles marry his daughter, Megara, and he soon had three sons. Hera, however, caused him to go mad and kill his children. When he recovered his sanity, he went to Delphi, seeking purification. The priestess told him to migrate to Mycenae, and perform whatever ten services King Eurystheus required. Something like this was fated to happen, because when Heracles was about to be born, Zeus declared that the next one of Perseus's descendants to be born would rule Mycenae. Hera then delayed Heracles' birth, while Eurystheus, a son of Sthenelus—son of Perseus—arrived prematurely.

Eurystheus first ordered Heracles to bring him the skin of the invulnerable lion of Nemea, on the isthmus of Corinth. Heracles chased the lion into a cave, where he choked it to death. Eurystheus was so frightened when Heracles returned with the lion slung over his shoulders that he had a bronze jar made for him to hide in under the earth.

Heracles was next ordered to kill the Hydra of Lerna, a marshy district nearby. The Hydra had a huge body with nine heads, eight of them mortal. Heracles wrestled the Hydra. He smashed its heads with his club—but when he smashed one head, two grew back. Also, a huge crab appeared and bit Heracles' foot. He killed the crab and then enlisted the help of his nephew, Iolaus, Iphicles' son. Iolaus set fire to a piece of wood, and burned the roots of the Hydra's heads as Heracles smashed them. Heracles cut off the immortal head and buried it under a boulder. He slit open the Hydra's body and dipped his arrows in its poison. Eurystheus said that the labor did not count since Iolaus helped Heracles.

The next labor, the third, was to capture the doe of the Cerynites, a river in southern Greece. She had golden antlers and was sacred to Artemis. Heracles chased her for a year and finally brought her down by wounding her with an arrow.

The fourth labor was to capture a boar that lived on Mount Erymanthus in Arcadia. While hunting it, Heracles was entertained by a centaur. Heracles encouraged him to open a jar of wine that belonged to all the centaurs in common. When he did so, a herd of centaurs showed up to protect their wine, and a battle ensued. Heracles chased them to the home of the wise and good centaur, Chiron, famous as a teacher of young heroes. While a group of centaurs cowered around Chiron, Heracles shot an arrow at them. It ended up grazing Chiron in the knee and causing an incurable hurt, much to Heracles' regret. Chiron wished to die, but he could not, for he was immortal. Prometheus offered himself to Zeus to be immortal in his stead, and so Chiron died. The other centaurs scattered. Heracles then tracked down the boar, and brought it to Mycenae.

The fifth labor was to cleanse the stables of Augeas in a single day. Augeas was a king of Elis in the western Peloponnesus and had many herds of cattle. Heracles appeared, and volunteered to clean his stables in return for one tenth of his herds. Augeas agreed. Heracles diverted two rivers, so that they cleaned the stables. Augeas, however, refused to pay up when he learned that the labor had been ordered by Eurystheus. On the other hand, Eurystheus refused to count it among the ten since Heracles had been working for profit.

Heracles' sixth labor was to chase a flock of birds away from Lake Stymphalia in Arcadia. Athena gave Heracles bronze rattles, with which he scared away the birds.

The seventh labor was to capture the Cretan bull. This was either the bull that ferried Europa to Crete for Zeus, or a bull that Poseidon magically produced out of the sea for King Minos. Heracles brought it to Mycenae and then released it to wander around in Greece.

For his eighth labor, Heracles and his comrades had to overcome King Diomedes of Thrace and his forces and capture his man-eating mares. He was successful as usual, killing Diomedes in battle. He released the mares on Mount Olympus, where they were killed by wild beasts.

For Heracles' ninth labor, he and his comrades had to get the belt of Hippolyta, the greatest of the Amazon warriors. Landing in Amazon territory on the shores of the Black Sea, Heracles met Hippolyta, and she agreed to give him her belt. While they talked, however, Hera convinced the other Amazons that Hippolyta was being abducted. They charged Heracles' ship. Seeing them coming, Heracles assumed that Hippolyta was trying to trick him. He killed her, took her belt, and sailed away.

On the return journey, Heracles dropped anchor at Troy. Apollo and Poseidon had recently built the walls of Troy for the Trojans, but their king, Laomedon, refused to pay them the wages that had been promised. Hence, Apollo inflicted a plague on the city, and Poseidon produced a sea monster to attack the Trojans. The monster rode waves onto the shore and snatched Trojans.

An oracle advised King Laomedon that he could rid the city of the monster only by sacrificing his daughter, Hesione. When Heracles arrived, Hesione was fastened to rocks on the shore. Heracles volunteered to kill the sea monster in return for the mares given to Laomedon by Zeus. These mares were compensation to Laomedon for his son, Ganymede, whom Zeus abducted.

Heracles killed the sea monster, but Laomedon refused to hand over the mares. Heracles sailed away, threatening to get revenge.

Heracles' tenth labor took him to the far west, where he had to capture the cattle of Geryon, a giant with three bodies joined at the waist. Geryon was accompanied by a herdsman and a two-headed dog. Heracles traveled west across Libya. When he finally crossed from Libya to Europe, he erected two great pillars. After this, he encountered and killed Geryon and took his cattle. He managed—with some difficulty—to drive the cattle back to Mycenae, where Eurystheus sacrificed them to Hera.

Eurystheus added two more labors since he felt that slaying the Hydra and cleansing the Augean stables should not count. The 11th labor was to go to Hyperborea, the land of the far north, to get the golden apples of the Hesperides (Daughters of the Evening). The apples were guarded by the four Hesperides and by a hundred-headed serpent. En route, Heracles encountered a Libyan king Antaeus, who used to kill strangers in wrestling matches. Antaeus gained strength when he was in contact with the earth because, as some say, he was a son of Gaea. Heracles killed him by holding him up in the air.

In Egypt, the king, Busiris, seized Heracles and tried to sacrifice him. There had been a famine in Egypt. A Cypriot seer prophesied that it would cease if the Egyptians sacrificed a foreigner every year. Busiris first sacrificed the seer and then kept up the custom with foreign travelers. At the altar, Heracles burst out of his bonds, and killed Busiris.

In the Caucasus Mountains, Heracles shot the eagle that was eating Prometheus's liver and released Prometheus. In return for Prometheus, Zeus accepted Chiron, who had agreed to die in his place.

In Hyperborea, acting on Prometheus's advice, Heracles asked Atlas to fetch the golden apples while he, Heracles, held up the sky. Atlas soon returned with the apples, but really did not want to resume holding up the sky. He volunteered to deliver the apples to Eurystheus. Heracles pretended to accept this arrangement, but asked Atlas to hold the sky momentarily while he put a cushion on his head. Atlas set the apples down, and received the sky. Heracles grabbed the apples and left.

The 12th—and final—labor was to bring Hades' dog, Cerberus, out of the underworld. Cerberus had three heads; his body was covered with snakes, and his tail was a serpent. Heracles entered the underworld at Taenarum in Laconia. Outside of Hades' gates, Theseus and his friend, Pirithous, were bound fast where they had been caught trying to abduct Persephone. Heracles freed Theseus, but was forced by an earthquake to abandon Pirithous.

Hades gave Heracles permission to take Cerberus, provided that he did not use any weapons. Heracles forced Cerberus into submission with a headlock, even though the snake in Cerberus's tail bit him.

After his labors, Heracles gave his wife, Megara, to Iolaus and went to Oechalia to seek the hand of Iole, daughter of King Eurytus. The king rejected him for fear that he would kill his children, as he had done in the past. Not long after, Iole's brother sought Heracles' help in looking for some stolen cattle. Heracles received him hospitably, but then went mad and killed him by throwing him off the walls of Tiryns.

After this murder, Heracles was afflicted with a dread disease. He sought help at the oracle of Delphi. When the priestess said that she could not help him, he began to plunder the temple and carry off the sacred tripod.[1]

---

1 In ancient Greece, the term "tripod" referred to a bronze cauldron sitting on three legs. Such tripods were common utensils. For some reason, the tripod also became a symbol of Apollo. A certain sacred tripod was a revered object in Apollo's temple at Delphi.

Apollo showed up to fight him, and Zeus threw a thunderbolt between them. Then, Heracles was given an oracle that he could be cured by being sold into slavery for three years.

Heracles' services were purchased by Omphale, queen of Lydia. At the end of three years, Heracles was cured. He then raised an army and sailed against Troy to get even with Laomedon. Telamon, the father of Ajax the Greater, was actually the first warrior in Heracles' army to break into Troy. Seeing this, Heracles was about to kill him so that he would not gain the reputation of being the superior soldier. Understanding the danger, Telamon began collecting stones. When Heracles paused to ask him what he was doing, Telamon said that he was building an altar in honor of "Heracles, the Glorious Victor." Heracles thanked him. He slew Laomedon and his sons, except for one who became known as Priam ("Bought") because Heracles allowed Princess Hesione to ransom him with her veil.

Heracles settled a series of scores on mainland Greece, making war on Augeas, Neleus of Pylos, and the Lacedaemonians. Then in the land of Calydon, he won the hand of the princess Deianira by defeating a rival suitor, the god of the Achelous River, in a wrestling match. The god assumed the shape of a bull during the fight. Heracles broke off one of his horns. Then, during a feast with his new father-in-law, Heracles accidentally killed a lad who was pouring water on his hands. Hence Heracles had to go into exile with his new bride. They planned to settle in Trachis.

En route to Trachis, they came to a river where the centaur, Nessus, ferried passengers across. He claimed that he was given the job by the gods because of his righteousness. Heracles crossed the river by himself but entrusted Deianira to Nessus. While Nessus was carrying her across, he tried to rape her. Hearing her scream, Heracles shot Nessus in the heart as he emerged from the water. Knowing that he was dying from the Hydra's poison on Heracles' arrow, Nessus told Deianira that she could make a love potion by mixing the blood from his wound with the semen that he had spilled on the ground. She collected some of these fluids and kept them with her.

In Trachis, Heracles raised an army to attack Oechalia and punish King Eurytus, Iole's father. He stormed the city, killing the king and his sons, and took Iole captive. Intending to offer sacrifice, he sent his herald, Lichas, home to Trachis to get fine clothing. Deianira learned about Iole from Lichas and smeared Nessus's supposed love charm on the tunic that was being packed for Heracles. As soon as Heracles put it on and warmed it with his body's heat, the poison of the Hydra began to eat into his skin. He lifted Lichas by his feet and threw him into the sea, killing him. When he tried to tear off the tunic, his flesh came with it. He was carried in misery to Trachis. When Deianira learned what happened, she hanged herself.

Heracles ordered his eldest son, Hyllus, to marry Iole when he came of age. He proceeded to Mount Oeta near Trachis, built a pyre, and gave orders to set it on fire. No one would do so except Poeas,[2] a passing shepherd. In gratitude, Heracles gave him his bow and arrows.

While the pyre was burning, thunder sounded, and Heracles floated up to heaven. He was made immortal, reconciled with Hera, and married her daughter, Hebe (Youth).

---

2   Poeas bequeathed Heracles' weapons to his son, Philoctetes, who used them in the Trojan War.

READING 3.5   The Courageous Harry Potter

Tom Morris

Harry Potter is certainly one of the most popular characters in the world. And he's using that popularity to teach us all some lessons about what's really needed for a good life. That's just the sort of wizard he is.

We're going to examine what may be Harry's single most striking quality. It's a personal characteristic much admired by the ancients. And we can learn a great deal about it by looking carefully at some of this young man's exploits during his first five years at the Hogwarts School of Witchcraft and Wizardry.

Magic and Virtue

The most salient feature of the J. K. Rowling novels about Harry Potter may well be their engaging portrayal of a world of magic existing distinct from, yet intermingled with our regular, or Muggle, world. But, however important magic might be to the vivid storytelling of the books, it is merely incidental to their philosophy. Most of us on occasion have heard other people say things like, "I wish I could just magically solve all my problems," or, "I'll try my best to deal with this problem, but remember, I'm no magician."

By looking at Hogwarts and its world, we can see that these common sentiments reflect a misunderstanding. Harry's daily reality is a world full of magic, and yet the people within it have loads of challenging problems just like folks in our world—except, they may have even more. And their problems are rarely solved merely by the use of magic, but rather by intelligence, planning, courage, determination, persistence, resourcefulness, fidelity, friendliness, and many other qualities traditionally known by the great philosophers as virtues. Magic for them is a tool, among many other problem-solving tools. But tools have to be used by people, and it's ultimately the character of the person using such a tool that determines how effectively it can be employed to deal with any difficulty. Rowling's aim in the Harry Potter books is not at all to convey to her many readers the importance of magic in the lives of her characters, but rather to display the magical importance of the classic virtues in their lives, and in any life.

The Virtues at Hogwarts

Hogwarts is a residential school. The original founders of the four student houses there valued different virtues, and wanted their respective residence halls to celebrate and encourage their favorite. Gryffindor House was founded for "the bravest," Ravenclaw, for "the cleverest," Hufflepuff, for "hard workers," and Slytherin, for those with "great ambition" (GF, p. 17). A student can of course be well endowed with more than one of these qualities, but it was the intent of the founders of these houses to give each student a place for the development of whatever might be his or her greatest strength or most distinctive quality.

When Harry Potter, Ron Weasley, and Hermione Granger arrive for their first day at school, each of them is assigned magically to Dumbledore's old house Gryffindor—the home of the brave. Harry seems to have it all—intelligence, diligence, and ambition. But he is put in the one house founded to recognize and support

Tom Morris, "The Courageous Harry Potter," *Harry Potter and Philosophy: If Aristotle Ran Hogwarts*, ed. David Baggett and Shawn E. Klein, pp. 9–21.

courage. And that's very interesting indeed, since the young Harry is a boy who experiences about as much fear as it's possible for someone his age to feel. In fact, Rowling goes out of her way to represent, in as vivid a manner as she can, Harry's visceral experience of the negative emotions and sensations centering on fear.

Feelings of Fear

Throughout the first five books, Rowling describes the emotions of all her main characters other than Harry from the outside, in terms of their overt behavior and other bodily displays. Only Harry's feelings are characterized from the inside, as if Rowling wants us to appreciate as vividly as possible what Harry goes through when confronted with great danger or even tremendous uncertainty. Let's glance at a few sample passages where the fear of other characters is portrayed:

> Gilderoy Lockhart's knees had given way. (CS, p. 303)

> Ron opened his mouth in horror. (CS, p. 331)

> Crabbe and Goyle were looking scared. (PA, p. 280)

But when it comes to Harry, fear and all associated emotions are described powerfully from the inside. Like many of us, Harry often feels fear in his midsection. Consider these statements:

> His stomach lurched. (CS, p. 138)

> Harry's stomach turned over ... (PA, p. 281)

> His insides were squirming. (OP, p. 122)

> Harry felt as though his insides had turned to ice. (SS, p. 212)

Sometimes, our young wizard-in-training experiences fear a bit higher, in his heart:

> Harry's heart gave a horrible jolt. (SS, p. 115)

> Harry stopped dead, his heart banging against his ribs. (PA, p. 256)

> It was as though an iron fist had clenched suddenly around Harry's heart. (SS, p. 259)

Occasionally, he faces danger beset with a sensation of numbness or paralysis:

> Feeling oddly as though his legs had turned to lead ... (SS, p. 116)

> Harry's whole body went numb. (CS, p. 80)

And as if this were not enough, there are a great many other manifestations of fear in Harry's body and mind as well:

> His mouth was very dry now. (OP, p. 778)

> Harry's brain seemed to have jammed. (CS, p. 314)

> Inside his head, all was icy and numb. (OP, p. 27)

Dozens more examples could be given. At a certain point, it can seem as if we're confronted with an equivalent of the Cowardly Lion (from another famous wizard context), or perhaps the Cowardly Lion Cub. Harry is certainly not someone insensible to danger, to put it very mildly. He recognizes it wherever it is and feels it deeply. Yet, he somehow always manages to overcome these visceral sensations, despite their strength, and embody the virtue of courage to the point of standing up to the greatest of adversaries, saving the day, and earning the accolades of people all around him. As little Dobby the house-elf exclaims:

> "Harry Potter is valiant and bold!" (CS, p. 16)

At the end of Book 4, headmaster Dumbledore says to Harry, simply this:

> "You have shown bravery beyond anything I could have expected of you." (GF, p. 695)

Coming from a man of great wisdom and discernment who customarily expects the best of nearly everyone, this is high praise indeed.

Harry's Recipe for Courage

What allows a quivering, fear-prone, and often terrified boy to face up to some of the greatest dangers of his time and prevail? It will be important to reflect for a moment on what courage is, and then look at how it is attained by such a sensitive soul as Harry.

Courage is doing what's right, not what's easy. It's doing what seems morally required, rather than what seems physically safe or socially expected. It's doing what's best, overall, rather than necessarily what's best for you. A courageous person properly perceives when there is danger and then overcomes the natural urge for self-preservation, self-protection, comfort, personal gain, or even the solicitude for guarding the feelings of others that might counsel avoidance of that threat.

The great philosopher Aristotle teaches us that courage is a midpoint between two extremes in our reaction to danger: the extreme of too little, which he characterizes as cowardice, and the extreme of too much, which he labels as rashness. We typically think of courage as the opposite of cowardice, but it's just as different from rashness. A courageous action is not the deed of a person insensible to danger, unaware of its presence, or reckless in the face of it. It is a motivated and measured response to perceived danger by a person who is willing to face that potential harm for the sake of securing or promoting a greater good. It's generated by a person's values, and the depth and intensity with which they are held, and it's to be displayed in a way that is proportionate to the needs of the situation.

Courage is a fundamental virtue, or strength, without which none of the other virtues could be exhibited properly in circumstances of perceived personal risk. An honest person, for example, has to have the courage of his convictions in circumstances where there is pressure to cover up and hide the truth. And you can't reliably show the virtue of persistence in a difficult and risky task if you let your courage falter.

It's fairly simple to come to at least a basic understanding of courage as a virtue, as well as to see that it is somehow relatively fundamental among the virtues. What's often harder is to grasp how it's to be cultivated and attained in difficult situations—the situations in which it is precisely most needed. But on this question, Harry Potter can teach us much. When we examine his many experiences of danger and fear, we can isolate several things that seem to be responsible for helping give him courage. We actually can find in Harry's encounters with danger five strategies for summoning the courage we need in difficult and even terribly frightening situations. It will be useful to list them first, and then see how they worked for Harry.

Harry Potter's Recipe for Courage

(1)   Prepare for the challenge
(2)   Surround yourself with support
(3)   Engage in positive self-talk
(4)   Focus on what's at stake
(5)   Take appropriate action

(1) *Prepare yourself for the challenge.* Nothing builds confidence and supports courage for a difficult undertaking like preparation. Listen to soldiers before a military action or athletes before a big game. You'll hear things like "We've worked hard to prepare for this, and we're just going to go in there now and do what we've been trained to do." Preparation is the first ingredient for confident and courageous action. Harry undergoes extensive preparation and practice for all his Quidditch matches. And it pays off. Before the final of three Triwizard Tournament Challenges that Harry has to face in the fourth book, he steadies his nerves and readies himself for action by remembering his preparation:

> He felt more confident about this task than either of the others. Difficult and dangerous though it would undoubtedly be, Moody was right: Harry had managed to find his way past monstrous creatures and enchanted barriers before now, and this time he had some notice, some chance to prepare himself for what lay ahead. (GF, p. 608)

And then again:

> Harry's nerves mounted as June the twenty-fourth drew closer, but they were not as bad as those he had felt before the first and second tasks. For one thing, he was confident that, this time, he had done everything in his power to prepare for the task. (GF, p. 610)

Preparation can inspire confidence and support courageous action.

Something should be said briefly about the relationship between courage and confidence, since they both have just been spoken about together, and Harry often displays them together. They are different, but closely related qualities.

Courage is a virtue. Confidence is an attitude. Courage is the fundamental disposition to act in support of great value, even in the face of great risk. Confidence is an attitude of positive expectation that a desired outcome will result from our actions. It's possible to be very confident in a situation where courage isn't even called for, and it's possible to be courageous in a situation where you can't be very confident at all that you'll prevail. So they are different qualities. But they are mutually supportive. Courageous action requires some level of confidence that the action chosen in response to a danger is the best one available, as well as that it has some reasonable chance of success. And the confidence needed for accessing your full potential for effective action is generated more easily in the life of a courageous person—one who is not overwhelmed by obstacles and threats. It is important to understand this connection because Harry often strengthens his courage by building his self-confidence in a situation. Preparation builds self-confidence more than anything else, and thereby enhances rational courage. Many things in Harry's life have prepared the way for his courageous deeds. And the same thing can be true in our lives. If you want to be courageous, be prepared.

(2) *Surround yourself with support.* The best preparation can ready us for almost any task at the level of skill, but that's sometimes not enough to elicit fully the feeling of confidence, and the disposition of courage, by itself. It's always hard to go it alone, especially in circumstances of great uncertainty or threat. If we have friends and associates who believe in us, and who express that belief to us, they can encourage and support us when we need it like nothing else can. This sort of support can then strengthen us in the courage we need when things are particularly difficult.

The best way to get supportive cheerleaders into our lives is to be a cheerleader for others. Harry supports his friends when they need him. Then, when he needs it, they are also there for him. Let me give a simple example. Before his first Quidditch match, Harry had a bad case of nerves.

> Harry felt terrible. (SS, p. 184)

As he walked out of the locker room to go on to the field, he found himself "hoping his knees weren't going to give way" (SS, p. 185). It was that bad. But then he saw something his friends had done to encourage him, and it had an immediate effect:

> Out of the corner of his eye he saw the fluttering banner high above, flashing Potter for President over the crowd. His heart skipped. He felt braver. (SS, p. 185)

At a later match, the Gryffindor team captain Oliver Wood gives his teammates a locker room pep talk, engaging their emotions and reminding them of their high level of preparation and competence (CS, p. 167). It has its intended effect. They win the match.

If we take an active role in encouraging other people around us when we see they need it, we will be preparing them to do the same for us when we are in need. Harry's friends mean a lot to him. He encourages them. And they encourage him. They also give him important forms of help. It's easier to be courageous and confident when we know we have the assistance of others. In fact, one of the most important themes of the Harry Potter stories is the great value of friendship.[1] Everything Harry is able to accomplish is rooted in the collaborative efforts of many. His friends help him. Some of the teachers help him. And the great Dumbledore often gives crucial assistance as well.

Just having other people helping out inspires more confidence and courage when we need it. But it's especially nice when they affirm their belief in us, thereby helping us to believe in ourselves. Before the second of three very dangerous challenges Harry must confront in *Goblet of Fire*, his huge, strong friend Hagrid speaks to him:

> "Yeh're goin' ter win," Hagrid growled, patting Harry's shoulder again, so that Harry actually felt himself sink a couple of inches into the soft ground. "I know it. I can feel it. *Yeh're goin' ter win, Harry.*" (GF, p. 485)

But the best intentions and wishes of others, along with their most heartfelt cheerleading, sometimes just doesn't convince us that we're up to the task of whatever challenge we are facing.

---

1   Harald Thorsrud's chapter in this volume explores this theme of friendship in Rowling's books.

The common room emptied slowly around Harry. People kept wishing him luck for the next morning in cheery, confident tones like Hagrid's, all of them apparently convinced that he was about to pull off another stunning performance like the one he had managed in the first task. Harry couldn't answer them, he just nodded, feeling as though there were a golfball stuck in his throat. (GF, p. 488)

We often need something more. It's not enough for others to express their belief in us. We need to convince ourselves that we're up to the task.

(3) *Engage in positive self-talk.* Sometimes, Harry tries to build other people's confidence by what he says, and at other times, he talks to his friends in a way that is actually aimed at building up his own inner courage as well. Having to leave Ron in a difficult situation and walk into a worse one, with fairly compelling evidence that he might not get out alive, Harry speaks to his friend, and in doing so, actually conveys a positive message to himself as well:

"See you in a bit," said Harry, trying to inject some confidence into his shaking voice. (CS, p. 304)

We are occasionally privy to Harry's inner thoughts. And in them, he sometimes seems to be working on beefing up his courage:

Did they think he couldn't look after himself? He'd escaped Lord Voldemort three times; he wasn't completely useless. ... (PA, p. 68)

Later, in his room alone at the Leaky Cauldron Inn, he uses the power of positive self-talk not just inwardly, but outwardly:

"I'm not going to be murdered," Harry said out loud.

"That's the spirit, dear," said his mirror sleepily. (PA, p. 68)

It matters what we tell ourselves in the privacy of our own minds, and in the solitude of our own rooms. Do we build ourselves up or tear ourselves down? Do we engage in persistently negative thinking, or do we employ positive self-affirmations to prepare ourselves to use our talents in the best possible ways? Positive thinking and positive self-talk cannot replace talent and preparation, but they can alter our psychology in such a way as to unlock our true potential when we engage in them carefully and appropriately. When Harry says "See you in a bit" or "I'm not going to be murdered," he need not be taken to be predicting the future, against whatever evidence to the contrary might exist, but he can rather be taken to be focusing his intentions, and mustering everything within him to move forward in a positive direction, refusing to allow himself to be held back by debilitating fear.

(4) *Focus on what's at stake.* The more important a situation is to us, the braver we tend to be in our response to danger, in order to protect, preserve, or promote what we consider to be of great and irreplaceable value. Harry will do incredibly courageous things to save the life of a friend. In one situation, he discovers a passageway, a large pipe that opens into an underground area where a huge snake has taken a young girl, the sister of his

best friend. Despite the grave danger involved and the likelihood of harm and even death, Harry is prepared to go down the pipe:

> He couldn't not go, not now that they had found the entrance to the chamber, not if there was even the faintest, slimmest, wildest chance that Ginny might be alive. (CS, p. 301)

He has no hesitation in deciding how to deal with the situation:

> "I'm going down there," he said. (CS, p. 301)

Great values cast out fear.

In the second challenge of three that Harry has to face at the Triwizard Tournament in his fourth year, he works hard to save his friends from a potential underwater grave without even thinking of fear. By focusing on what's at stake, he has no time to be delayed or detained by negative emotions. He just immediately takes the action he sees as necessary.

Some of the most courageous people in human history have later reported that they didn't feel particularly brave at the time of their great accomplishments, but that they just knew what they had to do and then did it. They were motivated to action by knowing what was at stake. Their convictions overcame their fear. They acted despite being scared, or else claim that they were just too busy to feel either scared or brave, in responding to the needs of the situation.

In some circumstances, preparation, the support of others, positive thinking, and considering the values that are at stake don't together generate any feeling of bravery at all. But the truly brave person doesn't wait for that to change before taking action. Courage is sometimes manifested only when the courageous action is already underway. The fifth strategy to produce and enhance courage is our last one, and sometimes the only one that works.

(5) *Take appropriate action.* Harry shows on many occasions the power of action. In one classroom situation, a large snake unexpectedly appears from the end of a wizard's wand, and moves toward one of Harry's fellow students, prepared to strike. Fear envelops the room.

> Harry wasn't sure what made him do it. He wasn't even aware of deciding to do it. All he knew was that his legs were carrying him forward as though he was on casters and that he had shouted stupidly at the snake, "Leave him alone!" And miraculously—inexplicably—the snake slumped to the floor, docile as a thick, black garden hose, its eyes now on Harry. Harry felt the fear drain out of him. (CS, p. 194)

When Harry and Ron first show up at the train station to catch the Hogwarts Express, the train to school, they are told the only way they can get to the proper departure point, platform nine and three-quarters, is to walk straight into what appears to be a solid brick wall. But appearances can be misleading. Sometimes our misgivings over a situation can be dispelled only when we take action. Ron's mother, Mrs. Weasley, gives this advice to the obviously anxious Harry:

> "Not to worry," she said. "All you have to do is walk straight at the barrier between platforms nine and ten. Don't stop and don't be scared you'll crash into it, that's very important. Best do it at a bit of a run if you're nervous. Go on, go now before Ron." (SS, p. 93)

A positive attitude is important, but it's getting into action that's most important of all.

Harry's Big Step of Faith

There is one sequence of events in Harry's very eventful life where we can see clearly the importance of both focusing on what's at stake in a dangerous situation and taking action before having any realistic assurance that it will be efficacious, or even that you yourself will emerge safe in the end. It's Harry's big step of faith.

He is in the third challenge of the Triwizard Tournament, making his way through a huge maze where many fearful dangers may stand between him and the ultimate goal. He sees a golden mist up ahead, across his path. He hesitates, not knowing what to expect of the mist, unsure whether it holds a powerful enchantment that could endanger him, and puzzled over how to proceed. He considers doubling back and trying another path. But then he hears a girl's scream from nearby, up ahead. He calls out the name of the female contestant and there is no response.

> There was silence. He stared all around him. What had happened to her? Her scream seemed to come from somewhere ahead. He took a deep breath and ran through the enchanted mist. (GF, p. 624)

But what happens as a result could never have been predicted.

> The world turned upside down. Harry was hanging from the ground, with his hair on end, his glasses dangling off his nose, threatening to fall into the bottomless sky. He clutched them to the end of his nose and hung there, terrified. It felt as though his feet were glued to the grass, which had now become the ceiling. Below him, the dark, star-spangled heavens stretched endlessly. He felt as though if he tried to move one of his feet, he would fall away from the earth completely.
>
> Think, he told himself, as all the blood rushed to his head, think. ... (GF, p. 624)

The situation looks bad. It is completely disorienting and very scary. It seems likely to Harry that any action on his part could make the situation much worse. But inaction would mean giving up any possibility of helping the girl who screamed. Harry does what he has to do—he steps out beyond the available evidence, in the manner of all heroes, and acts in courageous faith. The result is as startling as what had already happened:

> He shut his eyes, so he wouldn't be able to see the view of endless space below him, and pulled his right foot as hard as he could away from the grassy ceiling.
>
> Immediately, the world righted itself. Harry fell forward onto his knees onto the wonderfully solid ground. He felt temporarily limp with shock. He took a deep, steadying breath, then got up again and hurried forward, looking back over his shoulder as he ran away from the golden mist, which twinkled innocently at him in the moonlight. (GF, pp. 624–25)

Sometimes, when great values are at stake, you just have to take action, regardless of how you feel. That is the way of courage. That is a version of the famous "leap of faith" described by the great nineteenth century philosopher and father of existentialism, Søren Kierkegaard. It was Kierkegaard's insight that, when momentous values are at stake, thinking and reasoning about what we should do can take us only so far. The evidence available will never be fully sufficient for any truly important personal decision. As he says in his famous and seminal book, *Concluding Unscientific Postscript*, "reflection can be halted only by a leap."[2] It is this inner leap—in the present case involving only a small step—that Harry, in the company of every real hero, is willing to take.

Harry Potter shows how a young man vulnerable to all the fears that any of us ever experience can overcome those emotions and nobly press on to do what needs to be done. No one can guarantee that they will act with courage in any particular situation of danger. But we can position ourselves for such a response. We can do five things that will make it more likely. And that just means that we all have within our power to act in such a way as to cultivate the virtue of courage—a lesson we get from the remarkable and courageous Harry Potter.

---

2   Søren Kierkegaard, *Concluding Unscientific Postscript*, translated by David F. Swenson and Walter Lowrie (Princeton: Princeton University Press, 1968), p. 105.

Comprehension

Directions: Refer to the readings to respond correctly to the questions below.

1. What are some ways in which the wrath of Achilles alters the Trojan War? At the same time, what impact do the gods have in the outcome?
2. Having read the *Iliad*, think on the various points where a character displays both brutality and humanity. Do these opposing scenes condemn or vindicate the character in your view?
3. Once again, the *Odyssey* demonstrates that mankind is at the mercy of the gods. In what ways did the gods dictate the fate of Odysseus and his crew? In what ways was their fate ultimately due to their own actions?
4. Identify a positive and negative characteristic of Heracles. How do these traits personify the Greek idea of a hero and your own view of him today?
5. Does the way in which Morris outlines Harry Potter's avenues to courage make Harry seem more or less courageous? Would the Greeks agree that Harry is a hero?

Critical Thinking

Directions: Think about the ideas presented in the readings as you form your own answers to the questions below. When possible, use these ideas to support your answer.

1. Seeing Achilles's behavior throughout the *Iliad*, what are your feelings towards him? Can his actions be considered "heroic"? Given the divine actions and interference, ultimately what role do the mortals play in their own war?
2. How do you see determinism playing a role in the actions of the Greeks and Trojans in the *Iliad*?
3. Through the Homeric epics, both Odysseus and Agamemnon exhibited hubristic tendencies. Compare and contrast the fate of each character. Do you feel these are deserved?
4. How does Heracles epitomize what it means to be a Greek hero? In our society that scrutinizes every strength and flaw, is he still worthy of that title?
5. In what ways do you see the courage of the Greek heroes in Harry Potter? How, even, does Harry's courage surpass the Greeks?

Conclusion: As a Mirror (of Erised?) on Ourselves

. . . .

The previous readings have provided us various avenues of thought through which to understand and appreciate the mythology of the ancient and modern worlds. Unit I introduced the place of importance myths held and the roles they subsumed within ancient society. Mythological tales can elicit powerful reactions, as in the religious condemnation of Harry Potter, as well as critical thought of any lessons that may be learned from them. They serve as a basis from which to comprehend the culture in which they took place. Unit II touched on the true nature of the Greek gods, demanding obedience and subservience while ultimately failing to deliver motivation for such devotion apart from fear of their divine power. The divine myths also served to outline social structures for the Greeks, stressing a patrilocal structure through the oppression of female roles. The Wizarding World of Harry Potter readily differentiates itself in this regard through its strong female characters. Similarities still can be found, however, between the Greeks and Rowling's characters, for instance in the impact of the community on its hero.

Unit III continues this train of thought, focusing on the heroes of Greek myth. While the gods themselves formed the moral codes and guidelines for living, we see the mortal heroes supplying answers to why the world is as we see it and how we should navigate the obstacles of daily life. It is in Achilles, Odysseus, and Heracles that the Greeks found their most relatable counterparts (aside from their divine lineages), and this is also the case for Harry Potter and us muggles of today. Although the *Iliad*, *Odyssey*, Heracles's labors, and "He-who-must-not-be-named" represent much more formidable problems as compared our daily lives, how these heroes overcame the seemingly insurmountable serves as lessons to us all.

"Harry—yer a wizard." From the moment of Hagrid's revelation in *Harry Potter and the Philosopher's Stone*, our adolescent hero embarked on a journey into an unknown world vastly different from his familiar life with the Dursleys at 4 Privet Drive, Surrey. Harry's initiation into the Wizarding World begins at Diagon Alley. Although accessed through a doorway manifested from a brick wall, the bustling street provided familiarity to a typical English city center with a bookstore, pet store, and even a bank. The resemblances would end there for Harry as he toured Flourish and Blotts, Eeylops Owl Emporium, and Gringotts Wizarding Bank. Harry Potter's journey would take him through Hogwarts, the Forbidden

Forest, and the magical world beyond, but, ultimately, as he adventured, the trials and tribulations Harry experienced would reflect much of our own muggle world.

It is in the characters of Rowling's writings (and the cinematic versions) that the readers (or moviegoers) find much of themselves, experiencing the fear of new places, the excitement of new friendships, the butterflies of budding romance, and the adrenaline of sports. Although predominately full of divine or semidivine characters, the Greeks equally found semblance in the myths of their culture. How the *Harry Potter* tales of the modern world and the myths of the Greek world mirror the societies in which they were created allow for them to be vessels to topics of ethics and morality and instructions for navigating life.

We can see, for instance, that sometimes our desires can become that which in reality is not best for us. Rowling shows this in the Mirror of Erised. Harry just wants to be with his family, but he soon realizes that his familial loss is replaced by his pseudo-family of friends at Hogwarts. Ron wants success and fame in Quidditch, underscoring his jealousy of Harry. He eventually learns that achieving this does not ultimately make him happy, and Ron too finds the fulfillment he desires in his family and friends. In *Fantastic Beasts: The Crimes of Grindelwald*, Dumbledore sees his desire to be with Grindelwald but knows that this cannot become a reality owing to the vast separation that has formed between them and the sides they have chosen. Our desires can often lead to our detriment or downfall. Whether fame (Achilles), fortune (Midas), or immortality (Sisyphus), gaining one's earthly desire does not guarantee happiness. These stories can then serve equally as cautionary tales helping us make the right choices along the path of life.

How the myths of the Greek world have been adapted in modern society, particularly in the escapades of Harry Potter, reflect much of how our civilization has changed and adapted to the passage of time and the evolution of society. Whether it is the elimination of more risqué topics and scenes (such as the philandering exploits of Zeus) or the transfiguration of divine abilities to magical powers, these changes are not without purpose and influence from the culture in which they exist. It is through the capacity to understand the Greeks via their myths that we are better able to comprehend ourselves and our own tales. Looking at such a reflection in the mythological mirror of our own society better prepares us as we follow in the heroic footsteps of our past.

Printed in the USA
CPSIA information can be obtained
at www.ICGtesting.com
LVHW081522281123
765083LV00023B/76